D1079199

STAND

omen Changing the World

# HERE WE STAND
## Women Changing the World

Compiled and edited by

HELENA EARNSHAW
&
ANGHARAD PENRHYN JONES

HONNO

First published by Honno in 2014
'Ailsa Craig', Heol y Cawl, Dinas Powys, CF64 4AH

© The Contributors
© The Introduction: Helena Earnshaw & Angharad Penrhyn Jones

1 2 3 4 5 6 7 8 9 10

All rights reserved. No part of this book may be reproduced, stored in a retrieval system, or transmitted in any form, or by any means, electronic, mechanical, photocopying, recording or otherwise without the prior permission of the copyright owners.

A catalogue record for this book is available from the British Library.

ISBN 978-1-909983-02-1

Published with the financial support of the Welsh Books Council.
Cover photographs: image of Shauneen Lamb © Moorique Newman
Other images as credited in the book
Cover design: Laura Yates
Text design: Elaine Sharples
Printed by Bell & Bain Ltd, Glasgow

FSC
www.fsc.org

MIX
Paper from
responsible sources
FSC® C007785

So here I stand... one girl among many.
I speak – not for myself, but for all girls and boys.
I raise up my voice – not so that I can shout,
but so that those without a voice can be heard.

*Pakistani schoolgirl Malala Yousafzai's speech to the
United Nations, 12 July 2013*

| FINGAL COUNTY LIBRARIES | |
| --- | --- |
| FCL00000455293 | |
| Bertrams | 30/06/2014 |
| 305.4092 | £10.99 |
| BA | |

# Contents

*I did what I could:* **an introduction by the editors**     1

**1  Breaking the silence**     7
Jasvinder Sanghera on how she emerged from a
traumatic childhood to campaign against forced
marriage and honour killings.

**2  Nothing to hold me back**     29
Peace activist Sharyn Lock on how she was
changed by one Israeli bullet.

**3  Against the odds**     37
Helen Steel, one of the "McLibel Two", on standing
up to one of the world's largest corporations, and
dealing with the aftermath of her relationship with
an undercover policeman.

**4  The freedom of others**     63
Activist and artivist Skye Chirape on being forced
to flee her country because of her sexuality, and
having to battle her way out of a UK detention
centre.

**5  Fairness, justice, love**     73
Veteran campaigner Mary Sharkey on facing
down a police horse at Greenham, making food
parcels for the miners, and some hairy moments
with Women's Aid.

**6  My revolution**                                    **95**
   Children's rights campaigner and author
   Anuradha Vittachi on her part in the babymilk
   campaign, which sparked her own personal
   revolution.

**7  Who jumps first?**                                 **107**
   Disability rights activist and performance artist Liz
   Crow on a political awakening that happened in
   about 20 seconds flat, and why she took her
   wheelchair to the fourth plinth on Trafalgar
   Square.

**8  Drawing it out**                                   **133**
   Satirical cartoonist Kate Evans on bringing
   injustice into the light through her artwork.

**9  An act of defiance**                               **139**
   Jo Wilding on how she went from throwing fruit at
   Tony Blair to taking a circus to the children of Iraq
   during the invasion.

**10  Bearing witness**                                 **163**
   Camcorder activist Zoe Broughton writes about
   two decades of campaigning, including going
   undercover at an animal-testing laboratory.

**11  With my hammer**                                  **171**
   Nobel Peace Prize-nominee Angie Zelter on
   destroying a hawk jet, working with women in
   Palestine, and why she sees herself as a global
   citizen.

**12  Twyford rising**                                     193
    Poet Emma Must on how her attempt to save an
    ancient landscape from destruction left an
    indelible mark.

**13  Progression**                                        207
    Anti-racism activist Zita Holbourne on police
    brutality, the London riots, and the Olympics – and
    why she will never be silenced.

**14  For these are all our children**                     235
    Human rights lawyer Shauneen Lambe gives an
    email interview about working with death row
    inmates in the USA, and why she loves representing
    marginalised young people in the UK.

**15  Still here**                                         247
    Angharad Tomos writes about being imprisoned
    for her campaigns to protect her native language.

**16  In defence of life**                                 257
    Eileen Chubb on blowing the whistle on abuse in a
    care home and how, despite paying a huge
    personal price, she refused to give up the fight.

**17  Fire in my belly**                                   279
    Filmmaker Franny Armstrong on how she
    pioneered "crowdfunding" to make a climate
    change blockbuster, and why films are a powerful
    political tool.

**Contributor biographies**                                305

**About the editors**                                      315

# *I did what I could:*
# an introduction by the editors

The function of freedom, according to author Toni Morrison, is to free someone else. The 17 women featured in this anthology have done exactly this: they have used their freedom to try to ease the suffering of others. These are stories of women who are simultaneously ordinary (they work as teachers, gardeners, librarians) and remarkable (they are prepared to spend 10 years in prison to help prevent genocide on the other side of the world, or to face gunfire with no protection).

What is it that compels any of us to make a stand, to fight for what we believe in? Perhaps it is to do with the realisation that, as writer Deborah Levy puts it, "we are connected to each other's cruelty and to each other's kindness."* These women remind us of what it means to live in a state of connectedness with the world and other people. They are unable to turn their backs on injustice, to enjoy their liberty whilst others remain in captivity. Showing great physical, moral and political courage, in many cases they've suffered tremendous losses. They've had the temerity to take politics into their own hands, to shape it into something entirely their own, to challenge the status quo and risk abuse, rejection, imprisonment, and even death. Refusing to remain impotent in the face of oppression, they will not be derailed.

Our contributors cannot accept that the world is increasingly run, and ruined, by multinational corporations; that animals are tortured to satisfy human desires; or that beautiful ancient landscapes are devastated in order to cut commuting times for motorists. When they witness cruelty some feel, in the words of whistleblower Eileen Chubb, an emotion resembling "a cold rage". Others, like artist-activist Liz Crow, feel "bewilderment" as much as rage. While many bring an intellectual approach to their campaigns, their response can sometimes be more visceral than cerebral, or based on a complex interweaving of both thinking and feeling – McLibel campaigner Helen Steel says her politics stem from her "guts", and yet her fierce intellect helped her to stand up to one of the world's largest corporations. In all cases, perhaps it's fair to say that in facing up to injustice, our campaigners feel the fear, but do it anyway. And they become unstoppable.

Rebellious women have not been much celebrated in our society, but without radicals who are prepared to question social conventions and the legal system, women might not have the vote today and slavery might not have been abolished. How often we forget that many of the privileges we enjoy now have been fought for by ordinary citizens who collectively stood up to powerful elites. These outspoken people might have seemed ridiculous at the time – the suffragettes were labelled as dreamers, extremists, vandals – but with hindsight most of us can see that they represented a voice of reason in unreasonable times. And we believe that the women featured in this anthology – many of them lawbreakers with very loud voices – are not only reasonable but profoundly admirable.

Choosing which activists to include was a huge and daunting task: we had hundreds of inspiring female campaigners to choose from. We were keen to represent women of various ages and ethnic backgrounds from many different parts of the UK, and to cover a range of grassroots campaigns from the last four decades. We wanted to create a sense of the political landscape from the 1980s to the present day, as well as providing engaging portraits of women and their lives as activists. In this sense, the work was like completing a jigsaw puzzle, and inevitably, perhaps, there will be missing pieces.

We were looking for women who could speak truthfully about what it is like to have a passion to change the world for the better, and how that affects their lives – their jobs, their families, their physical and psychological health, and their children. How it has influenced them as women, what being a woman brings to their campaigning, and the intricate connections between the personal and the political.

We were interested, too, in the question of how a person becomes radicalised. We wanted to know whether the campaigners in this book were aware of having been changed by a single moment or event, or perhaps by a more drawn-out life experience. Maybe the process of becoming politicised had been a more subtle process for our contributor, a slow dawning over many years, whereby events and influences had accumulated in such a way that she had simply realised one day that she could no longer be politically passive: something had snapped inside her; she had to act, her personal revolution had begun. We discovered that whichever road led to her political awakening, each of the women had been irrevocably changed by the process: as one of them says, once your eyes have been opened, it's impossible to close them again.

Several themes came up again and again. Greenham

Common has left a lasting legacy and, predictably, features on many pages of this book. The relationship between motherhood and activism often crops up too: of those who've had children, many of our contributors said that since becoming mothers, they were no longer able to take the actions they'd taken in the past. Others, however, had been able to put themselves at risk time and time again thanks to the support of partners and extended families. A number of women spoke about the importance of both family and campaign networks and they were also attuned to the dangers of putting one person on a pedestal, of associating a particular campaign with one media-friendly activist and ignoring the less glamorous, behind-the-scenes efforts of the many other men and women who are catalysing change. Another recurring theme is the importance of seeing activism as a broad term which encompasses a range of approaches to achieving political traction. As one woman says, you don't have to chain yourself to a bus to qualify as an activist.

Half of the contributors have written their own testimonies; the other half were more comfortable being interviewed. To work with them has been a privilege. During our conversations there was laughter, tears, thoughtful silences. Perhaps more than anything, they have reminded us that to campaign on big-picture issues enlarges us as human beings, that egoistic and material concerns rarely lead to personal fulfilment. Many of them transmitted a sense of excitement about working collaboratively (something we as co-editors have also experienced whilst putting this book together), and they spoke of the unexpected pleasures of political resistance. Language activist Angharad Tomos, for instance, speaks of the "deep friendships" she has forged through 30 years of campaigning;

others talk about the creative and joyful aspects of fighting for change.

Editing their work wasn't always easy: you won't be surprised to read that many campaigners can be single-minded, stubborn and quite uncompromising. But their enthusiasm was infectious. We very much hope they will also affect you, the reader, and that they will inspire you to use your own freedom to free someone else. This doesn't mean that we should all feel pressured to smash a military jet or infiltrate an animal-testing laboratory. It could mean writing a letter, or attending a march. As Helen Suzman, anti-apartheid activist, says: "I did what I could, where I was, with what I had."

Our aim was to give voice to the passion and compassion that is in all of us. Each one of us has the potential to do good things in the world, and most of us actually long to do so. Every day many of us make small differences – picking up a piece of litter, teaching our children to share, holding open a door for a stranger. The women whose stories we've included may have committed extraordinarily courageous acts, but in all of them the impulse is the same: to help create a kinder world, to live in accordance with their deepest beliefs, to exist in a state of hope in spite of the brutalities and cruelties that surround us. Perhaps they would all agree with activist Howard Zinn when he says that:

"To be hopeful in bad times is not just foolishly romantic. It is based on the fact that human history is a history not only of cruelty, but also of compassion, sacrifice, courage, kindness. What we choose to emphasise in this complex history will determine our lives.

"If we see only the worst, it destroys our capacity to do something. If we remember those times and places – and there are so many – where people have behaved magnificently, this gives us the energy to act, and at least the possibility of sending this spinning top of a world in a different direction.

"And if we do act, in however small a way, we don't have to wait for some grand utopian future. The future is an infinite succession of presents, and to live now as we think human beings should live, in defiance of all that is bad around us, is itself a marvelous victory." **

**Helena Earnshaw and Angharad Penrhyn Jones**

* "*When we turn our back on human rights, we numb the knowing parts of our minds and make a space for something terrible to happen to someone else. We are connected to each other's cruelty and to each other's kindness.*" Deborah Levy, *Guardian*, 21 February, 2014

** Howard Zinn, *You Can't Be Neutral on a Moving Train: A personal history of our times*, as seen at
https://www.goodreads.com/author/quotes/1899.Howard_Zinn

# Breaking the silence

**Jasvinder Sanghera** on how she emerged from a traumatic childhood to campaign against forced marriage and honour killings.

*Interview by Angharad Penrhyn Jones*

*The title of your memoir is* Shame: *this is an important concept in the Sikh community you come from in Derby. Did you feel shame for being a girl? Would you say that you had a sense of inferiority from the beginning?*

I remember women would come to see my mother at the house, and they would pity her for having given birth to seven daughters. They would be tearful about that. The birth of a girl was this huge burden on our household. My mother would explain to us that it meant she had to get us married, she had to keep us in check so as not to dishonour and shame the family. When boys were born, they gave out *laddu*, which is an Asian sweet, but when girls were born that never happened, because giving out sweets is a sign of a celebration. I had one brother and he went to a better school than us. He went to one of the real high achieving schools in Derby.

Leabharlanna Fhine Gall

*Nobody expected you to get on in the world.*

Absolutely. My mother would always say to us growing up that we were a financial burden, so we'd be very mindful of that, and we were also mindful of the fact that we carried the family's honour on our shoulders, because as daughters we had the power to dishonour them. There were certain things that we were not allowed to do. We were not allowed to cut our hair, for example; we were not allowed to wear makeup, or date boys, or even talk to boys; we couldn't go to the school disco like our peers, or on school outings. Anything to do with integrating and being an independent thinker. We were not encouraged to educate ourselves, though our brother was educated to the point of being an engineer. We were told that where we were going, there wasn't a need for an education.

*Was your brother permitted to socialise outside the Sikh community?*

Oh, absolutely, my brother was dating a dual-heritage woman, who was half white, whose father was Asian, and my mother knew that. He even married her, whereas we had no choice in who we got to marry. We were expected to become dutiful wives and dutiful daughters-in-law, while he had all these freedoms. He was allowed to express himself through music – he was a big Bob Marley fan and he used to go to concerts and his music would be playing through the house. And he would always eat first, and when we had baths he always had the hot water first. We even had to serve him food.

*Did you feel a sense of resentment towards him?*

I certainly did. The fact that he was allowed to express himself and do the things that I yearned to do, like go on a bike, or go out with mates, just the normal adolescent things. But you're taught from birth to be subservient to the males in the family.

*Tell me about that moment when you were faced with a photo of the man you were expected to marry.*

The thing is, I watched my older sisters being married and taken out of education when they were fifteen. So when you're growing up and this is happening around you, it doesn't seem abnormal. So I didn't have a great shock when my mother sat me down when I came home from school, a 14-year-old girl, and very tactfully, very matter of fact, presented me with a photograph of the man that I'd been promised to from the age of eight. I just listened, and she said she was going to put the photograph on the mantelpiece, and that over time I would grow to like him. Now, because we were never allowed boyfriends, it was almost exciting to be given permission to like somebody of the opposite sex. But I didn't like the look of him: my first thought was, he's shorter than me. And he looked much older than me as well.

I went to school the next day as normal, but when I hit 15, the pressure started to mount, because my mother was preparing the wedding. As soon as I finished my GCSEs, people started coming to the house. There was a big trunk and they started filling it with clothes and towels. People would bring gifts and the wedding dress was brought as well. This wedding was being planned and it happened to be mine and I had this bird's eye view – that's how I'd describe it. I was looking down, feeling extremely disconnected from it all. And that's when I said, "I'm not marrying this stranger; I want to stay on in school." I was a really bright kid, I loved English, I really enjoyed religious education. So that's when I protested, and then I was physically abused, certainly psychologically abused. The emotional blackmail was horrendous – I loved my dad dearly, and my mother told me that if I didn't marry this man my dad would die of a heart attack and it would be my fault. She also said that I'd ruin my sisters' marriages, that their husbands would leave them and I'd cause shame for my family.

I should also say that my view of marriage was very negative. As a young girl I'd seen all my sisters suffering domestic violence. I'd be bundled into a car as a 10-year-old, and my mother would go to my sisters' houses to rescue them, and they'd have black eyes, cracked ribs and all sorts, and my mother would talk them into staying in that relationship. She'd never bring them back home. And that was my perception of marriage as a young person growing up: you got married and that's what happened to you.

In *Shame* I talk about how my mother would say that you have to think of your husband as a pan of milk. You put a pan of milk on the gas, you turn the gas on, and when it rises and it's going to bubble over, your job is to blow it down and to keep it calm, regardless. And that would be the analogy she would use, so no matter how abusive these husbands were, it was my sisters job to stay there, to make it work. Because divorce was a huge cause of shame and dishonour for the family. Everyone in the community would be telling them to make that marriage work.

*So the rights of the community are more important than the rights of the individual.*

Yes, and the reputation of the family. Which goes back to being a young person understanding that you carry a burden, a weight on your shoulders: you have the power to dishonour your family. So you have to be submissive, modest, agree to all the codes of honour and dishonour, and you take all that into your marriage. You're still playing that role.

*When you told your sisters you were not going to marry this man, how did they react?*

Every single one of them said to me, *"Teri ful lagi yah,"* which means, "Have you got flowers attached to you; are you different?" They had to go through with it, so why was I any different?

*Why were you different?*

My mother had to go to hospital to have me because I was born upside down. All her other children were born at home, and she was frightened of hospitals. So she would remind me from a very young age how I was difficult from birth, how I'd been born upside down, and landed on my feet. She'd constantly remind me of this difference. She used to call me a tomboy. Also I have a mole on my right cheek and none of my sisters have that. In our culture that's a bad sign, and she constantly tried to wipe it off. I used to say to her, "Mum, you can't wipe it off, it's there." And she'd scrub and scrub. When we went to relatives' houses or weddings, she'd try to cover it in powder. She said, "It's because you're different."

*You were marked out from the beginning.*

That's what she used to say. So I used to think, from the age of eight, that I might as well push the boundaries, because I'm different anyway. I think her telling me I was different helped.

*So it kind of backfired on her part.*

She did me a favour, actually, though she'll never know that. But yes, it made me question things.

I don't have any photographs from when I was young, bar one. When I left home they coloured my face in, they blackened it in all the photos, because I was somebody who'd blackened the family. So I don't have any photographs of me as a child, only one from when I was eight. And even as an eight-year-old girl, I was rebellious, and I cut my hair to have a fringe. You can see in the picture that it's really wonky! [Laughs.] But I wanted a fringe, because everybody else had a fringe. Later, when I was 15, I sneaked off to have my hair permed. I don't know how I was going to get away with that. [Laughs.] I used to have hair I could sit on, but my friends had perms in the very early 80s, so I wanted a perm. I wanted to fit in.

*Jasvinder's only surviving childhood picture.*

*Your father was more well-integrated in Derby, wasn't he?*

He was. My father would have a crafty cigarette and laugh things off. He'd never go to the temple unless he had to, whereas my mother used to go morning and night.

*Would you say they were they just going through the motions in their marriage or was there something deeper there?*

Well, again, my mother and father had this arranged marriage, although my mother was under the age of 16, and I question the word "arrangement" for a child. So it was an understanding. And I'm ashamed to say that women are perpetrators in cases of honour-based abuse and forced marriage and sometimes the women are the gatekeepers to maintaining the honour systems within their family. Some fathers are very active, hands on; they have a very strong presence and the women take a back seat. But in my childhood it was the other way round. My mother was the strong character. When I was taken out of education and locked in a room at home, I looked at my father and I said to him, "Help me." His face was so sad, but there was nothing he could do.

*That's interesting, because people might see it as a straightforward case of male oppression, but it's much more complicated than that.*

Absolutely. My father, I think, was a victim of the system himself. And he didn't have the power to stand up to my mother, because it wasn't just about my mother: it was about the approval of the wider community. So when I ran away from home and they disowned me, even if my father had wanted to accept me back, he would have struggled with that decision because it would have meant that everybody else would stop talking to him.

*So your family locked you up in a room, and said they wouldn't let you out unless you agreed to marry this man. You managed to escape through the window. Where did you go?*

I ran away to Newcastle with a friend's brother, Jassey. We literally closed our eyes and said, wherever our finger lands on the map, we'll go there. The thing is, I ran away hoping this would demonstrate to my family that I didn't want to

13

marry a stranger, and they'd let me come home. That's what I wanted. Looking back, I was very naïve.

Me and Jassey slept in the car for a number of weeks; we'd wash our faces in public toilets. I remember one night wanting to sleep on a park bench because it was more comfortable than the car. You have to remember that my family life had been comfortable. We were warm, we were fed, and all of a sudden I was so uncomfortable, and also being exposed to a world that I'd never been allowed to be a part of. I really struggled to get used to my freedom and independence. I didn't know how to manage that. I was extremely vulnerable. I was reported missing by my family and the police requested that I ring home. So I rang home and said to my mum, "Look, it's me, I want to come home." And she said, "You've got two choices. You can come back home, but marry who we say – or from this day forward you are dead in our eyes." And I chose the second option.

*You didn't agonise over that decision?*

It was a gut instinct. I knew if I went back, I would have to marry a stranger. But I never imagined my mum would say that I was dead in her eyes. And then you wake up the next morning and you know that you are never seeing a member of your family ever again, or where you lived, or any of the things that are familiar to you.

I would write to my family, send them birthday cards, but I never got anything back. Now I have no expectations of them whatsoever, so I don't feel the pain of not having had a birthday card in the last 30 years, I don't miss them as I used to. But I'm human. I still live in Derbyshire, my family still live in Derby and if I go to the town centre and I see them, they will physically walk away from me. But I don't go home and throw myself under a duvet in tears, I just get on with my day. There are certain times of my life where I do feel their absence. And my daughter Natasha's wedding last year was one of them. She had the big Indian wedding, and all the Asian families were there and there was no one on my side.

*So she married an Asian man?*

Yes. They are a beautiful family. I'd never experienced an Asian family that brings up their children with unconditional love and regard and the right to choose who they marry, so it was a challenge for me to accept that. I was very cynical. But Natasha's mother-in-law taught me a lot. And the thing about Indian weddings is that they are beautiful; our tradition and culture is beautiful. What I'm talking about in my own life is not part of tradition. It's not a tradition to force somebody to marry: that is abuse.

*You had a secret relationship for a while with your sister, Robina. She was absolutely trapped, wasn't she?*

We would talk in secret, and she would tell me about the abuse in her marriage. She suffered physical violence, psychological violence. I remember meeting her in secret in Leicester where she lived and hugging her at the coach station and she'd say, "Oh, don't hug me," because she had so many bruises around her ribs. You'd go to her house and you'd see the visible signs of domestic violence, like broken doors and windows. I remember saying to her, "Go and speak to mum and dad," because ultimately she was living her life for their approval. So she went to them and Mum said, "We'll call our local community leader."

Community leaders carry a lot of weight. They can be religious leaders, they can be councillors, they can be politicians, they can be a very high profile person in the corner shop.

And he was very clear: he said that our mother and father had only just started to lift their heads after the shame caused by me, and that if she failed to make her marriage work, it would kill her parents. That was his advice. And then a week after that, when I was working on my market stall in Bradford, this woman I knew came up to me and told me to ring home because something terrible had happened to my sister. I would have been about 22 at the time. So, I rang home and my mother said, "It's Robina, she's died, she's dead". I couldn't register this, and I thought, what do you mean, dead, how's she died? And my mother said, "She set herself on fire, she committed suicide."

And at that moment I remember saying to my mum, "I'm coming to the house right now." Because that moment of grief, you want to share. And she said, "Do not show your face here." But I still went. People were crying and hitting themselves with grief, but as I walked into rooms they would walk out, as if a bad smell had entered the room. And at the funeral, because Robina was so badly burned that you couldn't see her face, they just put a photograph on the lid. Our community leader was there, and all the other people that could have saved her. I had tried to save her and I wasn't even allowed to be at the funeral.

*What did you do with your grief and your anger and your trauma?*

Robina's death for me was the turning point, whereby I finally realised that my family were never going to accept me. So you stop living with the hope. And on that day I accepted that I was a victim and not a perpetrator, because before then I'd always felt that I'd done this bad thing to my family. I'd lived with this feeling that I was a bad person. And as a survivor, that moment is so important; you start to reclaim some of your sense of self-worth and respect and dignity. And that gave me the power to say, I'm not going to keep my head down any more, I'm not going to live in hiding any more, I'm not going to be afraid to show my face in Derby any more. The thing is, my sister couldn't come back. She's gone, Robina's gone for ever. And one of the things that my mother said to us was that we were never to speak about her again. So it was as if her memory had to be wiped clean.

*Because she'd dishonoured the family by committing suicide?*

It is my view that my mother would see Robina's suicide as being more honourable than for her to leave her husband. It certainly is a view that was compounded by community leaders who pressured her to go back to her husband.

*And is that why Robina did it, do you think – because it was the easiest way out?*

My sister was driven to commit suicide, without a doubt. She was completely isolated, she needed the approval of my family to leave her husband. She'd been conditioned to believe that if she left him, it would be a source of shame and could kill her parents, and this is why she took her own life.

*As an outsider, I see something very cult-like about it. The total indoctrination...*

Yes, absolutely. It's extreme. And that's the motivation we see with honour killings. This is my campaign at the moment, to remember a 17-year-old girl called Shafilea Ahmed, who was murdered by her own parents in Warrington. Nobody wants to talk about her, nobody in that community, not even the agencies that let her down. I went to her gravestone at the weekend and there she was, 17 years old, buried in the ground. Her parents buried her, when they knew they were responsible for her death, and on her stone it says, "To our beloved daughter." She was an A* GCSE student, her ambition was to be a barrister. But she was too westernised for her family. She went to five organisations and pleaded for help. They talked her into going back to her family time and time again. She said, "If you send me home they will force me to marry or even kill me. I'm scared I'm going to be killed." And nobody wants to talk about it. Shafilea's parents were convicted last year to 25 years each. But for me, what's important is that she went to five organisations. They all had opportunities to protect her, but they saw her as belonging to a different culture. Who talks about those girls; who is speaking for them?

*There was one bit in your memoir,* Shame, *that stood out for me, and that's where you talk about going to a Rape Crisis centre and for the first time speaking out about what had happened in your family. Until that point you say that openness had been like a foreign language to you; your mother had spun this web of secrecy around your family. So that was a turning point as well, being able to put your experience into words.*

We are taught to be silent. We understand that speaking to anybody outside your family is a cause of shame. Look at Shafilea Ahmed's murder – her siblings were told to watch as her mother and father murdered her. They maintained their silence for seven years. They witnessed their sister being suffocated and the only way we achieved a successful prosecution was through one sister breaking and saying, "I have to tell somebody..." But I understand the fear attached to speaking out.

*I was reading in the paper yesterday about Banaz [a girl murdered by her father and uncle in the UK] and according to the Iranian Kurdish Women's Rights organisations, this sort of case is actually on the rise.*

What you have to remember about cases like this – murders, forced marriages, honour-based abuse – is that we have multiple perpetrators, not one. With domestic violence it's usually partner to partner violence. In these cases, it's more the father, brother, sister, aunt, uncle – loads of people are involved and so it's a whole network of abuse. And not just in this country, but abroad also – there's a strong link. So imagine how isolated we are. Imagine how hidden we are. By virtue of the fact that it's hidden crime, we've got to increase the reporting. We're dealing with the tip of the iceberg, and beneath the iceberg there are hundreds of thousands we are yet to reach. So as with domestic violence, we want to see an increase in reporting to organisations. But the victim fears for her life, literally, because of the honour-based system network. And also the dilemma that you have in Britain, whereby some providers who are meant to protect you think this is part of your culture.

*And use the word "culture" rather than "abuse".*

Exactly. So when Banaz went to the police and said, "I'm going to be killed for kissing a boy at a Tube station," the person hearing that may not have had an understanding. It does challenge your belief and value systems: how can you believe that she's going to be killed for that? But she handed the police a list of the people that would kill her, and told them that if anything happened to her they should arrest these people. Top of her list was her father. So she told them what would happen to her, and she was seen as being melodramatic. Fantasising. If she had come to Karma Nirvana she would be alive today. So would Shafilea.

*If those two girls had come to Karma Nirvana, what would you have done?*

*Jasvinder Sanghera addressing a conference in 2011.*

We would have dealt with it as high risk and taken them into protection whereby they were away from their family. So they'd be placed somewhere away from their networks. If they were claiming benefits we would be making their National Insurance number sensitive, we would be taking them off computer systems, we would be putting in the infrastructure of support, including emotional support. But more importantly, we'd be advocating the risk of threat to life to the police. I've already dealt with two threats to kill this morning on the Karma Nirvana helpline. So, when we're taking those calls, very often other victims are going to organisations that downplay it, don't understand them, or fear being called racist, or fear offending the communities in treating it as abuse. So we become their voice. We would have said, on behalf of Banaz, or Shafilea, "This is a threat to life, this person needs protecting."

*How many girls in the UK are facing these dangers?*

We're told by the Crime Prosecution Service that there are twelve honour-related murders a year. Shafilea was murdered in 2003 – you think how many there's been since then. But what we've also been told by the Crime Prosecution Service is that they haven't got a handle on how many of the cases are honour-related. There could be far more because they're not being identified as being linked to honour. And they have no idea how many unmarked graves there are of British-born subjects abroad, or even in this country. Shafilea's parents shoved a carrier bag down her throat, suffocated her to death and she died, horrifically, and they dumped her body in the Lake District. Were it not for Mother Nature, her body may have never been found. There was a flood in the area which lifted her body up. Had that flood never happened, her body would never have been found and the parents would be walking around, free. So we have no idea.

*What would you say Karma Nirvana has achieved in the 21 years since you founded the organisation?*

One of my greatest achievements is breaking the silence of victims of forced marriages and honour-based abuse. Giving voice to an experience that no one was speaking about in 1993. I remember the first few years of being a campaigner, four... five years. I was lucky if I got one person in a room that was bothered to hear what I had to say. I had doors closed in my face, or people being polite and saying they'd call me and never calling me. But I knew I was speaking out not just about mine and Robina's experience. I always believed they were out there. And you have to remember, I hadn't met these survivors before, I was on my own. And the thing about victims is you always think you're the only one. So, for me the biggest achievement would be breaking the silence around this abuse.

*Tell me about your helpline.*

The helpline started in my front room in 1993. I used to pretend that I had this big flash organisation, but for the first six years it was just me and an answerphone. [Laughs.] We launched it formally in 2008, and since then the helpline has dealt with more than 30,000 calls and the number is increasing all the time. But I know Karma Nirvana has helped hundreds of thousands, because they're the ones that have reported to outside organisations. That's an achievement. And there will be a ripple effect because organisations are now developing platforms to speak about this; they're shaping policies and procedures. The other great achievement will be the criminalisation of forced marriage. I've been a huge campaigner for this, going backward and forward for 13 years asking Parliament to criminalise it. It didn't happen under the Labour government because they didn't want to offend communities. I was beaming with pride to hear the announcement of the new law in the Queen's Speech this year; it will come into effect in 2014.

I've sat in a circle with [the prime minister] David Cameron, and wherever I go I take survivors with me. They are the ones that matter. A survivor testimony is real, that's what you need to hear. So last year, Cameron agreed to give us a consultation on the criminalisation of forced marriage. And I said, "You're going to give us this, I'm really excited about it, but you've got to put it out to the public." Because last time, it was the usual suspects that were consulted – professionals, not survivors. So the home secretary opened it to the public for a consultation. I saw that as an opportunity to ask the public for their views, so Karma Nirvana went to the streets of Derby, Bradford, Manchester, Newcastle to gather opinion, and we did it on Twitter and Facebook. And we got around 5,500 responses. You look at the Home Office consultation and they got a few hundred. We were being proactive with the general public, because I don't think people recognise their own power. And people say to me, "Oh, you got to meet the prime minister," and I always say, "Anyone can meet the prime minister, he's accountable to us. That's what he's there for, he's not out of your reach." So then we went to Number 10 and handed the postbag in. And to be fair, he'd read *Shame* – he told me his head has been turned as a result of reading it, and that was one of the reasons he gave us a consultation. Then finally he announced it: it's going to be a criminal offence.

That happened in March this year. We took survivors with us and they shared their stories with David Cameron. I had to say to them, "He's just the prime minister, just tell him. Because when you speak, you are speaking for an army of women just like you, standing behind you, never forget that." They did it with immense courage and grace. Then he asked us what we felt needed to change, apart from the legal aspect – because the law is just one thing. I used that as an opportunity to talk about schools and how they have got to engage on this; it cannot be right that schools are refusing to put up posters about this issue, that headteachers are tearing down posters. That we can only get six schools across the UK to work with us.

*Why are they so resistant?*

Because they fear offending parents, the communities. We've still got a long way to go with schools.

*So would you like headteachers to be reprimanded for not dealing with missing children, for example? When Asian kids disappear off the school register and nobody asks why, do you think headteachers should be held to account?*

Absolutely. We've had two government enquiries about missing girls in education, because I also raised the question with [former prime minister] Gordon Brown in 2008. Over 100 went missing off one school roll and I pointed out that if 100 *white* kids went missing from education we'd be jumping up and down. Why are the same questions not being asked of South Asian children? I'd like to see the government do a campaign across society. Because we've gone from almost a social acceptance of domestic violence, with officers saying, "Oh, it's a domestic, we don't meddle in that," to a culture, thankfully, of zero tolerance. Forces now have domestic violence units, and this is a performance indicator in all police forces. I want to see exactly the same thing with forced marriage. At the moment we don't have a recording category in any police force for forced marriage, or honour-based violence.

*No category at all.*

No category at all. So we have no statistics. The law will create that awareness and statistics and it gives an organisation like Karma Nirvana and others more scope to hold people to account. The challenges haven't gone, it's a hard slog. We're having to cajole schools into working with us and explain why this is about child protection. You put posters up about bullying, drugs, safe sex, but putting up a poster of forced marriage, it's almost like a dirty word.

*So you're trying to break that taboo... You've achieved a huge amount, and it's really inspirational, but how do you keep going? What gives you energy to deal with this hard slog?*

In the beginning Karma Nirvana was my salvation, because it was somewhere to channel my anger about Robina. And then it became less about that. As time went on, my children became my motivation because, some days, you wake up and you don't feel like looking in the mirror, you feel crap inside and you have to take a platform and speak and you just... you have knocks but you've got to keep going. What keeps me going, what keeps me motivated, more than anything, is the sheer injustice; girls like Banaz, girls like Shafilea, those beautiful girls being killed.

*Would you make the same decision today if you had your time back - the decision to leave your family and community behind?*

Yes, because I have been allowed to watch my children grow into confident, independent human beings who will never inherit that legacy of abuse. I look at my daughter, Natasha - she's married a beautiful man in a beautiful family. She's married through choice. I remember on that day me and her father, my ex-partner, were there at the wedding, and when she had her first dance, we looked at each other and were both in tears. Her day arrived because of the decisions we made when I was 16. Because otherwise, I can tell you now, I would have been forced into marriage, I would have been pressured to force my children into marriage and I've seen it with my sisters and their children.

*You broke the cycle.*

Exactly. And when you are struggling, that's what you have to hold on to.

*Do you see yourself as campaigning as part of a broader movement of Asian feminists?*

When I wrote my book, my editor asked me who my audience was. And the first thing I said to him was, "If you think it's the Asian community, you're wrong." I said it's for every woman who's experienced rejection, divorce, homelessness, poverty, inequality, abuse, depression, or wanting to self-harm and commit suicide. Because we have an experience in common as women and the only way I've achieved things through the cause is by identifying like-minded women. They haven't been women from my community, I'm sorry to say. Most of them have been women from a white British community. Colour should be irrelevant. Because the problem with colour is what's caused the inequalities in the first place. There's this moral blindness attached to these cultural sensitivities that people pander to. And white professionals need to feel confident about speaking out. Wherever my team speak, we're appealing to their compassion. We want them to feel as confident as anyone else to respond to the problems. The days of Asian workers being wheeled out to deal with the Asian problem – those days have to go.

*You see this as a human rights issue, which cuts across all barriers.*

Exactly. Our chairperson, Kathy Row – she's white, middle class, had a privileged life. When she stands up and speaks she often gets asked, "How can you speak about this? You're white." And she says, "I can speak about this because I know it's wrong."

*Can you talk about the ways in which you've been threatened and intimidated because of your work?*

I've had panic alarms put in my house, reinforced locks put on my doors. I've had human faeces smeared on my office window, I've had notes left on my car. We've moved offices now and we operate on a PO Box number. I had a bomb threat once. I get hate mail, abusive tweets. Our website at Karma Nirvana is often hacked into and then people leave nasty messages. My daughter used to read some of the stuff on the internet and get really upset. Once she read that her mum should be fed to the dogs as war meat in Iraq. It's a protest, and the stronger and more effective you get in your voice, the more you're going to see it.

And the stuff I've been writing about is threatening. *Shame* was referred to as a lethal weapon in Parliament by one of the Baronesses. She threw the book in the air when it was being debated in the House of Lords, and said, "This is a lethal weapon." And that, for me, is a huge achievement, to see that a book was instrumental in shaping policy in the law.

*Do you think you'll ever stop fighting?*

I think I'll be doing this for the rest of my life. I can't imagine not doing it, because I would only stop if the problems were completely solved, and I can't see that happening. Last week, when ABC news were filming in my house, my son said to me: "You know, mum, we really admire what you do but we're very aware in our family there are three people." I said, "Three people?" And he said, "Us – the kids, and you, and the cause." [Laughs.] So if and when I ever meet anybody to settle down with in my life, who knows? They will have to marry the cause as well.

# Nothing to hold me back

Peace activist **Sharyn Lock** on how she was changed by one Israeli bullet.

I have tried to find a beginning for you. I went back as far as I could remember, and what I remember is knowing there was no difference between me and the children of Beirut, 1985: what they experienced, I imagined vividly. My mother taught me to be compassionate and my father taught me to be logical. The fundamentalist church I grew up in taught me that community is what sustains you, and then let me walk away easily, carrying the only fundamental beliefs that matter: that this earth is precious and all those living on it are my neighbours.

I should also attribute what my mother called my "over-developed conscience" to my appetite for Victorian novels. When I was 23, she mentioned that I had turned out quite a surprise to both my parents; surprised in turn, I replied that surely my being arrested for sitting in front of bulldozers was the inevitable result of my upbringing. She said that in fact they'd thought I might be a teacher or a doctor (and I now teach adult education and work as a midwife, so perhaps we were all right).

I was never particularly brave, but along with the Victorian novels, I read *The Lord of the Rings* avidly as a teenager (and this year was handfasted to someone who injured himself in his own imaginary sword fight at 16 – exactly the boy I dreamed of at the time), so I knew you didn't have to be brave: you just had to believe in good versus evil, and get on with it. When I first went to a protest site in Australia, where ancient forest was destroyed for woodchip, I was overwhelmed by the scale of both the beauty and the damage. I returned home with less skin and more capacity for both joy and grief. But I returned early because I was scared of crossing the line – if the police said "move" and I said "no", what might happen to me, to my life of order and safety?

It was in England that I discovered ideological "ancestors" to inspire me – the Diggers of 1649; the suffragettes; the international brigades that went to fight the fascists in Spain; my friend Helen's great uncle, the youngest lad allowed to join the Warsaw resistance against the Nazis; and my friend Oli's granddad who was sent to prison for refusing to kill on behalf of the state. I found the activist community which has been my home ever since, and it gave me all I needed to realise that the line I was scared of crossing was as imaginary as the distance between me and the majority of the world's inhabitants, who never had a choice in the first place. Which is kind of how I came to be shot on April Fool's Day, 2002, in Beit Jala, Palestine.

This is not a unique story: many international volunteers have been shot since then. And unlike them, I have no ill effects at all to endure. The eight fragmentation bullet pieces have settled down permanently throughout my abdomen, and frankly I'm pleased they did, since a non-fragmentation bullet, usually less damaging, would in my case have emerged through my spine. And I think the other injured volunteers would agree. if you want to hear the story of how the Israeli Army shoots unarmed people in Palestine, ask the schoolchild on the receiving end of a similar bullet; ask the Israeli teenager who does time for refusing to be the one firing it; ask the Gaza fisherman who was shot yesterday from an Israeli gunboat (his name is Saleem); ask the 17-year-old Gaza girl kneecapped by direct fire from across the border fence; ask the Israeli Physicians for Human Rights and the Palestinian Centre for Human Rights who document these shootings. But I thought I would tell you what happened to me because hearing other people's personal stories gave me enough conviction to live my own.

April 1st, 2002, my fourth day in Palestine with the International Solidarity Movement (ISM). We are in a suburban Palestinian neighbourhood, walking up the hill to Beit Jala, where the Israeli Occupation Force have been raiding houses and interrogating people. Anxious locals have asked the International Solidarity Movement volunteers to deliver food and first aid; after a disastrous suicide bombing in Netanya they expect a large scale Israeli military incursion as collective punishment (common, though illegal under international law), and a curfew, which may last weeks. Arafat's compound, elsewhere in the West Bank, has been surrounded, but here it is still quiet.

There aren't many Palestinians on the streets as we walk up the hill, but from their windows they wave and smile at us. We are carrying peace banners and strawberries we've just bought from the market, and a clarinet player in a red hat plays cheerful music. Until the two Israeli armoured personnel carriers appear, rolling down the hill and stopping several yards away, there is no sign of trouble. The soldier in the front vehicle gestures us away. We stop, put our hands in the air. Our negotiator steps forward to explain where we are wishing to go; this the soldiers will expect from previous volunteer work.

I don't remember seeing a gun. When I hear the first lot of bangs, I think, "They are using percussion grenades to scare us off, to make us think they are shooting." I've heard them before in Prague; they are startling, but I'm not frightened. We have our hands up, we are walking slowly backwards, and everyone is staying calm. No one is running. We are remembering our nonviolence training.

Even when several people in front of me suddenly seem to tumble back deeper into the group, I think, "They must be scared, so it's good they are away from the front." Everything is so quick, and shrapnel wounds are small, and the bleeding hasn't had a chance to start. It seems obvious now – if percussion grenades are designed to sound like gunshots, then of course, gunshots must sound like percussion grenades.

So when another series of bangs ring out, and simultaneously I feel a burning sensation in my middle, I am not very worried at first. "Okay," I think, "I'm wounded. This is going to be very *interesting*." I once read that Bertrand Russell said that the secret to happiness is being interested in as many things as possible. I had always remembered this, but I didn't know I had taken it to heart quite so thoroughly. However, my personal experience of dangerous situations is that time slows down so much that you have plenty of time for everything, even philosophising.

Next I think, "Well, I'd better get out of the front line now." I start to turn around, and then my legs collapse under me. Two Italians catch me, gently, as if they've been practising (they probably have) and carry me so smoothly in a fireman's lift to the Red Crescent ambulance accompanying us, that until I see the newspaper pictures later on I will assume I'd been in the arms of just one strong person.

I recall confused images of everyone still walking slowly backwards, holding hands, the Italian speakers pacing them with "Uno, due, tre." In our training we learnt that running away enables the soldiers to forget that we are their fellow humans and think of us as quarry. I also recall seeing that the ambulance is full, though mostly of people who can sit up. They squeeze me in crossways at the back, with my head in Mohammed's lap. Just before they shut the door I see Mick standing outside, and we have a daft conversation, with him saying, "Are you okay?" and me whispering hoarsely, "I'm fine."

I know at some point I do risk a glance down at the place my hands cover, half through my eyelashes, the way I try to censor grisly images when watching horror films. I see a little blood, but not too much. But by this time the burning is increasing, and I feel a weight slowly squashing me, becoming heavier and heavier, making it difficult to breathe. I have to shut my eyes just to concentrate on doing it.

"Perhaps my lungs have been damaged," I think. "That would be bad." (Later on, I find out it would have been appalling, because under those circumstances they sometimes puncture your chest immediately with the first hollow pointy thing anyone can find, so you don't drown in your own blood.) While breathing wasn't getting any harder, though, the sense of weight kept increasing (internal bleeding, someone later explained). "So it's not my lungs," I decide. "What's below my lungs?" I couldn't think. "What can it be? How can I have so little idea of my own anatomy? Is it something important? Do I need it? Do I have two of them?" I want more information.

"Mohammed," I croak, "I was hit by a piece of percussion grenade, was I?" "Ohhh, yes," says Mohammed. "A piece of percussion grenade. That's what it was. Absolutely, don't you worry. Just a piece of percussion grenade. No problem." For someone who has lots of occupation experience, he sounds very anxious. And now it occurs to me that actually I've been shot, with a real gun and a real bullet.

Oddly, this doesn't surprise me. I have long suspected someone would shoot me one day. "Am I dying?" I wonder. "I might be, right now. How do I feel about that?" This seems like an important question to ask myself. As is common for activists, sometimes I have found it very difficult to be alive in such a damaged world that I can't put right. Other times, considering risky situations, I have hoped that, if need be, I could somehow find within me the heroism of my own heroes. But if you have any sense of objectivity it is hard to take these thoughts seriously. Now, I might *be* dying. Is death in fact the worst thing that could happen to me? Am I scared?

No. I feel... only sadness. I feel that I would be very sad for my friends and family. For me, I feel... well, peaceful is the best word. I think quietly to myself that I have lived my 29 years trying to do my best. I am glad I came here, and if this is how I leave, then it feels like a good way to go.

By now we are at Beit Jala hospital. Here again, I only have images from the papers – someone manages to take a photo of me in the emergency room, being prodded at and making an awful face, for British newspaper readers to gaze at the next day. I whimper as they swing me off and on trolleys and bump me into lifts. They are in such a hurry. "Slow down," I want to say. "I'm managing, no need to rush on my account," but by this stage I can't even whisper.

In the lift, I suddenly have a thought that, for the first time, brings real fear with it. "Here I am in an occupied country, with curfews and closed military zones and shortages. *What if the hospital is out of anaesthetic?*" The longer I think about it, the more likely it seems. I know they run out of basic things; we'd been asked to bring in medical stuff if we could. There is no *way* I am going to be operated on without it. "Will they ask me? Will they give me the option? Can I say, no thanks, I prefer death?" – which I really, *really* do – "Will anyone speak English?"

With immense effort, I open my eyes, and find myself looking up from an operating table at a circle of faces in hospital masks. Distracted by the thought "It's just like on ER," I scarcely notice the pinprick to my arm. But swiftly, everything is fading. Beit Jala hospital does have anaesthetic after all.

The soldier who shot me also injured nine others with shrapnel, including an accompanying BBC journalist. The Israeli PR machine described the incident as "foreigners accidentally caught in crossfire", but considering that the only guns at the incident were held by Israeli soldiers and the only targets were ourselves, this was a lie as calculated as the shooting itself. The camera footage I have seen since shows the soldier checking in on his radio just before opening fire. It was the first time international volunteers were deliberately shot, and was the start of a series of attacks apparently designed to scare off the increasingly effective ISM and similar organisations. In fact, the number of volunteers increased.

After dark, while I was unconscious, Operation "Defensive Shield", the largest Israeli military incursion into the West Bank since 1967, reached Bethlehem, and the bombs began to fall. Many members of ISM were in bandages and all agreed that their status appeared to have dramatically changed. However, most decided they would continue to participate in the delivery of food and first aid, and also (bearing banners citing the Geneva Convention) accompany attempts by intrepid Red Crescent medics to bring ambulances to wounded civilians. But the Israeli army followed their usual policy and turned the ambulances back.

Not many people get the chance to seriously consider dying. What I discovered was that I really *am* willing to die for what I believe in. Not because I'm particularly heroic, but because what I believe in is worth dying for: justice, sustainability, peace, a decent future for the child I hope for. And Palestine had definitely captured my attention now. The intensive care ward I was held in remained virtually empty the whole week, since the civilians in the refugee camps, who desperately needed to be there, were not permitted ambulance rescue. Many did not survive even minor injuries. This shocked me into learning "far from help" first aid and planning my next volunteering visit. The first aid training indirectly set me on the path of becoming a healthcare professional.

And when, in 2008, I found myself meeting a collection of crazy and wonderful people who felt the only thing to do about the Israeli navy's blockade of Gaza was to find some fishing boats and sail right on past them, there was nothing to hold me back. But that's another story.

# Against the odds

**Helen Steel**, one of the "McLibel Two", on standing up to one of the world's largest corporations, and dealing with the aftermath of her relationship with an undercover policeman.

*Interview by Angharad Penrhyn Jones*

*You started campaigning at a young age. How did it all begin? What was the trigger?*

At secondary school my best friend and I wanted to study Agriculture O level, but we were told that only boys could do it. Eventually the school agreed we could go ahead if we could find boys willing to swap with us. Happily we managed to find some boys who wanted to learn to cook! So we learned about farming and helped with looking after the pigs, sheep and cows at school. One day the class went on a trip to the slaughterhouse, taking the school pigs. Seeing animals being slaughtered I was so horrified that I became a vegetarian. Then at an open evening for parents at my school my friend and I set up a mock-up life-size veal calf in a crate, and asked parents to sign a petition against veal crates, which at that time were legal in this country. I guess that was my first experience of activism. I was around 14 or 15.

When I went to sixth-form college I saw a poster for the Hunt Saboteurs Association and found out more about hunting. My friend and I started regularly going out hunt sabbing a local hare hunt. Sometimes we saw hares being ripped apart, which was sickening; other times we managed to stop them being killed and realised the value of taking action. Some of the people we came into contact with were vegans and I then became a vegan and was very involved with the animal rights movement, especially around factory farming and vivisection.

I also got involved with other environmental and social justice movements. When I was 17, I took part in a protest at Greenham Common airbase, where 30,000 women surrounded the base in opposition to nuclear weapons. It was an amazing and inspiring experience being among so many women taking action.

*Have you ever studied politics in a formal capacity?*

I haven't been to university or studied politics and my family wasn't particularly political. My dad was a union rep at his workplace but I'm not sure I was very conscious of what that meant at the time. My politics come from life, I suppose, things that I see in life. It's like a gut instinct. If I see injustice or oppression I want to fight it.

Taking part in protests against apartheid and staying in a pit village and joining picket lines during the miners' strike, through experiences like that I became aware of the injustices that are going on worldwide and how so many of those things are connected. Basically, most injustice is caused by the greed of a minority of the population, and their complete disregard for the effect that it has on other people, the environment, animals.

*Why did you become involved with London Greenpeace?*

I first came across London Greenpeace in the early 1980s. They had called for a day of action in the City of London, saying that this was essentially the heart of the war industry – people profiting from the sale and use of bombs and weapons around the world. But the protests were also about the multitude of injustices and oppression caused by capitalism. I took part in those protests and was inspired by the range of people and actions involved.

Then a few years later I went along to a London Greenpeace meeting and ended up getting involved. I liked the format, and I liked the people. It wasn't part of the bigger Greenpeace. It was an independent, open, non-hierarchical collective. Some campaigning groups can be dogmatic and everyone's got to hold exactly the same view, and it's all about people appealing to politicians to do something for us. London Greenpeace was much more open, with no obligation to get involved in everything, and also it was about taking action yourself rather than asking politicians to do stuff for you – DIY politics. They were a nice bunch of people doing useful stuff!

*Why did London Greenpeace decide to target McDonald's?*

I don't know what specifically kick-started the campaign as I wasn't involved with the group at that time. But I know there had been a lot of articles about the harmful effects of junk food, the destruction of rainforests for cattle rearing, the environmental impact of packaging, and about workers at McDonald's being poorly paid and not being allowed to join trade unions. There were protests – in Ireland, for example –

where workers tried to form unions and McDonald's put a lot of effort into preventing that.

During the trial McDonald's admitted they had a hit squad of top executives who'd fly in to a branch anywhere in the world if the workers were trying to set up a union. They were that desperate to prevent people from forming a union. It's such a tightly-controlled ship so I expect people picked up on some of that.

*I suppose McDonald's epitomised a lot of issues that people felt strongly about at the time, brought all those issues together.*

Yes, and I think another important thing was that McDonald's had a very high profile – they were constantly advertising, telling people how great they were, and when someone's really in your face like that, when they are actually doing lots of pretty bad stuff, it tends to grate. People aren't prepared to put up with that. They're going to say, "Hang on, let's get to the truth of what's going on."

So a small group of people within London Greenpeace produced a factsheet which essentially took a look at the overall effect of a multinational company, rather than just a single issue. They took what was in scientific and specialist journals and brought it into the public realm. This was probably the first time all this material had been collated and brought together in one place aimed at the general public. It was quite ground-breaking, really. And the campaign really struck a chord with the public. I know that whenever I went out leafleting about McDonald's the leaflets were always really popular. People wanted to know more.

*And McDonald's were very threatened by that. You were capturing the public imagination.*

Yes. If you spend several billion dollars every year on advertising, you want to make sure people have a certain opinion of you and you want them to keep coming back. You don't want anything that contradicts that. That's one of the interesting things the trial showed, when the trial was on there was a lot of negative publicity about McDonald's in national newspapers. It became mainstream, and I guess for the first time, the level of criticism about their practices reached slightly closer to the amount of McDonald's advertising people were exposed to. At that point you start to see the impacts. And after the trial, their profits went down.

To me, that really demonstrated how much society is influenced by advertising and corporate propaganda. And how much effort those in power have to put in to keep everybody behaving in ways which are actually detrimental to people and the environment. I guess that gives hope that it is worth doing something. A lot of the time people feel defeated, we're constantly told that people are selfish, they don't care, etc., but actually, people are behaving in those ways because they're being influenced by advertising and capitalist propaganda. And this isn't something that's impossible to change, it's not to do with innate human traits.

*How did you find out that you were being served libel writs over this factsheet?*

I got out of my partner's van outside his flat and as I stepped away from the van this guy approached me. He said, "Helen," and I had no idea who he was. I didn't say anything and he threw this envelope at my feet. When I opened it I saw it was the writ. I was really angry when I read it, I was like, "How dare you ask me to apologise for a whole load of things that are true! I'm not going to do that."

*Plenty of people have said sorry to McDonald's in the past. McDonald's threatened to sue at least 50 organisations in the 80s alone and all these organisations issued retractions and apologies. The* Guardian, *The BBC, Channel 4, and many, many others. What made you take such a massive risk? Why was it so difficult to say sorry?*

I was bullied when I was younger, and what I learned from that was that if you don't stand up to bullies they come back. They come back for more and they bully other people as well. Something I perceive as bullying really triggers something off in me! [Laughs.] It's such a clear case of bullying and intimidation – because they have financial muscle, they can use the legal system to walk all over you. It made me really angry.

*There were five of you, weren't there? You were all served libel writs, and three of you did end up apologising.*

Yes. Well, my instinctive reaction was to refuse to apologise. We then had to get legal advice, which wasn't easy because libel is such a specialised area of law and there aren't actually any legal aid libel lawyers – legal aid isn't available for libel claims. It tends to be a rich man's province. We were lucky enough to get help from Keir Starmer, who years later went on to become Director of Public Prosecutions. He offered to help us for free, which was fantastic, because we didn't have any money, never the mind the sort of money you'd need to fight a libel case. We met with Birnberg's solicitors and Keir, and essentially we were warned that we were on a hiding to nothing, fighting a libel case against a huge multinational corporation. It's very expensive, and complex, and the onus is on you to prove everything. You can have a peer-reviewed scientific article that says XYZ, but you can't bring that to court – you've actually got to bring the scientist to court to put the case forward, and all that costs money, you've got to pay for their time and all their expenses. So the advice we got was to put all our energies into a different campaign. They said we'd be fighting with our hands tied behind our backs, against top libel lawyers.

The other three people decided they didn't want to put themselves through that, which I totally understand. But it stuck in the throat with me to apologise for something that didn't deserve an apology, and one of the others, Dave, then agreed to come in with me, which is just as well because I definitely couldn't have done it on my own. [Laughs.] It was exhausting.

*It was a campaign for free speech, really, not just against McDonald's.*

Absolutely. There's a long and determined history by those in power to stifle the voices of people who want to create a fairer world. Because if the people succeed it means that those in power lose some of their privileges. So there's a lot at stake. And they put a lot of effort into trying to cling onto their privileges.

*And do you think the legal system as it is props that up?*

Of course. The legal system defends that power and privilege. That was something we realised quite early on with the case. During one of the first hearings we went to, we asked the master – early on you have a master rather than a judge – we asked him about the process and he said if we didn't know, we should be represented. And we said, "There's no legal aid, so how are we supposed to be represented?" He said that was essentially our problem. He wasn't interested in explaining what we had to do for this hearing. During the trial itself I can recall questioning one of McDonald's executives about why they didn't use some of their millions of profits to raise the wages of the staff, and the judge intervened and said that the shareholders wouldn't like that and whether we liked it or not we lived in a capitalist society. We realised that if it came down to our word against McDonald's, we would lose, because the establishment would back the powerful entity.

So we went for a strategy of trying to get admissions out of McDonald's witnesses, so that it became their corporate propaganda against what their witnesses had admitted in court. And that way, the court couldn't just dismiss our case. We were using their own statements against them.

In the end that worked well, with some very damning rulings against them – the judge ruled that McDonald's marketing had "pretended to a positive nutritional benefit which their food (high in fat and salt, etc.) did not match"; that they "exploit children" with their advertising strategy; are "culpably responsible for animal cruelty"; and "pay low wages, helping to depress wages in the catering trade." Then on appeal the court added to that, saying it was fair comment to say that McDonald's employees worldwide "do badly in terms of pay and conditions", and true that "if one eats enough McDonald's food, one's diet may well become high in fat, etc., with the very real risk of heart disease." However the court still ruled that we had libelled McDonald's over some points and said we should pay them £40,000 damages – which we refused to do – not that we had the money anyway!

*You were denied a jury trial. Why was that?*

McDonald's made an application for the trial to be heard without a jury, because they argued that the issues were too complex for ordinary members of the public to understand. And we said, hang on, we're ordinary members of the public, we're not represented. If we can't understand it, we can't have a fair trial. If we can understand it, then so can the jury. Essentially they knew a jury might well be sympathetic to our claims, and unsympathetic to the idea of this massive corporation trying to quash dissenting voices. A jury would be much more likely to see through their propaganda. We took that to an appeal and sadly lost.

*When you went into this case, did you have any sense that it would be such a mammoth task?*

[Laughs.] No. Initially McDonald's own estimates were that it would last just four or five weeks.

*At the time it was the longest trial in English history, wasn't it?*

That's right, yes. It was nearly three years from start to finish with 314 days in court. And there were pre-trial hearings too. If I'd known at the start how long it was going to take I might not have fought it. [Laughs.] It was absolutely exhausting. I wouldn't have apologised to McDonald's but I might have been prepared to go to jail.

*Would it really have come to that?*

Well, McDonald's were asking for an injunction to prevent us handing out leaflets. And obviously if you break an injunction you can be jailed. So, ultimately, they would have been asking for us to be jailed. But the defiance campaign meant that on the Saturday after the verdict, over 400,000 leaflets were distributed outside 500 of McDonald's 750 UK stores, and solidarity protests were held in over a dozen countries, McDonald's realised that if they tried to get us jailed it would backfire.

*Keir Starmer said that many top lawyers would have been proud to get the answers you got out of McDonald's witnesses. He said you grasped the complexities of the legal system very quickly and that he was left feeling humbled. And Mike Mansfield QC, a highly-acclaimed barrister, said he had undying admiration for you and Dave. Have you ever considered entering the legal profession?*

A few people asked me that, so I did think about it, but because there's such an imbalance of power I would find it incredibly frustrating and depressing to be part of it on a daily basis. I think I prefer to be out in the real world. There were a lot of times during the case when it was like being on another planet. We're standing there arguing about, for example, whether the minimum wage constitutes low pay. Of course it does, because it's the minimum wage! Of course it's low pay! Why should we have to spend hours in court arguing about that? I think I'd just get frustrated.

*Is it fair to say that the trial took over your whole life?*

For about four years, yes. I had very little time for anything else.

*How did you support yourself financially during the trial?*

For most of the trial I was working behind the bar in a nightclub on Friday and Saturday nights until three in the morning. During the week I'd get up at six to prepare questions for the cross-examination, be in the court all day, and then come home and work on the next lot of documents before going to bed. It was round the clock, really.

*How did you not burn out?*

[Laughs.] I don't know. There were a couple of points when I thought, I've had enough. I can't cope with this anymore. At that point it was definitely a good job there were two of us. And we had huge support from the public, writing letters of support, donating money, continuing protests, all that gave us strength to carry on. We had some help initially from people coming to court to take notes for us, and some legal advice on specific issues. But none of this made up for the fact that we didn't have a full legal team. McDonald's had two barristers in court – highly trained libel lawyers – and at least two solicitors, plus a host of other people to help them with logistics, and McDonald's themselves doing the PR. Essentially me and Dave were doing all of that. The support campaign was crucial in getting out leaflets and press releases, but we were involved in that as well. In terms of the legal stuff and all the processes around getting witness statements, getting witnesses to court, we did nearly all of it. We had a hundred-and-eighty witnesses from twenty countries. And we were compiling cross-examination questions and doing the cross-examining. So it was shattering. It was very hard to keep going sometimes. But the messages of support and solidarity from the public, and reports of protests around the world, kept us going.

*Was it exhilarating, in a way, interrogating executives from a massive corporation? It's not an opportunity most people get.*

That was one of the good things about the experience. Normally the people who run these corporations are completely unaccountable to the wider public, who are affected by their actions. But when they were in the witness box they had to answer our questions. And we could ask them about all sorts of things that normally they don't have to bother engaging with. Some of them were better than others at handling it. Some of them came out with ludicrous rubbish. Their environmental officer said something to the effect that it was an environmental benefit to dump waste because otherwise you'd be left with vast empty gravel pits around the country.

*[Laughs.] Did you manage to keep a straight face?*

It was difficult sometimes. What was the other one? Coca-Cola is nutritious because it's providing water and that's part of a balanced diet. Unbelievable.

*You'd think that would be thrown out of court.*

Well, yes. Actually, when you read the verdict you see how biased the legal system is because things they said that were utterly ludicrous were not ridiculed, whereas things that we said which were even slightly contestable were immediately dismissed. We had to work ten times harder to be taken seriously.

*What did you make of the media coverage of the trial?*

With a few exceptions, it was quite frustrating. The

*Independent* covered it quite consistently for quite a long time and published some very good articles about the evidence being given in court. But then it tailed off. The *Guardian* did some good stuff as well.

But it became really obvious that the media is mostly not interested in conveying the realities of the world that we live in. Their main focus is celebrity gossip and soap opera, diverting people away from things that affect their day to day lives. And when they covered our trial they often wanted to focus on what we were wearing, our appearance, etc., which was very frustrating,

*How did you feel about being in the limelight?*

I've never felt comfortable speaking in public, or on telly, or on the radio. But I became very conscious of the fact that it was just Dave doing the talking and that was so stereotypical, the man doing the talking. It wasn't what he wanted but my lack of confidence in speaking made it hard. So I essentially forced myself to talk to the media and over time it got a bit easier, but I still don't find it easy. I think this is something that affects a lot of people, but especially women, and so you end up with a certain subset of people expressing their views in public, and the more those views are expressed the more wider society assumes that they are the norm, even though a large proportion of the population is not speaking out about what it believes and may not agree. So I think it's really important that people find the confidence to speak out, so it's not just the views of people in power that filter into our subconscious.

*The trial must have tested your friendship with Dave.*

We had quite a few arguments. That's sort of inevitable in

any situation where you're thrown together with someone else and you've got to work with them intensely for a long time on something stressful. But it's important to see the bigger picture. We were working towards something we both felt strongly about and it was far more important to make sure that that was the focus of our anger and frustration, not each other. I remember Dave telling me at one stage that it's much easier to burn bridges than to build them. I think that's very true, and that's probably why we don't achieve as much as we could. Sometimes it's much easier to walk away from people than to work with them. But if we want to change things, to create a better world, we have to work with people we don't agree with 100 per cent on everything.

*What happened when McDonald's tried to settle with you out of court?*

Essentially they offered to make a substantial payment to a third party, a charity or something, which could be used to do work that we believed in – if we agreed to stop fighting the case.

They knew they were getting a lot of bad publicity, which is exactly what they didn't want. But one of the key things they wanted was for us to agree never to criticise them publicly again. They claimed this wasn't an infringement of our freedom of speech because we could still criticise McDonald's in private. [Laughs.] So I wrote back to them and said we'd consider their request if they agreed not to make any public recommendations for McDonald's food or advertise it, but that this wouldn't stop them from recommending it privately to their friends and neighbours. [Laughs.] They never replied. To be honest, it was a mixture of funny and insulting.

One of the guys they sent over was senior vice-president of McDonald's, but prior to working for McDonald's he'd been involved in psychological warfare operations. So that was quite an interesting choice of person to send over to talk to us. They've got quite a collection of people working for them, a lot of ex-police and ex-military.

*That doesn't go with the happy clown image...*

Exactly. But that's what they need, because they've got to control their image so tightly. We're bombarded with images that they are here for our benefit, giving us fantastic choice and pleasure. They don't want people to contemplate that really corporations are just about making as much money as possible at whatever cost to society and at whatever cost to the environment. If people did, then the vast majority of the public would reject that. But that's not the side that's portrayed.

*I love the footage [in the McLibel documentary] of you and Dave walking out of the courtroom on the final day. It's very moving. You both look so happy.*

[Laughs.] We were! It was the end!

*But you also look really self-possessed. How did you feel when the verdict came out?*

I felt very, very relieved that it was over. I thought it was fantastic that despite the overwhelming odds we'd managed to convince a judge that several of the issues in the factsheet were true. There was also frustration that we hadn't won on other issues. The odds were stacked against us and some issues were almost impossible to prove, like the link between the beef used in McDonald's burgers and the deforestation in Brazil. Getting witnesses to come from the other side of the world was difficult. McDonald's demanded that we should prove that particular cattle had grazed on a particular plot of land, that could then demonstrably have been used in a McDonald's burger. It

*Helen Steel and Dave Morris outside the High Court on the day the McLibel trial became the UK's longest libel trial. © Helen Steel*

was the same with nutrition: they wanted us to show that it was McDonald's food that had made someone obese rather than something else they'd eaten over a long period of time, but that's impossible.

*They might have won on a few technical points, but you and Dave captured the hearts and minds of the public, which arguably is a much more important thing. So it was a devastating verdict for McDonald's and it's been described as the worst corporate PR disaster in history.*

Yes, and I think the public knew that the criticisms were essentially true. They can see when the battle you're fighting is unfair. So I think we did win the battle for public opinion. And some of the issues the judge found against us were overturned in the Court of Appeal, like the link between their food and heart disease.

*George Ritzer [author of* Globalization*] said that from very small beginnings you created a worldwide movement.*

*After Eric Schlosser interviewed you about the trial he decided to write* Fast Food Nation, *which went on to become a global bestseller. Naomi Klein's* No Logo *also covered the trial. Then we had the success of the film* Supersize Me, *and the Slow Food movement, and José Bové's protests in France. Do you think you helped to catalyse a mass movement, a mass resistance to fast food and everything it represents?*

I think we were part of it. Certainly the trial helped to achieve much wider exposure of the issues. London Greenpeace didn't initiate the criticisms – those were being made by experts in their fields before LGP came along – but the trial brought the criticisms to the wider public. Obviously the trial received international media publicity, and also there was a mass defiance campaign with millions of the leaflets handed out around the world, in much greater numbers than before the case started. That really helped spread the debate about the fast food industry and the effect it's having on society.

*It turns out that McDonald's were spying on London Greenpeace. Can you talk about that?*

In the pre-trial hearings McDonald's served four witness statements from private investigators who said they'd been to meetings of London Greenpeace. They applied for their names to be kept secret, but in the end we succeeded in getting the names disclosed, and it was clear that they'd attended a lot more meetings than they'd covered in the statements. Eventually we realised there were at least seven private investigators over an 18-month period attending our meetings. Also the documents showed they'd stolen letters that had been sent to the group and made comments in their notes about the security of the building. We cross-examined them about it and one of them admitted that he'd broken into our office, using a credit card to get in through the lock. So they were using all sorts of underhand tactics. One of the female private investigators had a relationship with one of the men in the group. I was totally disgusted when I found out about that. This was before I found out about my ex-partner being an undercover police officer. She remained in the group after the writs were served and was spying on our discussions about how to fight the case and the campaign.

*One of the female spies broke ranks and joined you as a witness in court.*

Yes. By some amazing coincidence, she ended up on a nutrition course with Boo Armstrong, the sister of Franny, who was making a documentary about McLibel. The woman, Fran Tiller, ended up talking to Boo about how she felt really bad about what she'd done, spying on campaigners, not knowing that Boo's sister was connected to the case. And when we spoke to Fran she said she was absolutely willing to give evidence in court. She'd never felt comfortable about what she was doing – she actually thought the work we were doing as a group was good and shouldn't be interfered with.

*Were you aware that some members of the group seemed a bit... different?*

When you're working with other people you don't want to be suspicious of them, it can be really disruptive. But there was something a bit strange about some of them. They didn't seem to have any real politics. But there was nothing we could really put a finger on. It was my partner, who turned out to be an undercover copper, who first pointed a finger at the McDonald's spies. He phoned me one night and said that he'd been followed home, and then we tried to check out what was going on. One of the spies left soon after that, he may have realised he had been rumbled, but others continued and we didn't find out until the trial.

*Your partner at the time, John, was an undercover police officer working for the Special Demonstration Squad [SDS, a unit set up by the Metropolitan Police to infiltrate British protest groups, from 1968 to 2008]. So as a campaign group, you were being spied on not just by McDonald's, but by the state as well. Did you ever have suspicions about John, or did that revelation come much later?*

It was years later. John got involved with London Greenpeace not that long after I got involved, coming to meetings on a regular basis. And he would regularly offer to drive people home afterwards, which turns out to be a common tactic, because it's a good way to find out where people live. I was usually the last person to be dropped off and we'd end up having long conversations, getting to know each other quite well – or so I thought. We became closer and he asked me out a few times. We ended up in a relationship and became very, very close in a short space of time. I was surprised by how intense the feelings were, which is something the other women have said as well [the women who were manipulated into having sexual relationships with undercover police spies]. It seems the officers have been extensively trained in how to lie and manipulate emotions – they are very skilled at it.

After a while we rented a flat and lived together. We talked about buying a place somewhere rural, growing our own food and having children. Then he disappeared leaving a letter saying he had to sort his head out. He came back shortly after, but appeared to be going through some sort of a breakdown which continued on and off for the rest of our relationship. His story was that he had no one left in his life, that all his family had died and he had no siblings. The only other woman he'd loved had left him. He said he was terrified I was going to do the same thing. So his solution was to walk away from me to prevent it happening. He kept going and coming back and it was very draining emotionally. When he disappeared the final time I worried that he might even kill himself. The breakdown seems to be part of their exit strategy, because they did it to the other women as well. It's partly to do with making it believable that you've disappeared. If you suddenly vanish and don't contact anyone, people wonder what has happened and might become suspicious. But if you appear to have a mental breakdown before you go, they are more likely to think that explains your disappearance...

The whole thing was highly manipulative. I became really conscious of that when I re-read his letters recently, reading about his family and how he'd been abused, and now knowing that it wasn't true. These were not love letters, they were like psychological warfare – breaking you down so that you can't operate.

*So they were using very specific tactics and were trained to do this?*

There is a clear pattern in the letters they sent to us. Having spoken to Peter Francis [whistleblower from SDS], he said they didn't get formal classroom training. But they learned from each other using something like a mentoring system. So maybe somewhere along the way someone who's a deeply warped person has developed these strategies and then taught others, so it's gone down the line. So what you've got is one individual warped person becoming an entire warped institution. And it's institutionally sexist, the way they've been treating women. It's emotional manipulation and abuse.

*One activist went a step further than that and said she'd been raped by that institution, that she'd been raped by the state. Another activist referred to people having their phones hacked, and said that this was much worse, and that her body had been hacked. Do you feel equally strongly?*

Sometimes it's hard to know exactly how I feel about it. When I found out, I felt totally and utterly violated. There are some ways in which I feel it's like rape. And there are other ways in which it's different.

*It's a very unusual situation, isn't it? So presumably you don't have a framework within which to interpret it.*

That's true. When I finally tracked down John's marriage certificate and it said 'police officer', I can just remember my blood running cold, and feeling really, really, sick and trembling, and feeling really violated. And I remember being in a supermarket once and seeing someone who reminded me of John. When I came out of the supermarket and cycled down the road, I had this sudden overwhelming feeling of being utterly sick, and thinking that I'd had sex with a copper, and wondering whether he'd been reporting back on all of that, all of our relationship, whether they were all laughing and joking about it. That feeling of violation was... I don't know. [Starts crying.]

We didn't consent to that. In that sense it is like rape. But at the moment the sex took place it wasn't forced. I consented to that, but I didn't consent to having sex with a policeman who was trying to undermine the movements I was involved in, and I didn't consent to being in an intimate relationship with the state and having all my private life and thoughts shared with them.

*Is there any part of you that wonders if maybe John's feelings were real? Peter Francis [the former undercover agent and whistleblower] said that he doesn't know who he is anymore after his undercover operations. The spies lost their identities and became screwed-up themselves by their experiences. It's not straightforward, is it? Possibly they didn't know who they were.*

[Sighs.] I don't know. After John disappeared, all sorts of possibilities went through my mind to try to explain what had happened. One of them was that he had been an undercover police officer. That possibility meant I felt I couldn't talk to many people about what had happened, because then I'd be less likely to find out the truth. If my partner who I'd lived with could be an undercover police officer, then so could anyone else that I knew. And the more people I talked to, the more chance there was that it would get back to them and they'd make extra efforts to prevent me from finding him.

But I spoke to a few long-term friends, and one pointed out that even if he was a spy, it was still possible that he loved me. And for a long time I wanted to believe that that was true. Because it just seemed so cold-hearted and callous, to think that someone could behave this way towards another human being, that the entire relationship was a complete fabrication, that me and other women had been used in this way. I guess it was kind of comforting to believe that maybe they did genuinely love and care about us. But having gone through all his letters in the last year or two, and since finding out that many things in them are untrue, I've realised he was deliberately manipulating my emotions. Like he talks about his parents being dead when they were actually alive. He knew that I cared about him and was upset by what he was going through, he would have known that the letters would have distressed me, yet he went ahead, made it all up and sent it to me. That's not love, it's abuse.

*How long did it take you to get to the truth?*

He disappeared in 1992 and I finally had the confirmation that he was an undercover policeman in 2011. Almost 19 years.

*And he took the identity of a dead child.*

I'd heard about the "Day of the Jackal" – I knew of that method, where people pick up the identity of a child who's died. And one day I was passing St Catherine's house, where the register of births, deaths and marriages are kept, and had this instinctive feeling to go in there and look at the death records. I started from the year of his birth as I knew him, as John Barker. Eventually I found out he had been using the name of a child who'd died when he was eight years old. And that left me with this great void. I'd been living with someone for two years and I didn't even know who he was. I didn't even know his name. I didn't know anything about him. And it really throws all your other relationships into doubt. If you can live with someone for that length of time and not notice that they're not who they said they were, how can you be sure that anything going on around you is real? It threw my head in a total mess. How could I trust my own judgement?

*Have you and the other women who were violated in this way been able to support each other through this process?*

Yes, that's one of the fantastic things about the legal case that we're bringing [against the police]. We decided to bring the case because when the Mark Kennedy case was exposed [an undercover policeman who infiltrated environmental groups and had relationships with female campaigners], the line from the police was that this was very much about one rogue officer, that it was terrible what he'd done but he'd gone off and done his own thing. But they knew that there were lots of officers involved and other women who'd been abused in this way. I felt if the women came together to take a joint action, it would be much harder for them to carry on with this line. There are eight of us involved in this case, who had relationships with five different officers over a period spanning about 25 years. So they can't claim it was just a maverick officer. It becomes much more apparent that it's an institution doing this. It's a deliberate tactic.

It's been so helpful to hear the other women's experiences, to see the similarities in the tactics used and to realise that it wasn't your stupidity or naïvety or reckless indifference that caused you to be in this situation. It's the fact that they're deeply manipulative, trained liars, and they could pull the wool over anyone's eyes. You might start having doubts, as you might start having doubts in any relationships, but in this particular circumstance, they've got the whole state behind them to prop up those lies with false documents and so on, to make sure that you don't work out what's happening. And if you challenged them they would immediately be able to come up with some bullshit story that left you with enough doubt that you believed them.

*Do you think the police are still using sex to gain intelligence on protest groups?*

It's hard to say. Since we've brought the case they've put out conflicting messages. Some police and politicians have said it's outrageous and shouldn't happen, and others have said that they need to use these tactics because otherwise lives would be at risk. No one's given us a concrete example of how having sex with campaigners would save lives. Anyway, I should say that in a lot of ways we feel that it's the emotional intimacy of the relationships that is more damaging than the sexual aspect of it. That's what really messes with your mind.

The police have served a defence which mostly relies on them saying they can neither confirm nor deny that any of the men are undercover policemen. They want to try to sweep it under the carpet. They say they can't talk about it because they're worried about jeopardising the safety of these guys and future undercover officers. And of course, once you can't talk about it because it jeopardises people's safety, then you can't have a discussion about the harm it has caused, and so we can all forget about it, we can pretend it didn't happen.

My suspicion is that they'll continue with undercover relationships if they can, but they may be nervous at the moment because there's so much publicity about it, and there's more risk of them getting found out. I certainly think that if the pressure and publicity isn't kept up, they will go back to using it. So we're really determined to make sure it stays in the spotlight. We don't want to see it happen to anybody else.

*Who or what inspires you to campaign? Do you have any political role models?*

I take my inspiration from lots of people fighting against injustice and oppression around the world. You read stories in the paper or on the internet and you think, "Wow! These people did that and that's really impressive." That gives me the confidence to fight on and to remember that it *is* worth fighting on.

There was one thing I found inspiring recently. There used to be six hospitals in the borough that I live in, and now there's only one left – it's been converted to a mental health hospital – and they're trying to sell off two-thirds of the site. I'm involved in a campaign to stop this from happening. And what you encounter is a lot of comments like: "You've got to be realistic," or, "That's the way things are," or, "There's no point fighting, because you won't get anywhere." That's what people in power want you to believe, so you don't bother them with demands for change.

But I went for a walk near King's Cross recently, and there's a lovely little park there, Calthorpe Gardens, an oasis of calm, and space for children to play, in the middle of all these manic busy streets with all these tall buildings. At the entrance there's a plaque that says that in the 80s the site was earmarked for an office block, and that local people fought for this green space to be conserved. If they hadn't fought, there would be an office block on that site! That really inspired me, because it shows that it is possible, that people can make a difference. It just goes to show that it's always worth fighting, even when you think the odds are stacked against you.

# The freedom of others

Activist and artivist **Skye Chirape** on being forced to flee her country because of her sexuality, and having to battle her way out of a UK detention centre.

I had difficulties maintaining a sense of self in my own country. Growing up in Zimbabwe as a female, I often felt irrelevant, even within my extended family. As a lesbian my existence was not valid and, had I not left the country, my sexuality might have cost me jail time, "corrective" rape, forced marriage, banishment, beatings, or perhaps even death. Throughout my childhood and adolescence in Zimbabwe I did not come across one single portrayal of "gayness", "queerness" or "lesbianism" in the context of African-ness. Prior to leaving Zimbabwe, my identity did not have a language or name. I had never heard of the words gay or lesbian.

I began to have sexual feelings towards girls when I was about 12. I didn't understand why I had these feelings or what they meant. Nor could I comprehend why it was immoral to be attracted to a person of the same sex. There was no discourse about homosexuality around me: it was not discussed in the community or in the media, and so I had no framework in which to place these feelings. I had my first same-sex experience around this time. Unfortunately my maternal grandmother caught us. The head family members held a meeting. Following that meeting, my own mother beat me with the branch of a guava tree. Though no one spoke of what had happened, I sensed that I had committed a terrible sin. My family would now keep a close eye on my behaviour.

Due to my middle class and strict Christian upbringing, I found everyday life a challenge. My deceased father (a scientist) and mother (a former accountant) were bound by traditional customs which were stifling to me. That most of my maternal uncles were politicians, whose attitudes to gender roles were bound by patriarchal social systems, made me feel more isolated still.

I was vocal and opinionated, artistic and eccentric. My perceived rebelliousness resulted in punishment from my mother, since my actions were perceived to bring "shame" upon the family. I was not allowed to wear trousers, for example, and riled by this injustice, I would borrow my brother's oversized denim trousers and wear them to school. My mother would be furious. Also, when forced to cook, at times when I was supposed to be studying, I was merciless with the salt jar. My brothers were free to get on with their studies, but my needs were not perceived as being as important as theirs. Putting too much salt on the food was a form of protest. On those days no one could swallow my food, and I was lashed for it. I rarely shed a tear: by then I was used to beatings. I felt that by showing my vulnerability I would only bring satisfaction to my tormenters, so I trained myself to hide my emotions. Over the years I have learned to cry and am slowly learning to feel comfortable expressing my vulnerability.

The idea of questioning one's own gender role was

considered "uncultured". I have no qualms about other people choosing to take on conventional gender roles, but I wanted to do things differently. I did not wish to be boxed in by a particular gender role. *"Nhubu, uri nhubu yemwana"* (rabble rouser): those were my mother's words to me, and they have stained my childhood memories. My relationship with my mother has remained difficult to this day.

Many families in African societies are concerned about their positions in the community. Individual preferences don't often count: village traditions are all-important (hence the African proverb: "It takes a whole village to raise a child."). Anyone who is perceived to be going against the norm is viewed as a disgrace. In Zimbabwe, homosexuality is illegal, and therefore in the land I grew up in, my very existence is unlawful. It is unimaginable to think of expressing your sexuality in Zimbabwe, as there are no laws to protect you from violent retributions. Other visible queer people have refused to leave Zimbabwe and continue to fight.

While it is often claimed that homosexuality is un-African, studies by historians and anthropologists have revealed that same-sex relationships existed in pre-colonial Africa. Archives of oral storytelling have shown that people in same-sex unions, along with people of third gender, were considered to have mystical powers, and in Southern Africa they were respected in their roles as traditional healers. Various types of same-sex unions have existed throughout African history, embedded within the customs and traditions of many societies, ranging from informal, unsanctioned relationships to highly ritualised unions.

Boy wives and female husbands are prevalent in oral traditions of the Bantu tribes. In Southern Africa and the Nile region, women-to-women marriages between Sangomas and

Kalenjin people were also welcomed and accepted alongside heterosexual marriages. Mpho women maintained same-sex relations with other women and it appears that these relationships were not deemed threatening by their husbands. In the Ibgo tribe in Nigeria, there is evidence of the existence of female "husbands". In Zimbabwe, spiritual leaders believed sexuality to be related to spiritual powers and spiritual possessions.

Hence colonialism did not bring about homosexuality: homophobia appears to have been a by-product of colonialism, along with patriarchal systems of government, social stratification, and the introduction of a fundamentalist Christianity with its repressive moral codes.

Yet this idea that homosexuality is somehow un-African and non-existent is widely believed. The research figures are often cited by white academics, who have little knowledge of African cultures. How can we know how widespread homosexuality is in Africa, when many homosexuals live in hiding, when governments block reports from being published and consistently challenge the documenting of oral history?

South Africa's post-apartheid constitution was the first in the world to outlaw discrimination based on sexual orientation, and in 2006 South Africa became the fifth country in the world, and the first in Africa, to legalise same-sex marriage. Yet despite changes in the law, the black queer population still continues to experience homophobia and violence to a large extent. Human rights groups report ten cases per week in Cape Town alone. Since 2006, over 30 lesbians have been brutally raped and murdered. The looming anti-homosexuality bill in Uganda poses terrifying risks for the Ugandan gay, lesbian, bisexual and transgender community. In other countries across Africa church pulpits remain bastions of anti-gay rhetoric.

To suppress my sexuality would have been unimaginable, so I decided to leave Africa for the UK. Aged 20, having never travelled before, I went to London by myself. Being the fearless, independent spirit that I am, I was excited to leave home and to go out into the world. I arrived in England on a six month visitor's visa and enrolled at a college, making a hasty decision to study journalism. I was determined to raise awareness about important issues, but when I realised that I was going to be briefed on what issues to write about, I became disillusioned and walked away.

I signed up to do a psychology course, which was closer to my heart. My passion for psychology had been unearthed when I volunteered at a local children's home in Zimbabwe. I have always loved people. I attempt to live my life guided by the Ubuntu philosophy (human-ness/humanity): *I am well if you are well.*

During my second year of reading psychology at Thames Valley University, I sent off my passport to the Home Office department for a visa extension. In hindsight, I was naïve not to have made copies of my only source of ID. For seven years the Home Office withheld my passport and refrained from communicating with me. Every month I wrote to them. I sent faxes. I visited the Home Office's Lunar House in Croydon several times but was sent away. I sought the support of my local MP, and wrote to Number 10. Yet none of these interventions made a difference.

While sexual relations between men are illegal in Zimbabwe, sexual relations between women are not specifically legislated against. This has allowed the Home Office to conclude that many lesbians of Zimbabwean origin have not established a well-founded fear of persecution and that they do not qualify for asylum.

Without any evidence of identification it proved difficult to survive in London. It was a struggle to attend lectures when I had to undertake several menial jobs to fund my studies. As part of my psychology placement, I began working with children with autism; but as I was unable to apply for a CRB check, this work eventually became untenable.

Soon I was unemployable. I lost my only security – accommodation. My relationship ended. I was now poverty stricken. I had never experienced poverty until I arrived in the UK. I lost many friends; thankfully, others stood by me and even put me up on their couches for lengthy periods of time. Often I found myself seeking shelter on buses – the number 12 in particular. I felt vulnerable and exposed but I was determined to complete my studies. This often meant studying on the tube or sleeping in the university library. For years I struggled to stay sane.

Along with university staff and my employers, I contacted the Home Office over many years with regard to my passport. I never heard back from them. Then one day I received a letter identifying me as an illegal immigrant. I was to be deported! I was angered by this: I was not an illegal; the Home Office had made me illegal. On the advice of my solicitor, I decided to seek asylum, eight years after arriving in the UK. When my solicitor asked for the information the Home Office had on me, a huge folder of all my correspondence was included in the paperwork.

On the day I sought asylum at Lunar House, I was interviewed and kept waiting the whole day. Late at night, security bundled me into a barred-up security van. An immigration officer explained that they had run out of time to make a decision on my case, though I had been there from 6am. Next to me in the security van was a young, confused and tearful girl from Afghanistan. I wanted to reach out, but language was a barrier. I offered her a reassuring smile and hand. In the middle of the night, we were driven to what I now know was Dover. This is how my journey to an immigration detention centre began.

For almost 48 hours, I found myself amongst a few nervous-looking women of diverse cultural backgrounds, held in a solemn room with boarded-up windows. In the room next to us, men paced aimlessly like zombies, their eyes sorrowful. They made no eye contact; many wore expressions that pierced through my soul. Some had dried blood on their faces and were partially dressed. The nurse was patronising and violating. She asked intrusive questions as she searched my body, asking me about my sexual history, mental health history and my background. She spoke to me as if I was stupid. I had to strip naked. It did not feel right to me. I could not believe that such a place existed in England and that people could get such treatment in a so-called democratic country.

I am a resilient woman, and in the past I have overcome many upheavals. But I had never felt this vulnerable. I was one of the few women fluent in English and with any knowledge of immigration and human rights law, and it wasn't long before my instinct to fight kicked in. I began lending my mobile phone to the women, offering advice, calling their relatives on their behalf, attempting to translate the immigration laws, reassuring and supporting everyone around me. This experience became not just about me, but about all the people surrounding me. Their pain, fear, sorrow, anxiety and humiliation became my own.

My lawyer, Paul Ward, was amazing. I had the support of activists such as Peter Tatchell, Lady Phyll Opoku, Bisi Alimi, members of the UK Gay and Lesbian Immigration group (UKLGIG) and many friends fighting my corner. I was lucky to be in a relationship, and my then partner constantly topped up the credit on my phone.

The following day I was released. A week later I was relieved when a relative of the young Afghanistani girl rang my mobile to inform me that she was well and had also been released. The Home Office made the decision and gave me a three-year visa. I saw this as an insult. The decision to sit on my passport, and their failure to correspond with me, had contributed to all the challenges I had experienced as a "stateless" person. I had lost so much. I'd had to defer my Masters programme in Health Psychology in Edinburgh. I'd had to resign from my position as a behavioural therapist. I had lost my accommodation and become homeless. I had lost a sense of self. And then they had treated me like a criminal and a risk to society.

I declined the three-year visa and contested their decision. A few weeks after that, I decided to represent myself in an immigration court. It was the only way I could claim back power – to demand to be heard and to express my bitterness and horror at the way I'd been treated.

I received invaluable advice from a barrister I met through UKLGIG, one of the many unsung heroes of the resistance to human rights violations. The decision to represent myself in court proved empowering and fruitful. During the preliminary hearing, I was able to question the Home Office representative in court about my passport. They were ordered to return it to me as soon as they could; I received it within two days. I was fortunate to have an understanding judge who demanded the

Home Office provide me with his mobile number and notify me by the end of the working day on the whereabouts of my passport. On the day of the court case, the Home Office failed to turn up for the hearing. I was not surprised and neither was the judge. The court process increased my knowledge of the law and of the challenges many LGBTI asylum seekers face. This humbling and somewhat painful experience made me even more determined to continue fighting for other people in similar situations

I was present when the first ever UK Black Pride was set up, and I am currently their Arts Movement Curator. I am particularly drawn to Black Pride as it endeavours to raise awareness and visibility of the issues that affect the "black" community. It also creates a safe environment that is inclusive of marginalised communities from across the Caribbean, Asia, Africa, South American continents, etc. Over the years the mainstream Pride has been problematic: exclusive, racist, trans-phobic and hedonistic in nature. For example in 2010 when Noizyimage (an artivist organisation I co-founded) carried black coffins at Brighton Pride to highlight the death penalty and "corrective rape" facing LGBTI in different countries, the action was sidelined, the organisers saying that it was "taking the fun out of pride".

I believe that queer Africans are forced to straddle a queer culture which is documented, edited and archived by Europeans, a culture predominantly Euro-centric in its scope. It is crucial that we as queer "black" people tell our own stories, communicate our own narratives and document our own histories. We need to speak to the next generation, and to act as role models.

This is what I attempt to do through my work. My "artivism" has become a political response to the lack of visibility that forced me to live outside my own culture and to seek asylum in another country that I struggle to call 'home'. I believe it is crucial that we start fighting our invisibility as queer women from African countries, and that we use our own freedoms to enable the freedom of others. As a refugee I do not denounce Africa. I love my Africa. But I denounce the idea that homosexuality is not African, and the hatred and ignorance menacing most of African society.

I am a refugee who, simply, cannot go home because of my sexuality. For me, resistance is not a choice, a fashionable statement: it is a question of survival.

*Skye at an exhibition of Zanele Muholi's work.* © *Skye Chirape/Kay Hayward*

# Fairness, justice, love

Veteran campaigner **Mary Sharkey** on facing down a police horse at Greenham, making food parcels for the miners, and some hairy moments with Women's Aid.

*Interview by Angharad Penrhyn Jones*

*Mary, you've been politically active since the 1960s. What was the first campaign you worked on?*

I need to give you a wee bit of background. Livingston New Town had just been built [the fourth post-World War II new town to be built in Scotland, located between Edinburgh and Glasgow], and they were looking for people to move into it. Because I had a big family I was given the opportunity to move there, but I found that there were absolutely no facilities for the kids. My first need was for a playgroup for my youngest child, and it was the same for a lot of other mums. I got chatting to some neighbours, and people were complaining, and I said, "Well, let's do something." Somebody said, "Where would you start?" And I said, "I don't know, but I'll soon find out." I'd identified some premises on my doorstep, workers' huts and painters' huts which were no longer being used, so I suggested they could be used for a playgroup. I had to go and meet the chief executive of the Livingston Corporation. I was told by one of his colleagues that I should wear a skirt to the meeting – he said this guy had been a colonel in the army. So I got all dressed up, and I'm not normally someone to get dressed up. There was this huge guy towering above me, and I was really nervous. I said if they gave us the hut, we would do the work on it. And we got the hut! So this gave me a wee taste of campaigning, it kind of fired my belly a wee bit.

So my next venture had to be for the older kids, because they had no youth clubs to go to – there was nothing for them to do. I spoke to a few people, and we got a wee committee going, and then eventually we got a youth club. By that time I realised I was really enjoying myself, that I was getting a real kick out of all of this. And I ended up getting quite political. I joined the Labour Party, but I needed to do a bit more to stretch myself, so I applied to go to college to do a diploma in community education.

*How old were you then?*

I was 44 and I had seven children. So I went to Edinburgh to do this diploma, and while I was doing my diploma I got a placement with Glasgow Women's Aid. Now my marriage hadn't been all that great. It was an abusive marriage, I knew it wasn't right but I had no experience – I'd been with him since I was 19. So as usual with an abusive relationship, I tended to blame myself when things went wrong. When I went to Women's Aid, one of the lights turned on. I think I was a feminist all my life but that's when it first hit. It was amazing.

We had some hairy moments, hairy times, lots of laughs. But they took me to a disco one night, an all-women disco.

And I was just mesmerised by the camaraderie, the feeling in the room. That was my first real feeling of female solidarity. It was fantastic. That disco changed my life, actually. That disco and the women from Glasgow Women's Aid.

*Could you say more about those hairy moments you mentioned?*

We were going to pick up some furniture from a woman's house – the woman was staying at our refuge and she'd just been offered a house – and we'd asked the police to come with us. I'm going back to 1983, and in those days the police and Women's Aid didn't get on, because there was that old-fashioned attitude that what happened behind closed doors was nobody's business. It was not a good relationship. So basically we'd asked the police to meet us at the house because we knew there'd be trouble. And they'd agreed to meet us, but when we got there the police hadn't turned up. After 20 minutes I said, to hell with it, let's go. So we opened the gate and the door burst open and this guy came charging out with a baseball bat. [Laughs.] So we turned on our heels and ran like hell. There were lots of moments like that. When the police arrived they wouldn't let us into the house, they didn't think we had the right to pick up the woman's furniture, so we never got it.

Another time I went to a house with a social work student where an older man had been violent towards his daughter. We went to the house to get some stuff for the daughter and she came with us. This old man was sitting in the chair, and he was so pleased to see his daughter back home, though she wasn't speaking to him, and I said, "No, we're just here to collect some stuff." The daughter wanted a rug that was under his feet so I said to him, "Lift your feet, please!" And

I'm rolling up this rug, and the social worker said, "Are you not being a bit harsh? Look at him, he's so sad." And I said, "What about his daughter? He's abused her for years and years and now suddenly he's the world's most wonderful father." There were wee situations like that. Or picking kids up from school, running across the road to get them and piling them into cars. Stuff you'd never get away with now. In those days it was the only thing you could do. Women were desperate and very few women leave without their children. We were working by the skin of our teeth the whole time. You would beg, borrow and steal to keep the refuges going. Some of the houses we put the women in were terrible. You'd get stuff out of skips to put in the houses. But the women didn't care, they just had to get away.

*Did you identify with these women because of your own experiences at home?*

A wee bit, yes. But I was still living with my husband then, and I wasn't really ready at that point. Women have to be ready. That light bulb moment has to happen before you finally leave. Anyway, doing this work was my first experience of feminism, even though I didn't even know what it was. And from then on I was hooked.

I'll tell you the story of my husband, though. I began to realise there was something wrong with my marriage. I was bringing up all these kids basically on my own – although my husband was around, he spent most of his life on the golf course. He was a very controlling man. He was also a very macho man. I was there to be barefoot and pregnant in the kitchen, a good Catholic lassie. I was pregnant nine times in ten years. My mother-in-law once said, "What are you complaining about? You've got six beautiful kids." And I said,

"You know, I'd quite like to have a chandelier." [Laughs.] It was very much tongue-in-cheek. We couldn't afford a light bulb, never mind a chandelier. I'm going to have that chandelier one of these days!

With a family that size, we were always struggling for money. And I got a wee job in a local chip shop on the weekend. But my husband would never come home on time to take the kids. He was always on the golf course and he would never come home on time to let me start work at four o'clock. And I loved that job – it brought me a wee bit of money, and believe it or not, it was my social life! [Laughs.] But he was always late and I'd then get into trouble at work. So one particular Sunday, he still hadn't turned up, and I thought, I've bloody well had enough of this. There was one taxi in the village, and I had five kids at that point. So I marched them down the street, put all the bairns in the taxi and told the driver to take me to the golf course. When I got there someone told me my husband was on the ninth hole. So I walked up to the ninth hole with the five bairns and there were three other men there with my husband. They all looked up and I shouted, "Charlie, here's your fucking weans. You know perfectly well I've got a job to go to." I turned and walked back to the taxi and went to work. The whole night I thought, oh deary dear, what's going to happen when I get back home? I was terrified, thinking about what he'd do to me. And when I got in from work, I saw that all my clothes had been ripped into shreds, all around the house. He looked at me and said, "Don't you ever do that to me again, and you'll be packing in that job." I don't know where I got the courage, but I told him I wouldn't be packing it in. He said, "Who likes working in a chip shop?" I said, "I like working in the chip shop. And I'll tell you one thing, that wee job helps keep your fees paid on the golf course, and don't you forget that." And he was never late again. I think that was the first kind of personal-political statement I ever really made in my life.

It was really quite empowering, and it also gave me a push, because at that point they were building the new town, and they were advertising for people to apply for housing. So I put in an application form, for me and the kids. And five weeks later I was offered this spanking new five-bedroomed house. I thought, it has to be an omen. I never told him anything about it and I went and looked at this lovely new house and sat on bare floorboards for a long time and decided I was leaving him. I didn't ask for anything from him and I still don't know how I managed to get stuff together.

You have to remember that I was very much a woman of my generation. The woman was the good Catholic lassie bringing up the kids and the man was the master. It took me a long time to figure out that it really didn't have to be like that.

*What sort of household did you grow up in?*

I grew up in a strong working-class household, not a campaigning household. My father was killed in the mines when I was 14, and my mother went out to work. I was basically left to look after everything – I was the eldest girl. I was running everything, looking after the household and my four-year-old sister. I barely went to school. I hated it and resented it. I think I was a feminist then without realising it. I bitterly resented being in this role. Then eventually I went on to train as a nurse – again the good old tradition, women going into nursing. I didn't finish the training. I met my husband and married him at 19, to get away from it all. Straight from the frying pan into the fire.

I'm not a man hater at all, but the most important thing in my life is my independence, and wanting to get the message out that there's nothing a woman can't do that a man can do. Look at what happened during the war. Look at women's history. The women did everything when the men were away, and when the men came back they didn't know their wives, their kids. In the end, I suppose my feminism is about fairness, justice, love.

*Do you sometimes feel out of step with your generation in the decisions that you made in your life? Did you feel that other people disapproved of you?*

Of course! And especially my husband's family, because they were all very strong Catholic women living in households dominated by men. I don't think one of them was in what you might call a happy relationship. Aye, so it was all about that in those days, and part of my job now is to get a woman to believe that she does actually have a right to feel okay, that she can be her own person and you're not half a person because you don't have a man.

Anyway that's how I got to the new town, and that's where it all started for me. And after I left college I was asked to become a local councillor, because I was very active with the local Labour party. I really wasn't sure about it. It was all very well doing this campaigning but I didn't think I was intelligent enough to be a councillor.

*Were they mostly men on the local council?*

There were a couple of women but they were mostly men, yes. And the women who were there might as well have been men, because they were swayed by the men on every decision. They were very much women of their generation.

The decisions were made by the men. Anyway, I was persuaded to do it. And I was actually quite amazed at the response I got.

Before I became a councillor I had another light bulb moment, when I nearly died. I had a massive haemorrhage miscarrying a baby and I was at death's door and they gave me a blood transfusion. After that I thought, what if something had happened to me? I had five children, and I thought what would happen to all these bairns? So I thought I should start taking some precautions. I remember seeing the priest when I had number six, and he said, "Keep up the good work, Mary!" And I said, "I think a lot of this one, Father, because there aren't going to be any more." And he said, "Now, that's no way to speak, Mary!" But that's what things were like in those days, you know.

Anyway, I got elected to the council. Oh, I got my eyes opened then! That's when I went to Greenham Common. It was 1985, I think. That's another funny thing: in those days, equality was on the political agenda, so the council decided to form a women's committee. Now there weren't enough women to be on this women's committee. [Laughs.] So we had all these men, who had no more of a notion of being on a woman's committee than flying in the air. So they decided the women's committee would take place on a Tuesday afternoon at four o'clock. And I said, "Who the hell is going to be able to come to this committee at four o'clock on a weekday?" The chair, who was a man, couldn't see what the problem was. I had to remind him that the bairns needed picking up from school, needed their tea. So that was the kind of lip service that was paid to women's issues.

Now the MP for Livingston at the time was Robin Cook. He was very much against nuclear weapons, so the council got involved with CND and my next campaign was to get a group of us to go over to Greenham. And that was an amazing experience. We got a bus and went for a weekend when we knew they were bringing the missiles in and there was going to be a huge demonstration. There were thousands of women there, and seeing those women from all walks of life was incredible.

The camaraderie there, the feeling there, was amazing. Asian women, old women, young women, women with kids, teenage women, everybody there. A huge fence with banners all over it. And we were all camping and had campfires and it was just... amazing. The missiles were coming in on the Sunday, and on the Saturday there were police everywhere. Hundreds and hundreds of them. We got talking to some of them and one guy said to me he agreed with what we were doing. I said, "Aye, but when the call goes out, you're going to link arms with your pals. You're going to prevent us from demonstrating." He said he was just doing his job.

I was there with my friend Carol – a fantastic woman, very much into politics, but she loved to look good all the time. [Laughs.] So we'd all been singing around the campfire, it was about three in the morning, and I couldn't get to sleep because Carol was in the tent next to me and there was all this rustling going on. I said, "Carol, what are you doing?" She said, "I'm just trying to get my rollers in." [Laughs.] I told her to get some sleep, that no one would care what her hair looked like in the morning. But the next day she stepped out of that tent like someone from a band box. [Laughs.]

The Sunday morning was really serious. We were trying to stop these missiles from coming in and we had this daft idea that we really could do it. By that time there were more police arriving, hundreds and hundreds. Everybody tried to block all the gates but the police were just picking people up and moving us on. I remember being pinned up against a fence by a horse. That was the most terrifying experience of my life. The police were pushing us back with these horses, and I can still see that horse to this day. It was dribbling because the police was pulling on the bit. And I can remember this woman – I'll never forget. A wee woman, very slim, with grey hair, shouting up at a police officer who looked to me like he was a million miles up on the sky because he was sitting on a huge horse. And this wee woman shouting, "Officer, give me your number. I want your number immediately!" I couldn't believe how brave she was. By this time we were getting really scared. He could see that and he backed off a bit, and I have to be honest with you – I took to my heels and I ran. I was really frightened. This wee woman didn't give ground though. She stood her ground and it was quite amazing.

Greenham really opened my eyes. Seeing how different women were. One thing I remember is collecting money for Women's Aid – I was campaigning at the time to get Women's Aid set up in West Lothian. I went up to two women and asked them if they'd like to contribute, and this woman said, "How dare you? I will decide who I contribute to, and I certainly won't be contributing to that organisation." And I was so taken aback by it. I think the shock for me was realising that not everyone thought the same way as me. And that's another learning experience that you have to go through. You have to realise that not everyone thinks like you and learn to deal with that, to live with other people's ideas.

*Why do you think certain people might be prejudiced against Women's Aid?*

Because even now, people think that you're breaking up

families. And that families are basically patriarchal and should stay that way. At Women's Aid we base our ideas very much on a gendered analysis, which is about roles and responsibilities that have been handed down through the generations. I've got some fantastic literature, like the book *A History of Marriage*, that goes way back to 4BC, to Roman Romulus who declared the first law of marriage. And the first law of marriage declared that women should temper themselves to the rules of their men at all times. And that's where we believe that the sense of power and control, and the sense of entitlement, comes from. It's worth thinking about how we feminise our girls, and how we masculinise our boys. There's a fantastic book called *The Macho Paradox*, which is all about this. That's influenced me a lot.

*So how did your campaign go, to get Women's Aid in West Lothian?*

That was successful. But this was 1984, round about Christmas, and then another battle came up. I was sitting in the house with one of my daughters, reading the local paper, and I came across this wee square, a planning application. It was from an American corporation, Union Carbide. A chemical company wanting to come to Livingston. And two or three nights before that, the Bhopal disaster had happened in India, which had killed thousands and thousands of people.

*It was the world's biggest industrial disaster...*

Yes, and Union Carbide was responsible for that, and it's still having big effects now. And I read that planning application and thought, "Bastards. That'll be over my dead body." I was morally outraged. Now they weren't coming as a chemical plant, they were looking for storage facilities. It wasn't going to be a huge plant but they were going to be storing chemicals here. And the site they'd chosen was about 300 yards away from an old people's home. My daughter turned to me and said, "What are you going to do about it? You can't let that go." So I started a petition and went down to the church to speak to the minister and asked them to announce it on the Sunday. That was a big success. People stood up and said, "No way." Then it became a Livingston-wide campaign and it involved all the councillors. It was quite interesting because Robin Cook, our MP, was very ambivalent about it all, kind of sitting on the fence about it. He said it'd bring in 99 jobs. I told him I didn't give a fuck. And that's the exact language I used. I said it could bring in 9000 jobs and they would not be coming here. I said the company should be focusing on India and sorting out the terrible damage they'd done. I got into the local press and eventually we had all these public meetings in local schools and it was absolutely amazing. There were so many people at the meetings, lots of people had to stand outside. People were standing up and saying no.

*So people were outraged by what this company had done.*

People were absolutely outraged.

*And this was more important than bringing in jobs, even in an area of high unemployment?*

Yes, this was more important. But there was an element of fear as well. Because people had moved into this town to bring their kids up somewhere safe. But the majority of people did say that it was scandalous what this corporation had done to the people of India. So the pressure was really on Union Carbide. We invited them along to the public meetings and they came and all they did was dig themselves into a great hole. Because they were talking about worst case scenarios – an aeroplane crashing into the chemical containers. They did themselves no favours.

*Sounds like a bit of a PR disaster.*

[Laughs.] And the planning application deadline was getting nearer and nearer. Anyway, the upshot was that the planning application was rejected. We were all standing outside waiting for the result, and out they came and told us that the planning application hadn't been granted. Oh! Euphoria! That was about midday, and two hours later I got a phone call from ITV asking if I'd go on the telly! I said, "No way, no way am I going on the telly." Anyway, I ended up going on the telly. [Laughs.] I put on this fantastic red jacket, I'll always remember that. And the people at the television studio were fantastic – you could see they were all dead supportive. I told them it had been the most wonderful experience of democracy at work I'd ever seen.

*This was a case of people fighting a massive corporation with a lot of power and influence.*

Yes, and the people of Livingston won. It was interesting because we'd needed to work hard to convince Robin Cook, our MP, but I have to tell you this one: I got a phone call from him one day before the planning decision and he asked me if he could come and see me. So he came over to mine for some lunch. I didn't like the man, but he was a good politician. And to be fair, he did speak up against the Iraq war. Anyway we sat down and he said, "Could I have a wee word, Mary? I'd just like to say to you, Mary, do you think you could cool it a wee bit, with all this stuff you're doing?" I asked him why, and he said, "Well you're upstaging me." [Laughs.] I said to him, "Well why don't you come off the bloody fence and stand up for the people of Livingston. Stand up for the people of your constituency, because the people do not want this corporation coming to this town."

*He wanted to see which way the wind was blowing before committing either way. He was waiting to see what would happen.*

That's right, a typical bloody politician. And that was the problem for me when I was on the council – I wasn't a politician. I wasn't there just to do a day's work. I was always on the carpet because I was always breaking the party whip. I couldn't follow the party line when I thought it was wrong, and that was part of the problem. Anyway, eventually Robin Cook did stand up. He had two special surgeries and 500 people turned up to see him. And I said to him, does that not tell you something?

*So where did you go from there?*

The next campaign was the miners' strike, and against Thatcher. I hated the woman. I was all for the miners, because this was a mining area with a strong mining community. My father was killed in the shale mines, in a wee village not far from here, when I was 14. And also the strength of feeling for the miners – we had all these men out of work and all these women and kids... If it hadn't been for the women supporting the miners' strike, the men would have been back in the mines much quicker I think. We had these soup kitchens, we got involved in collecting money, and I did a deal with a local supermarket to help us set up a food parcel service in my house.

*Were you supported by the community as a whole?*

I would say that 97 per cent of people put money in those collection tins. So the women got together and did the parcels and did the shopping, and we did a lot of laughing. And over Christmas we did a lot of toys for the bairns. The guy who ran the supermarket was amazing – he used to throw in bags of sweeties for the bairns. We had wee concerts and stuff like that to raise money. It was an amazing time, the whole community coming together. And we used to go to the picket lines as well, we'd join the pickets at five in the morning.

*How did you look after your children during this period?*

By this time my kids were getting older, and my husband was back. But they loved it, they were all for it. In everything I did my kids were 100 per cent behind me.

*How long did the strike go on for?*

Nearly a year. And then they went back. Thatcher defeated them. It was interesting to see the police response to the strike. They basically loved it because they got loads and loads of overtime pay. I remember them saying to us, keep it up, keep this going for as long as it can, because it suits our pockets, you know? There were busloads of police all sitting on the sidelines. I had a friend who was a chief inspector and he told me, when the buses came in, not to lie on the ground. He told me if I did that the bus would run over me.

It was a great time but it must have been difficult for people as well. We were very anti-scab, but I remember being in a situation in college where there was a sit-in and a strike, and I didn't take part in it for my own selfish reasons. I knew that if I didn't pass my exams I wouldn't get my diploma. So I didn't get involved and I've always hated myself for it. But at least I got my diploma. And this journey has also been about finding me, finding what's right for me.

The miners' strike was great fun. The thing that saddened me was that all these women who'd come together and pulled together, when the strike was over everyone just went back into their houses again. I was really hoping something would come out of that, that it would grow into something else. But we have to accept people and the ways they process things in their lives. It's the same with women who go back to abusive husbands. It's taken me years to learn not to be judgemental, and I don't always manage it. But I do get frustrated and sad.

*You left the council in the end. Why?*

Yes, I did my four years and then I didn't stand for re-election because I really didn't enjoy it. I wasn't a politician. It was too hard to be fighting these men all the time. I thought when I went into it that I could possibly achieve more on the other side, but it's not true. You can actually achieve more by being a good strong campaigner and fighting for what you believe in, being on the outside of the system. That was a lesson for me.

After I left the council I got a job working for Falkirk Women's Aid. It was becoming more and more apparent that our relationship with the police had to change. The police hated us and we hated them. There was this amazing superintendent down the Stirling area and he came to see us one day and said he had a vision of a civilian worker from Women's Aid working with the police, building a strong partnership. He said his police officers needed better training to deal with these domestic situations, and also that the women who were being abused were very resistant to the police so they really needed a civilian working with them. There were situations where the police had to walk away from women and bairns who needed help. They needed someone who was not a police officer to go and speak to these women after the event and see if they could offer support. So he formed a wee steering group and went to the Central Scotland office to get a grant to set up this project. Then my ego kicked in, and I thought, I'm going to apply for that job. I did ask myself, who would want to work for the police? But I went for it, and I ended up doing the job for seven years. I went to work in the police family unit, which was mostly about child protection, and a large part of that was dealing with domestic abuse. So they needed someone not just to support the women but to raise awareness and change attitudes. And I loved every minute of it. The police were fantastic – they gave me a lot of scope to do what I needed to do. I got some amazing letters when I left, from some of the police officers I trained.

I took the referrals in the family unit from something like 200 a year to something like 2400 by the time I left. I made sure that if police attended a domestic and didn't put in a referral, then heads would roll and questions would be asked. So, eventually they got into the habit of it and every incident would be reported, and the woman would get a follow-up. But the unique thing about Central Scotland police was that they employed a civilian. I made sure that I had a lot of autonomy, that I wouldn't be reporting back to them every single thing a police officer would have to report. I said I had to be able to offer the women I was seeing a certain degree of confidentiality. I said if I went in the house and saw six televisions lying in the corner, I wouldn't be reporting that to them.

*Were people surprised by you taking this job? Because in all your campaigns you'd been facing the police on the other side, and been intimidated by the police on picket lines, and so on.*

Yes, yes. It was interesting – that woman I spoke to you about, Carol, the one who came with me to Greenham Common, I remember she couldn't believe her ears when I told her who I was working for. She said I was the last person she'd see working for the police. But I explained to her what it was all about. And anyway, the relationship between Women's Aid and the police has got stronger and stronger.

*So you helped change the culture within the police force.*

I was part of that, yes, changing the culture, certainly in Central Scotland. And other police forces started following what we were doing.

*The statistics in the UK are horrendous, in terms of women being murdered at home. What's the answer?*

There aren't enough refuges, for a start. In the whole of West Lothian, which is a huge area, made up of a lot of wee villages like this, there are 12 refuge spaces.

*12 beds?*

Yes, 12 beds. That's a communal space. In places like Glasgow and Edinburgh they have what you call single-occupancy refuges. We're still fighting the same battle now, for money, that I was fighting 30 years ago. We still fight every year to get money, and it's not nearly enough.

*It's not seen as a priority, politically.*

It looks as if it is, it looks as if it's high on the political agenda. But it's not translated into funding. It's all rhetoric, all words. We struggle all the time. And we get the council asking us why we turn women away. Sometimes it happens because we don't have space, but we also turn them away when they have addictions. We can't let women with drug or alcohol issues in because of the communal living arrangement, and we have kids in the refuge. A lot of the kids in the refuge have lived with it already – drunk fathers... If we had single-occupancy living we could take these women in and bring in the other services that are necessary to support them.

*That's very sad, because a lot of women seeking help are going to have addiction issues, aren't they? It's part of the whole problem.*

Yes, it's part of the whole spiral they're in. Some women will turn to alcohol or drugs but still be on automatic pilot when it comes to looking after their weans, you know? I had a daughter who died of drug addiction, and she had kids. So I know all about that... And we're very strictly governed by child protection as well. So obviously no men are allowed in. You'd be amazed by the number of women who sneak a man in, and that's an instant eviction when that happens, not just because of her safety, but everyone's safety. A lot of councils are setting up their own services now, domestic abuse support groups, but they're not offering refuges, and they only offer limited counselling for women. And the councils are so strapped now, it's really difficult. So instead of being easier 30 years down the line, it's getting more and more difficult.

*You're obviously a very resilient woman, fighting for so long. And you say you've lost a daughter too.*

Yes, I'd like to tell you about that because it's part of the whole thing. Look that's my beautiful girl. [Shows photo.] Now the interesting thing is, when she died, on Christmas day two years ago, it wasn't because of the drugs. She'd been clean for a long time. She was actually my biological granddaughter, but we legally adopted her when she was two. At the time my youngest was 11 and so this baby was a bonus. This beautiful baby girl came into my household and she was amazing. Her mother had a lot of problems and couldn't bring her up: she was only 16 when she had the baby. When the bairn was two, she met a man and wanted to get married, and this man didn't want to start married life with somebody else's wean. And that's when we adopted Tracy. For me she was a big bonus. I was still working, but I've always had lots of energy. I've worked since I was 15.

Anyway, Tracy grew up and she was a star, but when she was 15 she got into smoking weed, and eventually it spiralled into heroin. Then she had a baby boy and I ended up looking after him. Then she fell pregnant again, and again she couldn't sustain looking after the baby. She got worse and worse. She did manage to come off the drugs, and she'd been clean for two years, but in the end she died of bronchial pneumonia. They told us her immune system was shot to hell, basically because of the drugs. But I always used to say that about Tracy. I said one of two things will happen to her: she'll sort herself out, and she'll get clean, and she'll come home – or one day there'll be a knock on the door. And one day there was a knock on the door. [Starts crying.] However, she's home, and she's buried beside her father, because that was her wish.

So even if I come across as very strong and resilient, I have my moments. I really miss my daughter.

*Who inspires you to keep going at times like that?*

I'm very inspired by Maya Angelou. She came through the struggles in America. I admire all the black women and men in America who struggled for justice.

*What qualities do you think you need to be an effective campaigner?*

It takes a lot of guts. Sometimes it takes physical as well as emotional strength. And to refuse to take "no" for an answer. Determination. A firm belief in what you're doing. When I did training for the police on domestic violence issues, people said, "How can you do that?" But if you feel passionately about what you're doing, and you know it's the right thing, you can ignore the criticisms. Women need to recognise their own strength.

I love turtles. I say, "Behold the turtle, because she makes progress when she sticks her neck out." And my other motto: "The thing that stops us is the starting."

# My revolution

Children's rights campaigner and author
**Anuradha Vittachi** on her part in the babymilk
campaign, which sparked her own personal
revolution.

In 1982, my old life broke down and my new life – my real life
– broke through. I produced my first campaigning magazine,
saw through the painful relationship I'd clung to, stopped
hiding apologetically in the shadows, and met my soulmate.
It was a revolution.

But though revolutions erupt suddenly, they don't come
from nowhere. Whether it's the Arab Spring or individual
transformation, a revolution has roots. As actors say wryly, "I
was an 'overnight success' after twenty years."

My revolution was rooted in my childhood, in the fertile soil
of my father's journalism, which exposed unethical politicians
in Sri Lanka, the Philippines, Indonesia, India. His enemies
threatened to kidnap me to silence him. When I was 13, we
escaped by midnight plane to another Asian country emerging
from a bloodstained ethnic war, tanks still on its streets.

Growing up in such a febrile atmosphere took its toll.
When my English student friends were escaping dull
suburbia to explore the world, I escaped from the dangerous
world to hide in leafy Middle England. I wanted to bring

children up in a place where they would be free to worry about the usual childhood concerns, such as what to ask for from Father Christmas – not whether their mother would survive the secret police.

I hadn't yet learned that silencing one's voice was the most dangerous path one could take. Luckily, despite my best efforts to betray myself, my dad introduced me to *New Internationalist* (*NI*), a magazine exposing global injustice – and my revolutionary roots found rain.

My first job there was part-time, short term, and low paid, but it still felt like a homecoming. I loved listening to the argumentative, idealistic young journalists who formed NI's core editorial group. It echoed the evenings my dad and his friends had held forth about ethics, politics and journalism while I ate my dinner, napkin tucked into my school uniform collar, a haze of pipe-smoke swirling above my head.

The *NI* editors treated me like a kid sister, clueless but worth rescuing. I devoured every book they gave me, from *Freedom at Midnight* to the *Pedagogy of the Oppressed*. I was awestruck by their friends, especially the filmmaker who radiated so much energy when he burst into the room that I was rocked back on my heels by its force.

I clung to my job. Whatever impossible task the editors threw at me, I'd murmur, "Yes, no problem," and find a way to make it happen. The fizz and warmth at work were a far cry from the loneliness and fear that pervaded my domestic life, once the kids were asleep.

If my childhood values, reinforced by *NI*, were the kindling for my revolution, the spark that ignited it was a UNICEF press conference. Two campaigners from the International Baby Foods Action Network (IBFAN) explained why they were boycotting Nestlé.

Nestlé sales representatives were giving away free samples of infant formula to mothers in the global south. But newborns on formula don't suckle the breast to trigger milk production, so when the free formula ran out their mothers were trapped into buying the expensive, imported product, which cost around two weeks' family income *per tin*.

Naturally, many mothers diluted the formula to make it stretch – and the babies starved. Or the babies died of disease because formula didn't have the miraculous immunising properties of breastmilk. The mothers couldn't even afford enough fuel to make the water safe by boiling it – and the corporations knew this, but pushed their product regardless.

UNICEF reckoned (conservatively) that at least 1.5 million babies were dying each year directly because of the switch from breast to bottle. As many babies were dying every four years as the number of Jews murdered in the Holocaust. I had to help get the word out.

Back at the office, I announced that I wanted to produce an issue of the magazine myself, straight away. My topic would be baby milk, and I had to fly to Geneva to attend the World Health Assembly that afternoon.

"I need you to buy me a ticket." There was a stunned silence. "Please."

Eventually one editor murmured, "Well, it is about babies..." (A suitably soft topic for a soft young mum.) They consented.

I raced home to explain my departure to my children, aged six and seven. They thought hard, then asked: "Will it save babies?" I nodded – and they gave me a thumbs-up. I was so proud of their generosity. I packed hastily, gave them lots of kisses, handed them to someone they liked, and headed for the airport – to smack into my first hurdle.

My ticket had been made out in my professional (maiden) name. My passport was in my married name. The check-in agent refused point blank to let me through.

My dad had told me never to be fazed by bureaucrats standing in the way of good work. So I grabbed a copy of *NI* from my flight bag and pointed to the author photograph and name. "There," I said. "That's me, right?" He nodded. I flourished my passport. "And here's my passport, with my photo and married name. And they are obviously the same person, right? And that person is me, standing here, right?" He was so befuddled, he let me through.

In Geneva, the baby foods campaigners seemed like resistance fighters in war movies: hard-headed, well-informed, experienced, focused. They took me under their wing, organised my press accreditation, dinner, a bed, briefing papers. Overwhelmed, I couldn't take in a thing. But I felt fire in my belly and the relief of being in touch with my real self.

The World Health Assembly was voting on a critical resolution: an agreement to create an international code banning the marketing of formula. We held our breath – and let it out in whoops of joy when virtually the whole world agreed. There was only one shameful (shameless?) "no" – from the US.

I returned to the UK eager to commission articles and photographs, and to interview experts like Dr Zef Ebrahim of London's Tropical Health Unit. He taught me something wonderful: how breasts and babies constituted a marvellously complex, delicately regulated ecosystem.

Each individual baby, through suckling, signalled the breast to provide not just breast milk but the exact kinds and quantities of nutrients in that milk that were needed for her optimal growth – and even customised to each feed, providing more substance at breakfast, say, and a more thirst-quenching mix in the heat of the day.

If that were not miraculous enough, it also provided exactly the kinds of immunity she needed to combat the specific diseases prevalent in her locality.

No billionaire, said Dr Ebrahim, could afford a chemist's lab able to create artificial food and immunising agents half as tuned to suit his child! And yet the poorest mother on the planet could provide it for hers – until a babyfood corporation robbed her of this priceless start to her baby's life, and replaced it with a ticket to destruction.

He was unequivocal: "Whenever I am in a poor village and see a baby bottle, I reach inside my pocket for a death certificate."

I learned too about the hidden consequences suffered by the babies' older siblings, half-starved and thus more vulnerable to disease because 50 per cent of the family income had been wasted on formula.

The scale of the tragedy was far bigger than I'd realised. And it was not just a tragedy but an obscenity, because it was all so unnecessary. It was an anthropogenic disaster fabricated by corporations, motivated solely by profit, and destroying a natural ecosystem perfectly designed to nurture the next generation, the future of humankind.

Galvanised, I worked at top speed. But it was a terrible winter. Blizzards froze airports, delaying deliveries of key information from international baby foods campaigners. When the airports thawed, a postal strike delayed deliveries again. My ancient banger, unsafe in severe weather, skidded wildly across yards of ice on journeys to the office. When I finally pulled all the copy together, I sent it to the magazine's long-established printers with a deep sigh of relief.

They sent it straight back. What might the giant babymilk corporations do to them? We begged them to print it, but they wouldn't take the risk.

The editors tried every printer they could think of. Everyone said no. Finally Feb Edge, printers to *Private Eye*, the much-sued satirical magazine, agreed to take it on. Relief again.

But again, short-lived. The lawyers at Feb Edge stopped the print run of the cover *on the presses*. They'd decided it was too risky after all.

The refusal by Feb Edge sent a chill across the office. Was this issue also too risky for us? What had been seen as a soft edition for a novice editor had become the edgiest in the magazine's 17-year history.

I waxed passionate. "No way should this issue be silenced. I'll type every copy of the magazine at my kitchen table if necessary!" Until a senior editor intervened with cold logic: if Nestlé took us to court, the magazine would be wiped out – *even if we won*. The cost of standing trial for months would be enough to ruin us. And ruin would mean losing not only the magazine but everyone's jobs, and several of the editors' family homes. Was I still intent on publication? I sobered up, conscious of a double burden now: getting the magazine printed *and* making sure it wouldn't blow up in our faces.

New Internationalist *takes on Nestlé.*

You expect someone to be innocent until proven guilty, don't you? But if Nestle were to take us to court accusing us of libel, the onus would be on us to prove our innocence. And we would have to do that by proving the corporation's guilt, against the might of their lawyers. The McLibel trial, twelve years later, was to demonstrate just how exhausting and difficult that kind of confrontation would be.

The law seemed so absurd that my fellow editor kept arguing and the printer's representative kept arguing back. We were getting nowhere. And then I suddenly understood what the printer's real problem was. It wasn't the magazine's content: it was us.

"Are you assuming the content of this edition is some sort of juvenile rant?" I asked. "I know we look young, but you should know that everything here is based on hard evidence and corroborated by the world's top authorities. I can footnote every word."

I got a straight, hard look. "Ok, wait a moment." He called the libel lawyer and had a rapid conversation. Then he came back to me. "Can you get these world authorities to stand by you? In the dock?"

"Yes," I said. "No problem."

"List the six key points on which Nestlé could sue, and on each point get two world authorities to agree to stand trial with you. The barrister reckons that if you have people of this calibre to back you, Nestlé won't dare touch you because of the bad publicity. Probably."

"Probably," was near enough. As I stood up excitedly to leave, he added: "You have 48 hours."

48 hours. In 1980, with no email. No Google. And no status – just a rookie from a tiny magazine. I should have been panicking at the idea of asking these experts to stand trial with a nobody. But I forgot to be apologetic, because I wasn't

the point here: the babies were.

I went back to the office and picked up the phone. Two days later, I had all the agreements. These authorities cared more about the babies too.

Feb Edge kept their word. The magazine was finally published! It was now up to *NI*'s readers, especially the thousands connected to IBFAN, to make use of it in whatever diverse ways they wished – like the American academic who wrote to me to say the magazine was now "required reading" for her students at Amherst College.

But back at home, there was another hill to climb. My partner announced that he had taken on Nestlé as his newest client. I couldn't believe what I was hearing. Here I was, producing an issue revealing how Nestlé was putting profits before infant lives, and he was *helping* the multi-billion-dollar corporation?

And then I wondered why I was still so obedient to someone so totally disconnected from me, my work, my values? How could I be such a doormat?

These two different parts of me – the anxious, apologetic, dutiful young Asian mother and the unstoppable fighter for justice – finally looked each other in the eye. From that instant, there was no going back.

The late Polish journalist Ryszard Kapuscinski wrote: "All books about all revolutions begin with a chapter that describes the decay of tottering authority or the misery and sufferings of the people. They should begin with a psychological chapter, one that shows how a harassed, terrified man suddenly breaks his terror, stops being afraid. This unusual process demands illuminating. Man gets rid of fear and feels free."

Life, vibrant life, caught me up in its arms. A therapist

friend had once asked me what I really wanted to work on, and that filmmaker with the radiant energy had flashed into my mind. My friend urged me to call him but, crimson-faced at the thought of such boldness, I had laughed it off. Post-revolution, I was not only working with my joyous filmmaker, but also living with him. (Three action-packed decades later, it's still blissful.)

I discovered why I'd shirked from engaging with my power for so long: I'd confused *power* with *abusive power*. What a relief to learn that power didn't always have to mean domination – power over others, silencing, bullying.

As Einstein had pointed out: "You can't solve a problem with the same level of thinking that created the problem." Although oppositional heroics had their (limited) place, they just weren't attractive as a long-term solution. But what alternative was there? In the early 1990s a new kind of media, as ecosystemic as breastfeeding, showed another way.

The Grand Old Media were hierarchical, controlling and so money-guzzling that only billionaires could afford to own them. Plenty of people had critiqued the media for decades – with about as much effect as a Chihuahua barking at a giant's ankles. What actually brought the giant low was the friendly and innovative young Web: flat, informal, egalitarian, co-creative, cheap. It didn't bother to challenge the old giant, simply offered an alternative.

As did we. In 1994-5, we stopped making expensive documentaries and created OneWorld.org: the world's first global justice portal. We, along with the three thousand partner NGOs and progressive media organisations that quickly gathered around, could publish whatever we thought really mattered to the global family – without needing permission from anyone. OneWorld's purpose was to create an "enabling environment", where this networked community and their constituencies could connect, learn from one another, and take action if they wanted to. An astonishing number did. A 2004 survey showed that 47 per cent of its respondents had taken social action sparked by something they'd learned on OneWorld.

By 2006, OneWorld had taken a thrilling step: not just circulating information *about* a generation at risk in the global south, but innovating new mobile phone-based networks that enabled that generation – hundreds of thousands of African adolescents – to speak up and to get life-saving help directly. We were continuing the baby food campaigners' work of saving child lives, but in a whole new way. My dad would have been proud.

By now I was being invited to address the UN, to be the UK's civil society voice at the G8 Summit for digital inclusion, to speak alongside people I'd previously seen only on pedestals, like Amartya Sen or Susan George.

Luckily for my ego's health, I was sharply aware that these worldly successes were not mine. I was just one note on a piano, whose other notes included the IBFAN campaigners, the OneWorld team, my father, the *NI*, my kids, my partner. No-one can change the world alone, but it's amazing what a network can do.

The impact of networks working ecosystemically isn't easy to assess. They can't be judged in isolation or in a short timeframe. You'd have to include the initiatives of all the people whose creativity they've catalysed, probably over decades. My story is just one among thousands sparked and supported by IBFAN. And here's one more: my favourite.

In 1992, a hospital in a poverty-stricken quarter of Manila

– just the sort of overcrowded, under-resourced hospital that was targeted by the baby food corporations – was part of an emerging "baby-friendly" hospital network. Here, doctors and nurses ran outdoors and slammed the hospital gates shut whenever they saw a formula seller approaching.

They didn't have the money to hire enough breastfeeding counsellors. So they put the novice mothers in beds jammed right up against those of experienced mothers, who took charge as sisterly breastfeeding mentors. This mother-to-mother information exchange system ensured that every new mother relaxed and learned to breastfeed successfully.

"And how many newborns have died here since?" I asked a doctor, bracing myself, since the newborn mortality rate was painfully high in impoverished parts of the Philippines.

"With the exception of a few babies born with serious medical conditions unrelated to feeding – none," he said.

And when he saw how surprised and touched I was, how I hardly dared believe what I'd heard, he said again, "Not one. Every baby is alive."

# Who jumps first?

Disability rights activist and performance artist **Liz Crow** on a political awakening that happened in about 20 seconds flat, and why she took her wheelchair to the fourth plinth on Trafalgar Square.

*Interview by Angharad Penrhyn Jones*

*You don't talk about your impairment in very specific terms in public. Why is that?*

The disabled people's movement is premised on the concept of the social model and it's an incredibly liberating thing. Essentially the social model makes a split between impairment of the body, and social structures or the things that actually keep disabled people out of social life. For me, and I know this is the case for hundreds of thousands of others, that distinction has been transformative, and in many instances even life saving, because it shows our exclusion from society is fundamentally not about the way our bodies function, but about the structures that surround us.

My impairment is relevant, because I am ill and that has an impact on my life, but it takes a back seat. The primary focus of my campaigning work is the world out there because that can be changed. It's the social structures around us we can change, and it's much more relevant as an activist to put the emphasis on that.

*What story is the government trying to tell about disabled people at the moment, and how do we counter that story, those myths?*

Currently the story of anyone needing social support is one of the scrounger, the shirker, that they're too lazy to contribute to society and need punishing back to work. Disabled people are seen as being right at the core of that. Once upon a time we were the "deserving poor", which was hugely problematic, but now we've joined the even lower rank of the undeserving poor. [Laughs.] And there is no room in that story for the contributions we make.

You'd think that the Paralympics would have counteracted this, but actually it heightened it, because we ended up with these really strong contrasting images in the press and in government briefings: the sporting "superhumans", lauded wherever they went, and the benefit scroungers, the two set side by side, each exaggerating the other. Things were difficult before the Paralympics but got a lot worse during it and in the immediate aftermath.

With massive benefits changes and austerity coming in, I've seen a lot of things happening. There's been a turn in the press and the way that we've been portrayed, so whilst we've been routinely misrepresented in the past, suddenly the scrounger rhetoric is huge, with a really strong effect on myself and the people around me. Hate crime against disabled people has doubled since the coalition government came in. Like a lot of people, I'm aware of holding myself differently when I'm in the street, of trying to ease social contact with strangers – look them in the eye, smile excessively, and just ease that process. I know so many people who have experienced increased hostility: being confronted, receiving hostile comments, being spat on or subjected to physical violence.

I'd been an activist for a long time but I shifted to this area in direct response to current events. The government's claim was that austerity was a necessary response to the economic crisis, but it was quickly clear not only that austerity has a bad record as a financial solution, but also that it was an ideological move to dismantle the state, with a primary focus on the social security system.

In the thick of this, I knew that I would be assessed for the newly introduced Employment and Support Allowance. Like a lot of people I have an impairment that's very poorly defined and changeable day on day. The new system is even more problematic than the old one. Not only does it ignore the impact of social barriers, but it's also constructed for people with very quantifiable, fixed, recognisable, visible impairments. Anyone not falling into that category – generally the people who need the support most of all – fails the eligibility test and falls through the gaps because the system is incapable of recognising them. Initially, I decided I wanted to focus on the misinformed concepts built into the test, and implicit in deeply biased government briefings and press reporting. I decided to explore how what you see of me in public is not how I am behind closed doors. So where I edit myself to perform as this apparently well person in public, articulate and active, what you will never see is the preparation for that to be possible or the recovery needed afterwards. Without that full picture, you can't make a judgement about who I am or the support I need, but because that private side meets with such social disapproval, it's something I've kept under wraps for the best part of 30 years. In common with a lot of disabled people, basing any judgement about what I might be able to do, or whether I need a particular aspect of support, only on what is visible will be flawed and potentially dangerous.

*You're faced with social disapproval because you're lying in bed?*

Yes. Because I'm not productive in socially approved ways, because the aftermath of activity is not attractive, it doesn't communicate well, it isn't lively, it isn't all the things that get celebrated in society. If you imagine their opposite, that's how I am in private much of the time. And whilst I've hidden all of that for years, the dangers of the scrounger/fraudster rhetoric and its translation into hate crime and claimant deaths means I needed to start playing with those two stark contrasts and bringing them into a public space to trigger a deeper, more informed conversation.

That's what led me then to develop Bedding Out, a performance piece in which I took to my bed for 48 hours in an art gallery, live streamed and with a Twitter feed alongside, in order to convey that complexity and create a platform for discussion. Disabled people responded with visceral recognition of the public/private divide, that editing of self. And it created a platform for an incredible range of issues relating to benefits changes and their impact, representation, hate crime, protest, you name it.

Discussing this in public conversations held around the bed and in the Twitter feed, it became clear that the kind of questions we were looking at, the debates we were having, were not in the end about disability, but about much broader and deeper questions: what, as a society, are the values that are important to us, what kind of society do we want to live in, and what do we do to bring that about?

*So to critics who might say that performance art is a marginal, self-indulgent, middle-class pursuit...*

[Laughs.]

*What would you say to them?*

When you start doing a piece of work like this, there's always a risk it will be dismissed. It *can* be completely self indulgent, but equally if you don't do it, you can't know where it might lead, and this piece led to places I couldn't have imagined, got people discussing things and considering things at a depth that amazed me. Some of the journalists doing the more thoughtful reporting about benefits seized on *Bedding Out* because it gave them another way in to the issues. Disabled people, who'd felt so poorly and dangerously portrayed, said they felt represented and a lot of people new to the issues said they were presented with a story they simply hadn't heard. There's a risk involved with any of this kind of work, a risk that it'll be misinterpreted, a risk that you'll look foolish, and of course there's always the next project that doesn't work, but the power is in that risk, because it's only through risk that extraordinary and unpredictable things can happen.

When you're cutting through wire fences or blockading buses, there's risk. I don't draw a firm divide between that performance and the performances I have done in blockading buses. I think it's all connected because they're all about creating a compelling image, a symbol to encapsulate stories that are rarely told, and all of the time –

whether you call it art or activism – you need to be making judgements about message and presentation and how to respond to events as they unfold. All of it requires a sense of occasion and spectacle and symbol and how you make that work for the thing that you care so deeply about. I come from an arts background and so I call it performance quite comfortably and people who don't maybe call it something else, but I think they're entwined.

*Could you tell me about your performance piece in Trafalgar Square?*

The artist Anthony Gormley's work *One and Other* was appearing on Trafalgar Square's Fourth Plinth. Over a period of 100 days, 2,400 people were selected by draw and given one hour each on the plinth. I realised it was an opportunity to get disabled people represented, so I spread the word and threw my own name into the lottery, then forgot about it. But

*The poster for Liz Crow's* Resistance *Project.*

then my name was drawn out of the hat [laughs] and it was a non-transferable place, so if I didn't take it up it would be a lost opportunity. It coincided with the launch of my *Resistance* project, a film-based installation that looked at the Nazi campaign of mass murder that targeted disabled people and at how the values underpinning those horrific events remain absolutely contemporary. This was a hidden history, and even though it was the 70th anniversary year, the press did not report it. It was obvious this was the subject I needed to take onto the plinth and I needed an image either to convey the issues I was dealing with or to stop people in their tracks and cause them to ask questions – so not give all the answers, but to make people think, ask questions, in ways they hadn't done before. I was talking it through with a friend, chucking ideas around, and suddenly the idea came up that I should go up there in Nazi uniform. It was such an appalling thought that we burst out laughing, then took a breath and realised that the image, that uniform, with its swastika armband, combined with my wheelchair, made the piece.

*It's the incongruity of it.*

Yes. It creates an unresolvable image. There's this symbol of hate and this symbol of apparent vulnerability and dependence in the same image, and you can't square the two. I'd seen an image on the web that had played with something of those ideas, of a young Asian man wearing a red t-shirt with the Nazi swastika on it, looking to the camera and grinning. My response was visceral, like the rug being pulled out from me. I couldn't explain the mismatch between his expression, the image, the fact that he'd have been a target. I couldn't resolve it in any way and the image stayed with me, keeping me thinking, and I thought, if I could create a reaction like that in other people... I didn't finally decide to go ahead until four hours before my time slot because the prospect was so terrifying. I had no way of knowing if people would get what I was trying to do or whether they would throw bottles, and it could have been anything between the extremes really. And certainly I had a really good discussion about security with the organisers. [Laughs.] There were people looking out for me on the ground but for the hour on the plinth there wasn't a lot anybody could do to protect me, so it felt... it's probably the most risky thing I've ever done. It took a week for my heart rate to return to its usual level. I did think, "I can't do anything like that again," because it was *too* dangerous, and yet I'm glad I did it.

At the same time, a group of about 40 people from Direct Action Network (DAN) grouped loosely around the plinth, handing out leaflets. People were coming up and going, "What the fuck?" The first tweet was "WTF' [laughs] which was the same response that I'd had to that image on the internet. But the DANners knew the issues and at one point one of the women called up to me and said, "It's okay, Liz, they get it." They ran out of the leaflets in the first 10 minutes, but then strangers began passing leaflets on to each other, and in the Square and on Twitter, which was relatively new back then, there emerged these incredible conversations between people who, collaboratively, were able to make links between the historical and contemporary and fill in the gaps that the image deliberately left open.

Leabharlanna Fhine Gall

*One thing I'd like to bring up: we might think of disability as being something fixed, that you're either disabled or you're not, but anybody can become disabled. It's a very obvious point but it's something that physically-able people forget, that it could happen to any of us.*

Yes. If impairment doesn't happen to us it will surely happen to a family member or friend or colleague. It's the most ordinary of things. Bodies change over time, and when bodies change, what we discover is that we have created the social world in a very narrow way. It's very, very easy for people not to fit. A tiny shift in how your body functions means you no longer fit, because of social structures.

But this is something that we can change, and desperately need to change, because we lose so much by sidelining people. You can apply this to any equality issue, where people are losing opportunities to fulfil their potential and even losing their lives because of external structures. But society, too, is losing out. It seems extraordinary to have a society that needs every one of its resources, knowingly ignoring masses of those resources. There's no sense in it.

*I'm interested in how you became a disability rights campaigner in the first place. You said you've been doing it for many years – was there a sudden political awakening or did it coincide with you having problems with your health? What was the trajectory for you?*

It was a sudden political awakening that happened in about 20 seconds flat.

*Really?*

There's the before and the after, it's as simple as that.

[Laughs.] I had an impairment from the age of 10 but it was a very undefined, undiagnosed impairment which I was under pressure to pretend wasn't there. I didn't knowingly come across any other disabled people, so I was very isolated, and there was nobody to act as any kind of role model to advise or support me or tell me I was okay as I was. My family were brilliant, but my parents were so young, with no experience of battling bureaucracies or anything like that, so we were very much on our own. I was in mainstream education. I had a lot of difficulty writing because of pain. The school had no idea how to work with uncertainty or complexity in a system that required clarity and rubber stamping and they were unbelievably hostile. They asked me to leave rather than take exams, because it was a hassle for them. I had no learning support, so I would gather all my day's work and take it home in the evening and dictate it to my mum who gave up her job to support me during my O level years. I took exams but it was all down to my family fighting for it.

I got out of school as quickly as I could and managed to get into medical school. I was really excited. They knew I needed to dictate my exams and I got through the first term, but clearly the right person hadn't clocked it so they withdrew the exam provision and threw me out. I'd had a comfortable, secure upbringing and maybe that's the burden of a middle-class upbringing! You're taught to think that "with determination" anything's possible, and there's a long way to fall when you discover it's not so simple. I was struggling to get back into the med school and get the provision I needed, but was meeting a brick wall, seeing all these men who were my dad's age create walls where they weren't prepared to listen, reason, hear, and when I had to leave it wasn't simply that I'd lost my degree in medicine, it was bigger than that. I'd lost my compass if you like. I didn't understand any of the things I'd based my life on.

It was a time of being incredibly confused. I became a volunteer at the students' union for a while and happened to go on a weekend community action training. There was a brief session on disability equality training in which these two disabled women explained the social model.

And suddenly I had an explanation for all those years, suddenly there was a language that made sense. I'd got a word for what was happening, it was discrimination. That I'd got an impairment was a given, but there was all this other stuff, this discrimination, that didn't need to happen, and actually my primary distress and loss of opportunity wasn't from impairment but disability. Being able to name it changed everything. Shortly after, I became a disability equality trainer; that became my work, how I earned a living. I moved to London, got involved with the burgeoning disabled people's movement, the very beginning of the disability arts movement, and my life changed absolutely radically and much for the better.

*Did you feel that you were more equipped to face the bullying and the walls and the barriers?*

Yes, but I think it's more than that. I think I found my community. I found a second family really. And that instant recognition, where if you had a conversation with another disabled person there was so much that didn't have to be stated, that always had to be stated in the world outside, and that was an incredible release. I found a common explanation for what was happening and a common focus for what needed to change. And the late 80s was an exhilarating time.

It really was a kind of born-again feeling, like we could take on the world. And to some extent we did. We were the first, I suppose. There had been disability campaigners in the past but suddenly what we had was this mass movement, an international movement, and it felt that anything was possible. And some of the time I think it really was. We changed things with a rapidity never been seen before.

*Can you give me an example of something you changed?*

A really early protest was against ITV Telethon. Telethon was a television fundraiser that demeaned disabled people in order to raise money, often to fund essential services, such as education or community facilities, that most non-disabled people took as given. It was charity based and celebrity-driven, and portrayed people as objects of pity in order to release the purse strings. There was something so fundamentally wrong about that victimising process, yet people were not seeing the mismatch, just getting caught up in the razzmatazz of the event.

About 150 of us gathered at the television studios on London's South Bank. We had our own singer-songwriters there and we had a sound system so there was a great backdrop of songs, really inspiring, energising stuff, placards, chants, and we were visible en masse, which was a thing that just hadn't been seen back then. At a certain point all the celebrities started arriving. Some of them were quite unpleasant and derogatory towards us but then went into the studios, giving these cheesy grins to raise money for people like us. [Laughs.] So this whole mismatch carried on, and a couple of activists got into the audience and were flung out. Then at a certain point security put up all these high, six or seven-foot tall interlocking fences and we just went up to them, dozens of us, and started rocking them. And if you think of the image of disabled people as being dependent and weak and pitiful and all the stuff that they were putting on the TV screen and, with that number of us just rocking... The barricades went down. At which point they called the riot police, and all of this was just unheard of. If you think back to the earliest days of Greenham where male police officers didn't know what to do with women, physically didn't know how to manage female bodies. And then later they got over that and started—

*Started pulling them, pulling them by their hair...*

Absolutely. [Laughs.] They got over it quite quickly. But we were at that stage where they were scared of our bodies. And there were little tricks, like a woman with an artificial leg who loosened her leg when she was about to be carried off and that would cause a lot of fluster. [Laughs.] And just the pleasure that we took... I think that was what was so wonderful, some of what we were campaigning for was life and death stuff and yet the joy and the sense of liberation in what we were doing was just life defining, life changing. Just to be in that moment. And it was a moment really. It was a few years, around the early nineties, where I think incredible changes happened. And some of those changes were in ourselves, which was probably just as important as the measurable structural ones, because, where some people say, "I'm not an activist anymore," I think just being in the world as a politically conscious disabled person you are having an impact. I think anyone with any kind of politicisation can't help but be an activist, simply by doing the ordinary stuff they do. So by changing that, I suppose it's what they call consciousness raising, isn't it? By making those changes the ripples were going out from us into the wider world. But it was the most dramatic thing and Telethon ended soon after. It was a defining point for disabled activists, realising that we could have an impact, that our time had really come.

*When you talk about this, you seem really joyful and light – and isn't that part of what campaigning should be about? There should be joy in it and fun and humour. I think there's this image of activism of being a bit miserable and ascetic and self- sacrificing and punishing, and it can be very tough but it can also be playful.*

Yes. I think much of the joy has gone from current campaigning. There was a simplicity back then. People say things are better now, and in certain respects they are, but mostly they are more complicated. And when they're complicated it's hard to campaign, because what you need is simplicity of message. I mean, at rock bottom, the stuff that we've always dealt with is incredibly simple – what is the value of a human life? Is one human life more valuable than another? Because that's embedded in our structures at the moment. The issues now are the same issues as then and the same issues as 150 years ago, but they've got a lot muddier in the way they're enacted.

If I think back to then I can remember, just as an example, being in East London, coming out of college, needing to get a taxi back home to South London at a time when there was no such thing as accessible public transport, so a taxi was the only way I could travel. For three hours taxis drove past me and refused to take me, and that was standard. That stuff still happens now but a little less. Theoretically, there's legislation we can call on now, but then it was completely legal and defended as reasonable. The level of behaviour and the attitude toward disabled people was so extreme that the college also managed to remove my place on the basis that I was a fire hazard. I have lost more college places than most people have had cooked dinners, and it's all been discrimination based, but back then it was all allowed to happen so easily, it was *normal*. And what many people felt towards me, simply for existing, was a profound sense of pity, unmitigated pity, that my life must be so awful it was amazing I was choosing to be alive.

Attitudes like this still exist, they still get expressed to me sometimes by complete strangers, but then it was wall-to-wall. But actually when it's that blatant, it's easy to confront, whereas now, most people know that stating that stuff isn't really acceptable or appropriate. It doesn't necessarily mean they don't think it, but they don't express it in the same clear way and therefore it isn't exposed for you to tackle with the same clarity.

And where we've made significant progress on some of the more visible and practical issues, I realise now that, relatively, they were the easy ones. You know, there are more disabled people now who are in employment, maybe have families, can get around on transport, relative to 30 years or so ago. But those are the very public and visible things to fight. The things that are much harder, nebulous and hidden, are about our value in society: do we deserve to live?

*Liz taking part in a bus blockade.*

Do we deserve to continue our lives? Do we even deserve to have lives in the first place? We need to find ways to confront these most fundamental questions, to demand the right to life, from conception to natural death, because they are absolutely out of sight, out of mind. There's more need than ever for activist momentum, not to feel that, phew, well it's better than it used to be, because although these issues are much harder to organise on, they are the ones that everything else traces back to: whether we are of sufficient value even to be here.

But I think there was a joyfulness in those early days because there was this whole new discovery of community, of the power and potential we had, and that simplicity ran through it. All through the 90s we were doing big bus blockades and, again, that was exhilarating. The idea that one wheelchair user can wheel into the road, put up their hand and hold up a double-decker bus and all the traffic behind it for a reason that's absolutely clear and compelling, and in the process of that, yes, annoy some people, but really change the minds of some others, is just extraordinary. I mean, everybody should have that experience of what life can be! [Laughs.] It's absolutely brilliant. But, I think for a time, as a movement, we've lost our way. A lot of our organisations have floundered through loss of funding. The political context shifted so that, where in the 80s and 90s there was a "wall" of opposition to hit against, when Labour came in, instead of that wall, it was like dealing with blancmange. There wasn't that same thing to hit against. You could recognise things that were fundamentally wrong, policies going through that were damaging, but the crystal clarity that had been there before was gone. And the current government, instead of announcing one clear policy change at a time, introduced a scattergun approach which has been very effective in dissipating a united and focused opposition. That's some of what we're struggling with now.

In the bus blockades our tactic was really obvious: the transport system is inaccessible, you go and you block the transport system. But if you decide to move on to something like institutional living, why so many people are forced from their own homes into institutions, do you carry on stopping buses? It's the most visible, public tactic we had but I think we have gone past the point where blockading a road gives the return that's needed, it's not direct enough to communicate on broader issues, but we still haven't found a replacement. I still don't know what that replacement is, for that particular issue or for others, the non-transport issues if you like. There was a beautiful clarity to it. It was a gift. The very first bus blockade people held up a banner saying: "At last, disabled people are catching buses" and it hit the front page of national newspapers.

*Were you there?*

I wasn't at that one, no. I was going through an extremely ill phase. But it fed me, knowing it was happening. It was a powerful thing to experience direct action as a spectator, knowing that next time I'm out there, I might be sustaining other people in the same way. Over the years, I have had to move in and out of that kind of direct action and, these days, much of that way of action isn't practical for me. But I also think we need to keep inventing new and imaginative approaches, and part of that comes back to making sure the artists are present. It's not that they're the only ones that can provide imagination but sometimes they bring in a spark or a new perspective and just release some new and striking way of doing it.

I think one of the things we need to do is get back to the absolute basics of why we're activists, what it is we're trying to do. I guess at the core, it's about communication, whether we're communicating hidden or invisible lives or communicating an injustice or a solution to it. When I'm in front of the bus, it's about communicating to the people on the bus and the driver of the bus and the other people stuck in traffic or passing by and, ideally, with the media, getting it out to more people, communicating that public transport that excludes a community is not public, until ultimately we build pressure on the policy and law makers to effect change. And whether it's direct action or a work of art or a piece of writing, it's always about communicating.

*Isn't the difficulty partly that we're all so much more scattered now than we used to be, with the rise of the internet, so that it's harder to get a message across? It's a complicated thing, because the internet itself can be a powerful political tool, but the public is so much more diffuse.*

I might have given you a different answer two days ago. I've just started reading a book about how we've become used to talking more than listening, and I think the internet feeds that. I don't know that it's entirely responsible but there's a pattern of parallel voices just shouting into the dark: one voice shouting that austerity is necessary, that there's great injustice that not everyone is working and the taxpayer is subsidising idleness and fraud, and then us, the opposition, going, "Well, actually, here's why people are out of work, here's why most of the population is a benefit claimant, here's the true fraud rate and the truth about tax avoidance," but the risk is that you've got all these voices yelling in parallel and no one at all is hearing what the other is saying.

*So there's a lot more noise.*

There's much more noise, and if we're all busy making the noise, then who hears it? Not just who can filter their way through it, but if everyone is making noise then they're not even trying to hear.

On the other hand, I think social media at its best gets beyond the shouting and can allow conversations between people who might never actually meet. This is what I saw in *Bedding Out*, where extraordinarily deep and thoughtful and deeply supportive conversations took place between friends and strangers, both around the bed and through a range of social media. When it works, it can be transformative.

The book I mentioned is called *The Art of Listening*, by Les Back. I'm at the beginning of it, but his introduction has grabbed me. His thesis seems to be about the role of sociology in an age that wants certainty, and the need to embrace the fact that actually life is uncertain: your life will be different from mine, therefore we can't necessarily extrapolate from your life and know how mine will go, sometimes we have to accept not knowing. And I think we need to devise an activism or a way of expressing art or whatever that works with uncertainty instead of shying away from it. Maybe in some way that links with the issue of risk as well, and when I say risk, I mean uncertainty. I can't be sure how the onlooker will react to my work but actually if I leave the interpretation open they have to go more deeply into themselves in asking questions and finding a position than if I just say what they ought to be thinking. In *Bedding Out*, people seized the idea and kind of ran with it and made it work for them. And I think where projects such as that reach people and start to change their minds, preferably in the direction I'm hoping for, that change might well be far more profound.

*And by telling people what to think, arguably they become further entrenched in their own positions – so it can become counterproductive.*

Yes, that's the risk. I keep referring to bus blockades, but you could substitute different actions in there. And when we were doing the blockades with that clear image, clear rationale and so on, there would of course have been some people we alienated, but it's about trying to weigh up the costs and the benefits. If you judge that you'll probably reach more people, shift things more than you will do damage, that's the point at which you might make the decision to go ahead. But you're highly unlikely to sweep everybody along with you. The risk is that you will entrench some people into a more polarised viewpoint. I think we need to acknowledge those risks, that they *do* exist, and then allow them to inform the decisions we make.

*I wanted to ask you about the collective response to the coalition government's attack on the disabled. With the Spartacus campaign, DPAC [Disabled People Against the Cuts], Black Triangle, and others. Tell me about the way people have banded together recently and your part in that groundswell of resistance.*

I wouldn't say it's an entirely united front. There are different perspectives, different degrees of politicisation, and that has its tensions. There is an attempt at the moment to define a kind of core to which those different groups can subscribe, to define the values that can reliably inform everybody's work. This recent campaigning and activism has been really interesting in that a whole new swathe of disabled people has come out of the woodwork. Some of that links to the internet because there are people now able to be activists, to be present through the internet, in ways they can't be physically present in the broader world, and that's really exciting. So you've got people with more extreme or complicated impairments, who spend most of their time at home, maybe in their beds, who have become incredible activists, creating far-reaching campaign work. We're getting those new perspectives coming in and shifting the way we work to become more inclusive. So if there is still a movement of disabled people, and that's a big debate that goes on, it's becoming more representative than in the past. I find that very exciting. If you look across the range of activism, it covers everything from the more traditional campaigners, the letter writers writing to newspapers, MPs, creating petitions and so on, through to the more radical wing of doing blockades and all of that stuff, and everything between. And there are crossovers between the work of some of those groups so that different approaches feed and reinforce each other.

I don't know if this is typical of activism as a whole but I think there's always been a divide in the disabled people's movement between activists, artists, and academics. I don't fully understand their resistance to each other since I kind of move between all three and think the cross-fertilisation of ideas and support the three communities can give each other are critically important. The night I performed on the plinth really underlined that for me, where the academic work underpinned what I did through historical and contemporary evidence... gave it gravitas. The artistic side communicated that to new audiences, and the activism came through the people on the Square reaching out to the public and the people who have since seized the image and used it to push forward debate and change.

*That relates back to what you were saying about how we need to take different approaches in order to achieve political change.*

Yes. If we think about the people that we're trying to reach, they range enormously in the lives they lead, in levels of education and literacy, in the kinds of thinking they do, whether they're very cognitive-based or creative/emotional. Such different ways of being mean we need lots of ways of communicating. If you pick blockades as your sole form of action, you'll reach some people but fail to reach others, whereas if you go for multiple approaches, which might be creative writing or dense academic study, or it might be poetry or theatre or whatever, you'll reach many more. If we're to be effective we need to call on everything we have at our disposal.

*That's a very positive idea because it suggests that there's a role for everybody. It's important to talk about all the different ways in which we can become active and make interventions.*

Activism is more about how driven you are or what your starting point is or your clarity of purpose, rather than the tools that you use. Somebody recently wrote about my work, saying I'd recently turned to activism through the plinth and other performance. And I was thinking, no, actually, all the film work I did before was activism. It was more subtle activism, but it all has a role. Sometimes it's necessary to be confrontational and sometimes it's vital to be subtle and nuanced. Our task is to find effective tactics for different situations, different modes of communication.

*People have said to me, "Oh, I could never be an activist," and what they mean by this is they could never blockade a bus.*

It's just one strand. People have also said to me: "Why do you do all this confrontational stuff, why don't you write letters?" But who says I don't? The confrontational stuff is just the most visible – I'm out of sight when I'm writing a letter or signing a petition, but I do that too where I think it's useful. I imagine most activists pull on different strands – it's simply that some are more visible than others, some are more headline grabbing. If you climb up the outside of a very tall office block you probably get a headline. If you write a letter to your local MP you probably don't. But they are both a form of activism since they both actively pursue change.

*You've been politically active for 30 years. Are you able to identify anything that sustains you, motivates you, keeps you going? What stops you from stopping?*

I think what stops me from stopping is that new stuff comes up. What I keep saying is that my next piece of work is going to be fun, it's going to make me laugh, it's going to be light, and then something else comes up so I deal with Nazis. [Laughs.] Or contemporary echoes of that. I get driven by the urgency of it. It's about lives on the line. People are dying in large numbers because of current policy, while others are finding they're hardly living. It's as simple as that, how can I not keep going?

There is a lot of trauma amongst people because of current political decisions. There are people dying unnecessarily, whether it's because the support they need is withdrawn, whether they're being driven back to work in ways damaging to their health, or whether the stresses they're being placed under are driving them to suicide. People are dying. It's known to the government and they're ploughing on anyway. And when you see that, how can you not keep protesting and looking for solutions?

I think it's important to recognise what activism does for *us*, as well, that in focusing on what's out there, we can feed ourselves. When I started doing disability equality training, I was able to take the horrible everyday things that were happening to me, these everyday insults, and turn them around. When something bad happened, instead of feeling it just as a personal attack, I was able to think, "I can use that." I can use it as an example in the next training so that people can understand that social process of discrimination and then understand their role in dismantling it. It was a really liberating experience for me to be able to make use of what was happening to me. I might be there in a room and people even think I was this dynamic trainer, but outside I was still getting all of the crap that all disabled people do. The difference between me and lots of others was that there was somewhere to go with it, to turn it around and use it.

And I think that was the case with *Resistance*. I was dealing with a really difficult history, with the fact that really difficult things were happening, currently, politically, to disabled people, and I was able to do something constructive with it. The idea of using a history that was so hopeless in a way that just might change things for the future was really significant. If I had looked purely at the history perhaps I couldn't have dealt with it, but that I might be able to turn aspects of it around, to apply it for some better purpose, changed everything.

Physically I need to look at how I'm an activist, because my illness is quite problematic if I'm trying to do the more physically demanding forms and emotionally the relentlessness of it can take a toll. I suppose I'm asking myself questions about the different ways it's possible to be effective as an activist, whether there are ways that take less of a personal toll and are still effective. A more gentle way of being an activist. Rebecca Solnit's book *Hope in the Dark* is wonderful. She talks about how, as activists, we need to live what we're working towards, that it's no good saying, for example, "Well, I know we exclude lots of people from our campaigning but it's so urgent. Once we've sorted this issue then we'll look at including all these other people." You can't do that because it's a fundamental contradiction of what you're working for. You can't create this utopian world having excluded people on the way there because it will be flawed.

*And quite dystopian. [Laughs.]*

Yes, exactly! So what we need to do is start looking at how *we* function in the world and using that as a way to communicate the changes we want to see. And living better becomes a part of our activism, even if it's not the most direct and visible part of it. It gives an integrity to the work.

Also the collaborative nature of activism is critical. We hear about Gandhi and Martin Luther King – extraordinary leaders though they were, they didn't do it on their own, they were never a single person creating those changes. It's rare to be able to say, "I – or even 'we' – did that... I made that change," because what we create are ripples, where the work of many people combines to make change. That can be hard because, however long you work, it's not often you really know whether you've had an impact. In the end it's a leap of faith, a determination to keep on living what we're working towards. And maybe that's something I need to look at: how do we create a bedrock of resilience in the population so that all of us learn how to recognise injustice and have what it takes to answer back? How do we support each other to take that leap of faith and not wait for others to do it first, not wait to see if it's effective but just do it anyway because it matters enough?

The thing that came out of *Resistance* for me was this question that people ask so often about the holocaust: what makes ordinary people commit such evil? But the question that came from the project for me was what makes ordinary people commit such *good*. It was ordinary people who turned those events around. Even in the desperation of the disabled people's holocaust, the beginning of ending those events came from disabled people. Even when they knew they couldn't save themselves, it was disabled people who alerted the wider population until they were compelled to protest. They didn't wait to resist until they saw someone else doing it first. It's a tangled web of who jumps first, and actually you just need to jump, and you'll bring other people with you.

# Drawing it out

Satirical cartoonist **Kate Evans** on bringing injustice into the light through her artwork.

"Give a shit" is my first published cartoon. I was a student in Brighton, living in a housing co-op, and it was an incredibly fortuitous place to start out as a cartoonist in pre-internet days. There was a postcard publisher living in the flat above, and another cartoonist in the flat opposite who collaborated with me on zines. Everything had to be photocopied, so all my work was black and white. Looking back through my cartoons now, I see a point where it all bursts into colour, when the web freed me from that constraint. But I miss the black-and-white days of photocopied zines, printed alternative press, and radical bookshops.

"Give a shit" is an example of subvertising. Body image is such an important topic, for young women especially. It's great to be able to twist a repressive "thinspo" slogan and reclaim it for all body sizes. I'm still really proud of it. Years later, my sister saw it propped against the mirror on an Australian lesbian TV drama. I'd decided by this point that I was going to aim high, for World Cartoon Domination. And since my postcard made it to Australia, presumably I've achieved that.

In the 90s, my work was directly linked to activism. I was living in a tree and resisting road building and opencast mines, and I started doing cartoon reportage – reports of direct action in comic form. I did them mainly because I thought they were funny, and people liked them, but I also wanted to shatter the media stereotype of activists as "other", as "eco-warriors". We're all just people, whether we set out to save the planet or not.

So this set me on the road to doing comics about serious things. I like taking an abstract subject and rendering it comprehensible: if they're being entertained, readers don't realise they're being educated. I think the best example of this was my full-length comic book, *Funny Weather*, about climate change. It's a very difficult subject to make funny. I finally hit on the idea of the climate modellers (all serious scientists in reality) making models of the world using Play-Doh, glue, and balsa wood. And the comic got steadily more bonkers from there.

"NHSplc" is a very recent cartoon. I've read primary parliamentary legislation before in an effort to understand what's being proposed – it's so hard to find out what the government is actually up to. So much for democracy! But in this case, the research had been done for me and printed in an academic summary in the British Medical Journal. The reality of the Health and Social Care Act is so drastically different to what was reported in the mainstream media. The Tories sold the Bill to the public as being about "GP choice", completely disguising the fact that they'd organised the wholesale sell-off of our beloved National Health Service. The BBC didn't even have the courage to interrogate the lie. The cartoon has had a lot of exposure on my blog, and several grassroots "Save the NHS" groups have reprinted it. I'm pleased that my work helps, but I wish it wasn't necessary. Why should we need to learn about subjects as serious as free medical services, or climate change, from a cartoonist? That's so sketchy. Pun intended.

# An act of defiance

**Jo Wilding** on how she went from throwing fruit at Tony Blair to taking a circus to the children of Iraq during the invasion.

*Interview by Angharad Penrhyn Jones*

*You first went to Iraq in 2001, when you were just 25. What took you there?*

I went to a talk by Joanne Baker who had been to Iraq twice and was about to go for a third time, taking items that would break the sanctions. This means that you took things in without applying for an export licence: vitamins, medical supplies, and so on. She was saying that 5,000 extra children a month were dying as a result of the sanctions. So I started campaigning on this issue. As part of that two of us went and threw squashy fruit at Tony Blair when he came to Bristol and shouted: "How many kids have you killed in Iraq today, Tony?"

I don't generally think it's appropriate to throw things at people but it felt like a pretty desperate situation. The sanctions had been in place for over a decade by then and despite all the civilian deaths and the lack of impact on the Iraqi regime, there was no real reporting about the sanctions in the media. We wanted to do something which couldn't be ignored. If we'd stood with a banner, it would have gone unnoticed, but because of the fruit, the question about sanctions killing children was in all the press that day and the next. Then we were interviewed about the sanctions and the same issues were reported again during the trial because I raised them in my defence, so I think more people knew about the sanctions as a result.

*Did you hit your target?*

Yes, my friend Bee hit him on the shoulder with a tomato and that was on the front page of all the papers. I got him on the tie with a tangerine. [Laughs.] That wiped the smile off his face! So we got charged with a public order offence and a journalist said to me, "Well, how do you know that this is happening in Iraq?" And I think I just felt it was time that I went there to see for myself exactly what was happening and to take supplies to ordinary people in defiance of the sanctions.

*Were you doing it as an individual or as part of an organisation?*

It was very difficult then to get a visa to Iraq – you had to be invited by an organisation. Voices in the Wilderness were taking delegations every three or four months from the UK and the States, so my friend Jenny Gaiawyn and I decided to apply to join a delegation. You could only get a 10-day visa so that was the longest you could go for.

*What did you learn whilst you were there?*

It was all really confusing. Iraq in August is stiflingly hot anyway. But also there was a lot that I couldn't quite understand. No one would say straight out what they actually thought about things because of the dictatorship, and you knew you couldn't ask them certain things. You couldn't say, "What do you think about Saddam?" But people were really friendly. So we met and talked to a lot of people and we were taken to hospitals to deliver the medical supplies. And while of course that was what the Iraqi government wanted us to see and tell people about, at the same time it was appalling and shocking. For example, there was a ward where children suffering from thalassemia and sickle cell anaemia were treated. They needed blood transfusions regularly but they also needed bone marrow transplants to survive long term. So you could see the littlest children were still quite bright and chirpy and energetic and as you went around the room the older children were just lying on the bed weak and emaciated and being fanned by the family members because the air conditioning didn't work. And the doctors said, "We know how to do bone marrow transplants, we've done them for years, but we can't do them now because we haven't got the equipment, we can't create a sterile environment, we can't store the bone marrow from donors." So there was nothing they could do to save these children, even though they knew how to do it.

*You went back in 2003, when it was clear that Iraq would be invaded.*

Yes, in February. We arrived in Iraq on the day of the big march over here, when more than a million marched against the war.

*Did you find it quite motivating when you arrived, knowing there had been the biggest march ever in UK history in protest against the invasion?*

It was a little while later that we knew about it. But people did mention it to us. And when we were in the hospital during the bombing, a man said to me that they were thankful to people all over the world, but especially in the UK and America. I was just completely humbled that with his son critically ill he could find it in his heart to thank us. But it also inspired me that the march was so huge that people in Iraq knew about it, and that it had meant something to them.

The other thing that was really inspiring was seeing the student walk-outs, and seeing the kids walking out of school in the UK and demonstrating. It was just amazing that so many people of all generations were taking action. It was the first time we'd seen kids taking action like that, in my memory.

*Was there a sense of shame around being British when you were in Iraq?*

We kept on apologising to people and they were saying, "Well, we understand that it's the government and that the government and the people are not the same." They understood that the sanctions were not the will of the ordinary people of the UK. Because the Iraqis understood about not wanting to be identified with the government, they carried that over to us as well and didn't blame us.

*So did you feel welcome there?*

I did, I did. People were really friendly. And at that time Iraq was very safe. Of course everything is double-edged. It was safe because the punishments for any crime were so extreme and because there was such a lot of surveillance everywhere. But there really was little crime and women could walk around the streets safely, we could drive back from places late at night, and we never felt in danger. Baghdad was a very beautiful city. You could go up on flat roofs and see all these domes and minarets rising up above this carpet of palm trees.

*I'm assuming it's changed a lot since then.*

Yes. A lot of the trees were cut down for military purposes, so the Americans could see across expanses. And obviously a lot of places have been damaged as well. I haven't been back since April 2004, so things will have changed again since then. But also the security has changed, in that people were not going out at night by November 2003, because of carjacking and kidnapping and so on, and for the first time a lot of women felt they had to cover their hair or wear an abaya to cover their normal clothes when they went out.

*How did your family feel about you going out there during the invasion?*

They were proud of what I did, but obviously it was really worrying. I think they would have much preferred that I hadn't been there.

*Did you ever feel that your life was genuinely in danger?*

Yes, and no. During the bombing obviously you don't feel completely safe. Nothing fell that close to us because all the foreigners had to stay in three different places. So other than the human shield group, who were in various different locations around the city, everybody foreign was staying in these specific places, and there weren't any bombs dropped that close to us. We were in a much safer position than the average Iraqi.

*But you were, in fact, kidnapped.*

Yes, though that was much later, when I went back. I went in February 2003 and left at the beginning of April because we were told to leave by what was left of the Iraqi government. And then I went back in November 2003 and was there until about the beginning of May 2004. It was when we went into Fallujah in April 2004 that we got detained. There were no demands for a ransom, or threats, so it wasn't a kidnapping in that sense, although at the time we didn't know that that wasn't going to happen. During the invasion there were no kidnappings, it didn't start until later. There were rumours and people came up with stories but there were never any actual threats to us as foreigners.

*It must have crossed your mind when you were detained that you might never get out.*

Yes. Fallujah was an entirely different situation and we felt that our lives were in danger quite a lot of the time, because there was completely indiscriminate bombing going on by the American forces. We were trying to take supplies to the hospitals and get people out that needed to leave. We were asked to try and get to a woman who was in premature labour. She was in a part of the town that was controlled by the US, so the Iraqis couldn't just drive an ambulance to her and bring her to the clinic. And when I say the clinic, this was like an ordinary doctors' surgery. The main hospital was not accessible to them and the second one was operating, but was down what they called "sniper alley" so they couldn't get people to and from the hospital safely. So we were just going to bring her to this clinic where there were doctors but no equipment. The blood banks were stored in what had been a

*Bullet holes in the windscreen of an ambulance transporting casualties in Iraq.*

Coca-Cola fridge and warmed up under the hot tap and the electricity was going off in the middle of emergency operations.

So we went out to try and get to this woman, waving our passports, but it was just getting dark and the Americans didn't see that we were foreigners and they fired at the ambulance. I was sitting by the window and the mirror casing shattered and a bit of it scooted across my hand and I shrieked, just because it made me jump. And they were firing and you could see the line of the tracer bullets coming and at that point I didn't feel particularly safe. But what I did was start singing, because I realised that the person driving the ambulance was a bit panicked and the first thing that came into my head was to sing a song. [Laughs.] He reacted then, put the ambulance into reverse and got out. In hindsight, obviously our lives were in danger at that point – bullets were hitting the ambulance.

*I suppose you never really know how you are going to react until you are put in a situation like that.*

Yes, your reactions aren't necessarily what you would expect. We went back to Baghdad the next day, taking casualties, then we came back a couple of days later and tried to carry on doing the same sort of thing. We tried to get supplies to the hospital and the Americans were firing. And so then we tried to leave Fallujah because we weren't actually doing anything useful and tensions were getting higher. The doctors at the clinic told us we weren't safe anymore. As we were leaving, the Americans started firing over the car and the locals in the houses behind us started firing back and that was when one of the gunmen jumped into the car and we were taken prisoner. I didn't think that we were at first. Jenny was saying, "Well, we're hostages now, aren't we?" and I was saying, "Oh it's all right, they're just showing us a safe way out of the town," and then Ghareeb, the guy who'd taken us there, took off his glasses thinking they were going to blindfold him. And that was when I got scared, thinking that we were going to be blindfolded and separated from one another.

*And that's something we've all seen on the news, isn't it?*

Yes. There had been one kidnapping, then – a group of Japanese people including one who had been feeding the street children. They'd gone somewhere near Fallujah a few days earlier and the three of them had been kidnapped and were being shown on TV with machetes held to their throats. So that was the point that I felt scared. They tied the hands of the men but they didn't touch any of the women.

We were taken to a house and there was a man who was obviously in some sort of authority, middle-aged, very dignified, very smart and clean, while everyone else was grubby after days of fighting. He told the young men to go and make us some tea. They had their faces covered apart from their eyes, you could see from their eyes that they were really young, and they had Kalashnikovs over their shoulders. We could hear them giggling in the kitchen and we thought, are they giggling because they are masked up, carrying Kalashnikovs and yet making tea for a bunch of women? [Laughs.] And then Jenny started to feel sick – it was very hot in there – and they brought a pillow and a blanket and were very tenderly tucking her in.

They asked what we were doing in Fallujah, and we said we'd been escorting ambulances and bringing medical supplies. They managed to verify that story with the clinic that we'd been at and then we were released. They came to us in the evening and said they were going to take us back into Baghdad, but they couldn't do it then, in the dark, because someone might kidnap us. And we went, "Oh, we're not kidnapped now, OK." [Laughs.] From their point of view it was really risky driving into Baghdad because when they went through checkpoints, American checkpoints, they would be in danger. It was brave of them to take us. So it was a really bizarre journey where at times we would have to be the ones that were visible and at times they would have to be the ones that were visible. So much was made of foreigners being kidnapped but Iraqis were being kidnapped all the time, or being arrested with nobody told where they were – they would simply disappear, and it just wasn't news. There's that complete imbalance of value put on different lives.

*When you went back, you took a circus – why was it helpful to take a circus act to Iraq? Some people might say this was quite a whimsical thing to do under the circumstances.*

The children had been through so much that they weren't behaving like children any more. They would play kidnappers and hold imaginary machetes to one another's throats and make sawing actions. When you took them pens and paper they drew pictures of airplanes bombing houses or tanks firing missiles, that was what was filling their heads. And the adults had all been through so much that they couldn't help the kids in that way. So playfulness was one thing we could give them. They were the best equipped to work out ways of distributing aid, they were the best equipped to decide how they wanted things rebuilt and restructured. But playfulness and silliness they really didn't have in them anymore. And we met two Iraqi theatre groups that were trying to do similar things and we were able to join up with them and work with them and support them. We carried on supporting one of them, Happy Family, after we got back, until two of their members were murdered in 2006 and they all had to flee the country. It was because they were working with children of all different sects and different backgrounds. That was almost a revolutionary thing to do, certainly for them at that time.

But you would see the reaction from people when we would turn up in a squatter camp, for example, and the kids had nothing – no school, no sanitation, absolutely nothing. We would turn up and do a show and then play with them, and people said to us, these children haven't laughed since before the war. They were really laughing from their bellies.

I remember one woman saying to us, "It makes me feel like there's still hope." And we worked with a group of street children, from when they were in a street shelter, right through to when they moved into a long-term orphanage. And the credit for them staying there goes to a lot of people, but I think we really helped because it was something they really looked forward to, when we turned up and played with them. Although it sounds really trivial, clowning and playing just gave people a morale boost. It gave the children a little bit of their childhood back.

There were a huge amount of mental health problems arising because there was nothing for people. No counselling, no help, no respite – and no light relief. The theatres were closing, the TV stations were closing, concerts were not happening any more. Every bit of light relief was being wiped out.

*I suppose circus routines are a universal language that transcend cultural and age barriers – everybody can enjoy those sorts of games.*

Yes. We put together a show that didn't have any words in and a lot of it was just silly slapstick, with sounds that were easily understood. There was a bit where I was on stilts and I swiped Luis's hat and ran off with it,

*Jo and fellow clown, Peat, in action.*

and he would get one child on his shoulders and then a bigger child on his shoulders – just silly slapstick chasing around. All very simple but quite universal.

*It must have been exhilarating at times.*

It was. I remember being in bed in the morning and the alarm would go off, and I'd be so exhausted it would almost be painful to move. But the first thing we did in the show was shout, "Hello!" to the kids, who'd shout "Hello!" back. Then we would shout, "Boomchucka!" and they would all shout it back, and you'd get this great swell of really excited voices shouting, and that was the moment, it was like an energy shot. That would keep you going.

*Where did the idea come from in the first place?*

Back in the middle of the war, we'd been going round the hospitals interviewing casualties of the bombings and there was this family who'd left Baghdad and gone to stay with relatives in farmland outside the city because they thought it would be safer. So there was a whole extended family staying there and the house had been bombed. The family members were all in the hospital and there was a young man who'd just got married – a lot of people were getting married because they didn't want to die unmarried, so there was a whole spate of weddings before the war. His new wife was not with them, she was buried in the rubble. And while we were there they told him that she had died. And there was a woman with four children. One of the children had died, one had serious head and leg injuries and then there was this little boy, who was four, Mohammed, and he had minor shrapnel wounds in his head and his hands. He was obviously completely traumatised and just not reacting to anything except being put down and then he would cry for his mum. And this guy who was with us, Shane, sat down on the floor and started drawing a picture, and Mohammed watched him drawing it. And then he got out some bubbles and started blowing bubbles. And Mohammed was watching them, following them with his eyes. Then he put out his hand and popped a bubble and he smiled.

That just stayed with me, seeing how the bubble made such an impact on that little boy at such a time. And I was at the Big Green Gathering in the summer and I saw someone with a giant bubble blower. I was already planning to go back and I thought, I want to take one of those back to Iraq with me. I was thinking about Mohammed. And then I walked through to the circus field and went, "Actually, I want to take one of *those* to Iraq." [Laughs.] I was telling my friend Sam about it and he said, "Oh, that's a great idea, I'll set up a website." So we put out this call on the internet. It said, "We want to take a circus to Iraq: it will be really dangerous, you won't get paid, you won't be able to get insurance, let us know if you want to join us." [Laughs.] Bizarrely enough, there were enough crazy people out there to put together a little circus.

*Where did you take the circus?*

We went to schools and youth centres. There were a lot of squatter camps where people were living in very insecure accommodation. People had been made homeless for all sorts of reasons: their houses being bombed, or landlords evicting them because social housing wasn't being paid for. Or they'd travelled up to Baghdad because of insecurity in their home area. There were a lot of Palestinians living in Iraq and some people felt they'd lived relatively privileged lives because Saddam's government had taken care of them

*Children in Iraq playing the "parachute game".*

wanting to make a point about Palestine and Israel. So a lot of Palestinians had been made homeless and were living in big camps. In some of the more traditional tent camps you'd see refugees, we went to quite a few of those. There was a shelter for street children, we went and played with them and then we carried on working with them when they were moved into an orphanage. There were quite a few orphanages about so we went to those. Also hospitals, children's hospitals.

*How did you cope with seeing children dying?*

My blog really helped with that in a way, because it was a chance to pour it all out. And we had each other to talk to.

*Do you think now that you have children you would feel differently about it? Obviously I understand that you might not be able to go to war zones, now that you are a mother, but do you think psychologically you would find it harder?*

Yes, I think so. I think once you've got kids it's all the more unbearable to see something happening to someone else's. And I remember when I was giving birth, thinking back to the woman that we didn't get to in Fallujah, because the ambulance was shot at. She was on her own without electricity, without water, without medical care. It must have been absolutely terrifying. And the labour was premature, so I can't imagine how she would have managed to keep the baby safe, if she did manage to give birth. It must have been utterly appalling, and that's just one story. When I came back I do remember feeling incredibly lucky. I used to cycle to the university just feeling so lucky that I could not only have an education but that I could get there and back safely and that nobody was going to tell me what I should wear. The electricity probably wasn't going to go off in the middle of my exams.

*You mentioned your blog earlier. Could you talk a bit about the citizen journalism that you did, and how that took off?*

When I went back in February 2003, I just started writing down what I saw and the things people were telling me, just to communicate to people outside about what was happening. In the UK we were only hearing about military figures or political figures and what they had to say about the war, and nothing about ordinary people and how they felt about it all. I started off by emailing the stories out to a few people, and then turning it into a blog made more sense. Throughout the war the blog was getting reprinted, being put in the *Bristol Evening Post* and on the *Guardian*'s website. And that really broadened the readership because a lot of people in the States were looking to the British media for a more accurate picture of what was going on. So that was how it started getting read more globally.

*What was your response to that?*

It was a surprise. I had no idea whether people were really interested in what was going on in Iraq. And no idea that things got read and then got passed on. It seemed like there was a real hunger for information. The internet was very limited then [in Iraq] – you had to be in an internet centre in one of the hotels to be able to get access, it was very difficult to have it at home. But what I realised was that actually these young people had all these ways of getting round these restrictions on the internet. Because of the sanctions none of them had credit cards, so they'd say, "There's a site that tells you this that or the other, only there's a firewall, but you can break that firewall if you have this or that software and you can't get that without a credit card so you have to go this way..." It was like this kind of secret passageway through the hidden bits of the internet to get to the information that they wanted.

*That's quite a hopeful thing, that there's a way round these obstacles.*

Yes. Incredibly dangerous, though, because if you were caught doing it, as an Iraqi, you could have got yourself and your family in a lot of trouble. And so that was why people had to be very careful in their use of the internet, be very careful about telling people they had a blog. But in the end blogs became a way for middle class Iraqis to communicate with the rest of the world, in the immediate aftermath.

I didn't know until I got back to the UK in April 2003 about the "Baghdad Blogger", Salam Pax, and that his blog was being really widely read. He would have been in serious trouble with the Iraqi government if he'd been caught.

*Your blogs were not only circulated, but the material you came up with was used in different ways. That must have been quite rewarding, to know that your work was feeding into other people's projects.*

Yes, and what I really loved about it, actually, was listening to people and taking notes and putting it out on the internet. And then those stories just travelled – they got passed on from person to person and got turned into other things. So somebody made some graffiti stencils about Fallujah, somebody else wrote a poem, and somebody else wrote a song, and other people made pamphlets which included bits of my blogs. And there were two plays. So people were giving me their stories to pass on to other people. And I loved that, that you could tell the stories and they would travel and let a lot more people know what was happening.

*And it's a way of bypassing the mass media, the propaganda, the misinformation – a way of filling in the gaps.*

The first time there was a house bombed in Baghdad, all the journalists were taken there on a bus and it was massive news. And with the second and third and fourth and fifth, there was declining interest. And then when they thought a hospital had been bombed there was great excitement because that was news again. But it turned out it was a market place, not a hospital, and it wasn't quite such news. That is the way that news operates. It doesn't treat ordinary people with ordinary stories as being particularly newsworthy.

And there was also the whole thing about casualties not being counted. Obviously it was beyond the scope of what I could do there to count the people that had died. But just telling the stories of families who had lost people at a particular bombing incident was quite an important thing to do. We went to try and find the family of little Mohammed, the boy we'd met in the hospital. Most houses don't have an address in the way that we do here, more descriptive addresses. So we followed these instructions and we ended up in a completely different bombed house, where a completely different family had been destroyed, and this young boy had been staying with another family member and that evening his family home was hit by a bomb and everybody in it was killed, so he came back to find he was without parents and brothers and sisters. After they'd told us their story we said how sorry we were and they thanked us for coming. They said nobody had asked them about it – not the government, not the Americans. Nobody had heard this story. That kind of story never fits into the news agenda. But actually I think it is really important to people to tell their stories.

*It's an obvious thing to say, but news value is always about what's new.*

Yes, novel things, or something that's more extreme than the last thing.

*Or things that affect powerful interests...*

Yes.

*What was the saddest thing you witnessed in Iraq, and what was the most positive or hopeful thing that you saw?*

I think the most positive things were when people said to us, "We haven't seen the children laugh like that, from their bellies, since before the war." And one man said to us, "My son wants to be a clown now. He draws you and he imitates you." And seeing children who a few minutes earlier had been drawing pictures of tanks and airplanes drawing pictures of clowns and jugglers. I think that's probably the most hopeful thing I saw.

The saddest things... [Sighs.] In the hospital in Fallujah there was a little boy brought in, the family came in and said he'd been shot by a sniper. They'd been trying to leave the house and get out of Fallujah and he and his sister were both shot by a sniper. As they brought the child in from the car you could see that he had wet himself, and as they were operating on him the lights all went out and David gave them a torch to operate by, and somebody was holding a lighter for them to see by. We didn't see him die, but he did die, and the women, the mother and the family, were all brought into the office at the clinic and they were screaming and crying and hitting their chests in grief. It's only one of lots and lots of the same story in Fallujah but that was one that we saw and were part of.

And also the hordes of refugees, internally displaced people from Fallujah camping in dusty fields in Baghdad, and seeing the shock on the children's faces. They were quite manic because we turned up to play with them – basically they'd had nothing until then and although on the surface they seemed happy and excited, it was painful to see their response to what they'd gone through.

Also getting letters from people in the States saying, "Why don't you write about all the good things that we're doing, like the fact that girls are going to school now?" And thinking, you don't understand what this country used to be. Girls were going to school, the children were off the streets and were not begging, they were all in school and girls were in high positions, qualifying as doctors. Regardless of your class background, if you were a talented student you could go abroad and study for higher degrees and PhDs. Of course that doesn't take into account the political questions, but Iraq wasn't this very backward country. It had quite a large measure of equality for women, they didn't have to walk around with their heads covered. There was a complete lack of understanding of the country Iraq used to be. And how much they've lost.

*If we could go back in time a bit... How did you get involved in activism in the first place? You obviously didn't go from being a completely conventional person to visiting Iraq with a circus. Were you political as a child or as a teenager?*

I wasn't political at all as a child or a teenager, and nor were my parents. I did lots of sport at school. I always cared, I had a conscience, and if I saw that people or animals were being mistreated I used to write letters to my MP and things like that. And the first thing that I remember was seeing something about Vietnamese boat people on TV – they were all in this locked camp and there were children and it wasn't safe. And they had appallingly frightening journeys to get there. So I wrote a letter to my MP. I think I was 12.

Then I did a Master's degree in exercise and health science and I was thinking I would go into health promotion and educate people about how to avoid having heart attacks. I was researching nutritional deficiency in children in low-income families and realised that actually the reasons for good and bad health were much more collective and political than about individual lifestyle choices. I looked into it further, into the quality of housing and the way the benefits system is set up. I looked at the way the planning system actually takes people's health out of their own hands to a large degree, by concentrating the housing in one place and access to affordable and healthy food in another. So, if you were relying on a bus to get yourself and a toddler and a baby to the shop, you weren't going to be bringing back bagfuls of fruit, you were going to be bringing back things that last a long time, cost very little and don't weigh too much. So I finished the Master's degree thinking that if I wanted to help people or to make a difference to people's lives, it wasn't going to be by telling them to do some exercise or eat more fruit.

I worked part-time and looked for voluntary things to do. Bristol Friends of the Earth picked up the phone first and were enthusiastic and said, yes, come in there are lots of things you can do. So I got involved with them and their campaign against a quarry in Ashton Court – a public park in Bristol. It was where I used to ride my bike and it was just beautiful, the wildest bit of the park, but there were plans to extend the quarry into it. So that was how I got into environmental campaigning. It was while I was down a tunnel on a road protest in Essex that my friend Jenny started telling me all about the peace campaigning work that she'd done and then from there I met Joanne Baker who gave the talk on sanctions.

*And that changed the course of your life.*

[Laughs.] Yes. That's how I ended up in Iraq.

*In terms of "winning" campaigns, you said in a piece that I read: "I don't see it as two poles of winning and losing and only those two possibilities, I see it as a whole array of possibilities in between." And that's something that [author and activist] Rebecca Solnit has written about as well, that there's a real danger in seeing it as two poles. Because the achievements aren't always obvious – the results aren't always measurable. What keeps you going, then, when you can't see those intangible achievements?*

I remember when Rachel Corrie was killed in Palestine I wrote something about it on my blog. My friend was working with very vulnerable teenagers in a secure hospital and she was reading selected parts of what I had written. She said there was this girl who wrote her a letter afterwards, saying that she'd made the decision not to try and kill herself any more: she was going to live, and she was going to try and make the best of herself. Because it was the first time she'd ever heard of people putting their lives on the line to protect other people, and here she was trying to kill herself for no reason at all. It really inspired her to turn her life around. It was such a lovely thing to be told, because you would normally never know that something had made a difference to somebody in that way. And you just never know what effect you're having. You could look at millions of people marching on the streets, and the fact that it still didn't stop the war. If you look at it that way it's really depressing and disempowering. But you can't see what would have happened if that hadn't gone on. How many countries might we have invaded since then, if it hadn't been for the degree of opposition that was shown? Maybe they didn't back down on that invasion, but maybe it influenced decisions that have been made since then.

*You've also used the metaphor of a chisel breaking the façade of the status quo. You say everyone's got a chisel, you've just got to work out what yours is. I think that's a really inspiring thought, because not everybody's got the guts to do the kind of campaigning that you've done.*

I think everybody's got skills, and if you beat yourself up about what you can't do then you're not going to find your own way of doing things. And it might be writing or performing, or it might be to do with direct action. It might be that you're brilliant at rousing other people to a fury. It might be that you're good at gardening and inspiring young people to grow things and becoming less reliant on fossil fuels. There's so much out there that's problematic and so much out there that's possible and doable.

It might be as simple as what you buy or don't buy, or how you travel, or where you travel to, or signing up to campaigns, or starting campaigns, or it might be performing or creating artwork or explaining links between what people do here and what happens in the Bangladeshi flood plains. I think everybody can do something, whether it's in their own lives or whether it's influencing other people. Often there'll be somebody else who's already doing something that you can join up with, so you don't have to reinvent the wheel every time. It's all out there. But as I was saying earlier, you have to be aware that you can't see the results of what you do a lot of the time, and so you have to do it not because you expect an easy win in the traditional sense, but because it's the right thing to do.

# Bearing witness

Camcorder activist **Zoe Broughton** writes about two decades of campaigning, including going undercover at an animal-testing laboratory.

The convoy of vans loaded with activists and camping equipment mounted the grass verge of the military base at 2:30am, establishing a peace camp along the perimeter fence at the Atomic Weapons Establishment, Burghfield. Police arrived. I wore my press card on a cord hung round my neck and was left alone. I filmed till nearly 5 a.m., slept for a couple of hours, resumed filming in the morning and then headed home to edit and upload the footage, posting it online just before midnight. My video was used to explain the issues and show the camp as peaceful and welcoming to a wider audience.

I became a campaigning video journalist over twenty years ago, and a lot has changed in that time. When I started, we filmed on Video 8 tapes and used a massive and expensive computer for editing. Nowadays, I edit on a laptop which fits into my camera bag; and when filming actions, such as those at Burghfield, I even make mini-films on my iPhone, allowing me to upload my footage onto the web almost instantly.

In 1993 I helped found the alternative news organisation Undercurrents with three others. Two of them were experienced but disillusioned with the broadcast media and two of us were prepared to stay at the campaign sites, ready with a camera to catch the action. We created the first activist video magazine – made up of a compilation of documentaries and news round-ups of protest, initially from around the UK, and later globally. Our aim was "to show the news you don't see on the news," which we screened at festivals and events, also distributing the VHS tapes by post.

Working on my first documentary involved spending months filming the M11 protest in East London – the campaigners wanted the government to rethink their road expansion plans, pointing out that all the evidence showed that more roads leads to more cars, more journeys and more pollution. The road would also cut through a long-established East London community.

While campaigners were evicted from the first street of houses, I was barricaded into a small room with two other women, one of whom had lived there for fourteen years. The wall cavities had been filled with concrete; the ceiling and floor had several old doors nailed to them, making it the place that would hold out the longest. The women put their arms down stretches of pipe, and these tubes were encased in concrete into an old washing machine, so it would be extremely difficult to drag the women away.

We knew the bailiffs were getting close but were still startled when a pneumatic drill broke through the wall. The women stayed strong, shouting for the men to be careful as the room filled with rubble and a cloud of dust.

While the bailiffs were breaking in, I kept changing the videotapes, hoping to get some footage out. I hid tapes down my socks and knickers. Eventually I was told to leave and was forcibly carried out by riot police. I kept the camera running as I was being carried, giving me a tracking shot through the police lines.

On the other side of the road a press pen had been set up by the police to keep the media safely away from the action. The only images the press could capture was of protestors being removed from the buildings and taken through the police lines.

Once I'd been let go, I approached the ITN crew, pulling the tapes from my knickers and socks. We started negotiating the sale of my footage. The images of the women holding strong inside the room made it onto the six o'clock news.

This was a crucial moment for me. I loved getting the issue seen by thousands of people, helping them to understand the protestors' point of view. I have sold my footage and made videos for campaign groups ever since, enabling me to make a small but sufficient living.

I believe that video is a powerful nonviolent weapon – it has the power to change the way people think. Undercurrents was partly funded by Small World Productions, who make films for development and environment NGOs. In the autumn of 1996, I was called into one of the Small World offices, sworn to secrecy and asked if I would try to get a job in Europe's largest animal-testing company, Huntingdon Life Sciences (HLS). Small World had secured a TV commission based on other people's research. I was to go inside and film the day-to-day happenings inside the lab. It was to be my first venture working undercover.

I applied for a job advertised in the local paper, went through an interview, and was asked to start work shortly afterwards. For the first two weeks I couldn't film covertly: unless you can prove it is in the public interest, this breaches privacy laws. So I wrote a detailed diary of the goings on, sometimes on scraps of paper I'd fold small into my trouser pocket. Occasionally I would scribble brief notes on my stomach in the toilet. We applied to OFCOM and were granted a licence to film. I was wired-up with a camera built into a pen.

At first I was excited, but working with beagle puppies and dogs, whom I grew to love, was emotionally exhausting. During stressful test days, puppies squealed and were shouted at, shaken and hit. The images I filmed still have the power to shock and I have to be careful to warn audiences when screening the footage.

Huntingdon Life Sciences were asked to reply to allegations both about animal cruelty and about technicians taking short cuts in measuring out and administering doses. It would be my word against theirs – except they were unaware that I had caught it on videotape.

When the film was finally edited, my main worry was that the cruelty I had witnessed would simply continue, that the film wouldn't change anything.

It was screened on Channel 4 on March 26th 1997. The response was amazing. The local police arrested two of the lab technicians and by September two of the HLS employees had admitted to charges under the Protection of Animals Act of "cruelly terrifying dogs".

On 24th July 1997, the Home Office minister, George Howarth, told Parliament in a written answer: "Shortcomings relating to the care, treatment and handling of animals, and delegation of health checking to new staff of undetermined competence, demonstrate that the establishment was not appropriately staffed and that the animals were not at all times provided with adequate care." He revoked the company's license to operate with effect from November 30th

1997 unless 16 conditions could be met.

Huntingdon Life Sciences is a contract testing laboratory and some of their clients stopped using them. The share price collapsed from 126p down to 54p in a matter of weeks.

The company did meet the conditions set. Ten years later I tried to book a visit to HLS with a camera – I could have shown how they have changed and what goes on there now, but they refused. I am *persona non grata*.

I spent the next few years working undercover. I investigated animal cruelty for Compassion in World Farming. I looked into horse markets, foot-and-mouth disease, and long-distance animal transport. It was a bizarre job for a vegetarian, working side-by-side with those dealing out the cruelty. But I knew that that if I gathered video evidence I might play a part in stopping it. Often I was scared. I'm not a brave person; I often can't eat before going undercover. I've been held at gunpoint by police in Italy and had my car stoned by angry abattoir workers. But how else can we show a wider audience that this is going on? This is the reality of the meat on our plates.

I spent weeks working as an egg-packer in factory chicken farms, and gathered footage showing five chickens crammed into a cage where they can never stretch their wings. I filmed a bird stuck onto an electric wire, put there to keep them from pecking at their eggs as they are conveyed away. The video was sent to every MEP before a vote on the phasing out of battery cages. They voted in favour of a gradual discontinuation of that method of battery farming.

I have made films on other issues too, and in dangerous parts of the world. A personal passion for the people of Burma and their ongoing struggle for freedom led me to accompany a Burmese friend who, having gained his refugee status, wanted to travel to the refugee camps in Thailand to see if he could find any of his comrades from the 1988 uprising. (This was a peaceful student protest, mowed down with machine guns by the Burmese Military.) I had assumed this would be a safe trip, but ended up helping to deliver medical equipment to the camps and being smuggled across the river in the middle of the night into Burma. There I experienced, first-hand, the relentless stress of listening out for the Burmese military, which could approach at any time. It made me empathise with the exhausting fear of those living in conflict areas of the world, especially those with children to protect.

Now that I have my own children I would not consider working in such violent places. I spend more time editing at the dining room table, working when my children are in school and when they sleep at night.

I recently travelled to Northern Canada for 16 days to film a documentary about tar sands oil extraction. This was the longest I'd been away from my children. My husband of 11 years looked after them whilst I was away and did more than his fair share of the childcare and domestic chores when, on my return, I worked crazy hours to condense the 90 tapes into a coherent one-hour story. When we put the credits onto the film I credited him with childcare. He vetoed this, however, not wanting a man thanked for doing his share until the partners of male filmmakers are also acknowledged for giving them the space and support to do their jobs.

Since 1997 I have worked as a freelance videographer for Greenpeace. I've filmed for 26 hours from a speed boat on the Thames, while protestors stopped coal being unloaded from a ship delivering to the Kingsnorth power station. I arrived home from the action at 4 a.m. and did the school run a few hours later, not mentioning my other world.

Tonight, while I sit here writing, I think of my comrades, who tried to scale an oil rig in the Arctic and have just been sentenced to two months on remand in a Russian prison. I could easily have been the one filming that action. Friends have lost their freedom and are being kept from their young families, but the images they got out and their efforts to save the Arctic are being seen around the world. My daughter Matilda has just produced a stunning piece of homework on the Arctic where she mentions that Mummy's friends are being held in prison. I wonder what her teacher made of this.

Filming protest is not an easy career. Over the years I have earned very little and have risked arrest and injury. But I strongly believe that campaigners need filmmakers to protect them and to get their stories heard. Injustice hates a witness, and it particularly hates a witness with a video camera.

*Zoe on the front line of a protest.*

# With my hammer

Nobel Peace Prize-nominee **Angie Zelter** on destroying a hawk jet, working with women in Palestine, and why she sees herself as a global citizen.

*Interview by Angharad Penrhyn Jones*

*You've been campaigning for over 30 years now. When did you first became politicised?*

I didn't come from a political family. My dad is Armenian but we never talked about his country, or the genocide of the Armenians – and I was the first to go to university. Then at the end of my degree I came across the very first copy of the *Ecologist* and read about acid rain and nuclear weapons and climate change. I hadn't been aware of these issues at all and I thought, I've had a university education and I haven't heard about any of this. And that's what really turned me around. So my education actually started when I left the education system.

*You went to Cameroon shortly after university. What were you doing there?*

Well, when I was at school someone came to talk about their

171

experiences of doing Voluntary Services Overseas (VSO), and I thought, "Wow, that's something I really want to do." Then, during my last year at university, I met Arnold, my future husband, and we decided that we would like to do VSO together. Arnold was offered a job with the Overseas Development Office in Cameroon and I thought I'd find a job when I got over there. I was only 21 and it was a huge culture shock – for a start, I didn't know that colonialism still existed and how racist whites could be. Everybody had servants and the whole idea was anathema to me. I refused to live like this, which cut me off a bit from the other expats. After I'd been out there six months, I decided to have a party for all the people I'd met, but it was a disaster – the whites were at one end, the blacks at the other end, and I was in tears. There were all these white expats having such racist conversations about their black servants and I couldn't bear it. I thought, "God, what have I come in to?"

But in that first year I got to know this Cameroonian, and he said, "Why are you here?" And I said, "Well I've always wanted to help, there is so much poverty here in Africa, I've come to help." I was so naïve! He said, "How do think you can help? Where do you think our problems come from?" That really got me thinking. There were banana and coffee and cocoa plantations owned by companies that were controlled by Britain and all the wealth was drained away to the UK and France – Cameroon is an incredibly rich part of the world and nobody needs to be hungry. There was a lot of poverty and the riches were just being siphoned off. The exploitation was absolutely amazing. So at the end of the three-year contract we decided to leave and try to create change in our own country.

*What did you do when you returned to the UK?*

It was the beginning of the 80s and it was the time when people were very concerned about nuclear weapons. So I got involved with the local peace group in north Norfolk. The first thing we did was organise an action around Parliament on nuclear weapons and international law, where we chained ourselves to the railings. I also went to Greenham Common Peace Camp with them.

*Why did the issue of nuclear weapons capture you so completely?*

It was the height of the Cold War and there was a fear, a genuine fear, that the world could just be blown up. And of course we knew about the possibility of a nuclear winter, how if a certain number of missiles went off it would change the climate drastically and there would be huge starvation.

*Tell me about your experience at Greenham. How did it influence you?*

I think Greenham influenced me by giving me the confidence to do things in any way that felt right. In my first court case, for instance, I was up with a group of women and everyone was representing themselves in really different ways. Some women were completely quiet in court, some shouted, some did poetry, so I realised there's no right or wrong way to do this – you just had to be true to yourself.

My kids were quite young so I only went to Greenham for two or three days at a time. Sometimes I took my kids, sometimes I didn't. There were all kinds of women there. There were some who wanted an all-female environment to be in, and it was a whole lifestyle thing for them. Some mentally handicapped people with major problems – our society doesn't have any spaces for them so they would hang out there. Some highly political and articulate women. Some that were particularly nasty to men, but I think most of them had had really bad experiences with men and this was a safe place for them to vent. I stayed at Orange Gate, because that was the friendliest place for women like me who were married and had families.

*What did you make of the decision-making process at Greenham? Within your campaigns you generally seem to take a non-hierarchical, consensus based approach to making decisions.*

It felt like a very natural thing to do. I still have this idealistic vision that if you spend enough time on it, and you are willing to really listen to the other person's point of view, you should be able to find something that satisfies you both. Not a compromise, which is unsatisfactory, or a majority decision which leaves a whole section of society unrepresented. We've used it with groups in Palestine more recently, and used with good heart and compassion it's a great way to work. So everything I've done really since those early days has tried to be consensus based.

*In Greenham, was there something about being with women only that nourished you?*

Yes, I think so. I've never been a person who was put down very easily by men anyway; I've always been quite a confident person. But it was such an exciting time to be there. It wasn't just being with women, it was also that people were protesting seriously day after day, year after year after year, which I don't find happens very often now in the UK. I've recently been over to Gangjeong, on the island of Jeju in South Korea, and I thought, yes, this is what we need to do again back in the UK. The whole village has been protesting the building of a naval base that will be used by the US in its coming war with China. It is an inspiring place and reminded me how powerful resistance can be when you really put your heart and soul and mind into it and work with whole communities.

And in a way, that's what I felt when I was at Greenham. We were thinking all the time about all the different political problems, so that's where I learnt to link many of the issues. To me, almost any of the social change issues are intrinsically linked with the others.

There was also this motto that really had an impact on me, especially as I had a family and was mostly at home, and it was "Carry Greenham Home". I realised that I had all these US bases near me, in north Norfolk, and so I started the Snowball Civil Disobedience Campaign. I still meet people who say they took part in it. I had this idea of linking up an action locally with the steps for disarmament that were being talked about internationally. So I thought, let's take a symbolic action which nevertheless is serious enough to be seen as criminal damage, so something they can't ignore. The fences are what keeps the public from thinking about or seeing what's really going on inside these military bases and I thought, well, cutting one strand of wire is quite symbolic, and it's not going to be too difficult to get people to do that but it is an act of civil disobedience that cannot be ignored

There were three steps: you do the action, you get more people to do it and you write a letter to the government and ask them to take a step towards nuclear disarmament. And we also had an open letter that went to the government telling them what we were going to do. Right from early on I wanted everything to be accountable and non-violent. Because ultimately the things you are doing have to be in accordance with the end that you want. If we want government to be accountable then we should also be accountable.

*Do you think the world is safer now than it was, in terms of nuclear weapons?*

No. In Britain we think that the Cold War is at an end and therefore we are safer, but consider the proliferation that has taken place. From the five original nuclear weapon countries that signed the Non-Proliferation Treaty, there are now eight, including Israel, a country that is engaged in ethnic cleansing and human rights abuses, and whose threats are now leading to other countries in the Middle East wanting to develop their own nukes. It's also become much clearer over the last decade just how much nuclear pollution there is. People aren't aware of the number of nuclear submarines that have sunk, for instance. And the infrastructure of those submarines is being breached now because some of them have been under the water for decades and the fissile material is leaking out. The links between civil nuclear reactors and the military nuclear programmes are also making us much less secure.

*You've also campaigned a great deal on the arms trade. How did you get involved in this issue?*

I've always been concerned about the arms trade; it seems to me to be a terrible thing that people earn their money by selling arms when you know that those states are going to use them for repressive means or for exploitation of other countries. I'd heard about East Timor and that whole tribes were being destroyed by our Hawk jets, and it took me back to this Cameroonian, who made me think that I should go back home and deal with the causes and what my country was doing. And I thought, this is a British company and we are selling arms to a repressive regime.

The Ploughshares movement was talking about doing something about arms exports, so I was invited in. And we decided that we would like as a women's group to disarm some Hawk jets and prevent them from being exported. We ended up being a group of 10 women and taking a year to prepare for the action.

*Were you at all daunted? Did you hesitate at all?*

No, not really. I'm not very easily daunted if I think it's the right thing to do. When I was thinking of doing the Malaysian anti-logging action, in support of the Penan people who wanted to stop the logging of their ancient rainforest home, I was coming up to 40 and I said to Arnold, "Look, I'm thinking of doing this action, and it could be just a week in prison or it could be a long time, years." And it was very hard, he didn't really want me to go away because of the uncertainty.

*Was he an activist as well?*

No, he wasn't, but in the early days we had to think very carefully about the children. We decided that one person had to be around for the kids and to keep the family going, earn the money. But we used to talk about things, we'd plan things together and then I would do them. My parents-in-law were also part of the network of support as we lived in an extended family. My children always had at least three adults around, which allowed me much more freedom of action than many other mothers. I was very lucky.

*Did your family keep you strong, psychologically?*

The family I married into, yes, because they were highly political themselves, so they understood. My own family, no. My stepmother was shocked about the whole thing. I can remember her ringing me up when I came out of prison and I was in tears by the end. She was saying, "How could you leave your children?" My kids asked me why I was crying, and when I told them they were really angry. They said, "Why is she worrying about us? We're fine." But she was very unhappy about all this political activity. The only time she started respecting my activism was when Trident Ploughshares got the Right Livelihood Award and I went to Oslo to receive it. It was getting external recognition that helped her understand and I thought that was very sad.

*Tell me about the Hawk action itself.*

Of the 10 of us, it wasn't until quite late in the whole process that we decided that only four could risk arrest. The other six for all sorts of reasons couldn't – having very young children or not being able to take leave from their jobs, etc. So they had to be kept quiet and secret. Then we had to work out who would do what, and after lots of debates I decided to stay on the outside and do the press work. So four of us were the open disarmers and the other six were providing support. When we got the peace prize from the International Peace Bureau I purposely gave my bit to Rowan and Ricarda, the two people on the outside who'd done the most support work. I thought it was wrong that only the four of us got it, as the supporters are just as important and vital as the open disarmers.

I think it's really unhelpful to put people on a pedestal, whatever the action or the event. There are always hundreds of people who make things happen – it's not just about the person who's known in the media, the person who's arrested or imprisoned. Actually it's much easier going to prison than doing all the support work behind the scenes, because that just goes on and on.

*Yes, in this media-driven world it's very easy to forget about the people behind the scenes. Still, you could have faced 10 years in jail. Were you able to get your head around that?*

The four of us could have gone to jail for 10 years, yes. As for getting my head around it – yes, I could. And I did. And by that time, the kids were at university, so that was not an issue for me.

I'd already spent time in prison, unlike the other three, and in our lead up to it we were exchanging information about how we would cope with it. I just thought, I'll use that time as education. I'll learn another language. I also knew I could get a bit depressed, I knew I'd have to cope with that, but I was already beginning to learn how to be myself in prison. One of our group would not have survived the 10 years in prison, – she was already getting really depressed and it was a real worry about what we would be able to do to support her if we got a long prison sentence. She hadn't had experience of prison before. It's a good idea before doing a big action to check whether you're claustrophobic for instance, and how you're actually going to deal with it mentally, but of course, until you actually experience it, you do not really know how it will affect you.

*What was the thing you found the hardest about prison?*

The visual impairment, really. You don't have anything

around you apart from walls. You get out occasionally for exercise. And the silly mind games that the prison officers play on you, and the dependency and institutionalisation that you succumb to because you are not allowed to take responsibility for much and are treated like children. The other thing that happens when you're inside is that you get emotionally distanced and cut off from people. It took me quite a long time after that to relate properly to people again. Also some of the other prisoners that you meet are very disturbed. And the other thing is just the inequity of the whole thing. Most of the women I met in prison had been sexually or physically abused as kids.

*It's quite an eye-opener, I suppose.*

Oh yes, I think everyone should go in for a short period of time – it's one of our institutions, and we need to know what's going on in our society. Prisons should be much more open to investigation – there are many abuses going on inside.

It was actually during that six months that I started writing prison reports. We were locked up for a very long time, they had a staff shortage, and sometimes we didn't get out to wash for days on end. You were allowed out for about five minutes to get your food, take it back into your cell and eat it. And that was it. We were really cut off from everything. So I did a survey amongst the other prisoners on the rare occasion when we were let out and able to talk to others and I got a written report out to an MP about the situation. Then the next thing, I was hauled before the governor and told I could face years in prison for breaking the rules. I didn't know that as a prisoner you are not allowed to write reports or do surveys inside. I said I didn't believe they could give me extra years just like that, they'd have to take me to court and if they did I would tell everyone what was going on in their prison. They never did charge me, but that was quite scary for a while.

Ever since then, whenever I've gone in for any longer than a few days at a time, I do a report. I say to the prison warders, "I just want you to know that while I'm in here I shall be doing a report, I don't want it to be underhand." I've had the prison ombudsman writing thanking me for my work because they are getting an honest report written by an articulate person right inside the system.

*Did you manage to get these stories out to the press?*

Yes, one of the reports I did has been used by the press in Scotland, about all the wrongs going on at Cornton Vale prison. For instance, there is a lot of prejudice in Scottish jail against Irish prisoners, and when the relatives of an Irish prisoner came over, the prison staff would lie and say they were not in the prison, that they'd been moved. And there is quite a lot of racism against Afro-Caribbeans in the prison system. Also at some point over the last 30 years it changed from being only women staff to having men in women's jails, and I think that was a really bad innovation. I've witnessed, for instance, the sexual abuse going on, with prison officers going into women's cells and having sex with them.

*Tell me about the time you were assaulted in prison.*

We had decided, five Trident Ploughshares activists inside for a month at the start of the anti-Trident campaign, to demonstrate against the fourth Trident submarine being launched. If we'd been on the outside we would be doing a demonstration, so why shouldn't we as prisoners do the same? We planned that we would make banners on a certain day, hang them outside our prison cell windows and not eat or drink or go from our cells, just for one day, as a protest. We were in different cells, but we discussed it in the exercise yard. We made banners by tearing bits out of newspapers and using our toothpaste to stick it onto a prison sheet, and then we hung them out of the window. And then we all wrote a little note explaining what we were doing so that when the prison guards came in we would just hand them the note. So when the prison officers came in the morning and told me to come out of my cell, I just shook my head and gave them the note. They came back and said I had to go to a disciplinary hearing. I just shook my head and that's when they assaulted me and dragged me out of the cell. They really hurt my wrists and I was screaming by the end. I didn't speak but I was screaming in pain. And they shoved me in a cell and several male officers took all my clothes off me and left me naked in the cell. The doctor came after a while, because I was in quite a lot of pain.

*After the Hawk action you chose to represent yourself in court. Why?*

Because I wanted to understand what's going on and I don't understand legal jargon. I always try to represent myself. The people who represent you don't often know about the issues or why you are doing things, and a lot of lawyers are so busy they don't even get the facts right. I also think that's something I got from Greenham, having seen all those women doing it themselves.

*Were you surprised when you were acquitted?*

Yes, and no. I think I was the only one of the 10 Seeds of Hope women who said right from the start that we could win this, because I'd already had a lot of court experience. I insisted right from the start that we had the pamphlet, that we had the video and that we used the right language. I said, "Don't talk about damaging the plane, talk about disarming the plane. And don't talk about wanting to get publicity for the cause – that's not why you are doing it. You're doing it to protect people, to prevent the plane from committing more genocide, to prevent crime."

I remember the judge in one of my Snowball cases saying we didn't have any legal right to cut the fences. We were using the Criminal Damage Act to say that we had a right to prevent crime, and he said, "How can you prevent crime by cutting a wire?" He pointed out that it made no sense. And then he said, "You'd do much better if you destroyed a plane or something." And I thought, yes that's a really good idea... I bet he lived to regret that. He probably never knew actually. I wish he did. [Laughs.] He would have been quite shocked.

*You had some great witnesses in court. One of them won a Nobel Peace Prize.*

Yes, brilliant witnesses, and absolutely vital. [War correspondent and author] John Pilger, Professor Paul Rogers, [human rights activist] Carmel Budiardjo, and also José Ramos Horta, the East Timorese foreign secretary in exile. José was particularly important. I can remember asking him in the court, "Can you explain what those Hawk jets did, and is it true that whole tribes were eradicated?" He was starting to answer when the judge shouted at him, "Yes or no?" and hardly gave him any chance to speak. I was absolutely devastated by that. I said to him as he left the court, "I'm apologising for the way you have been treated in this court, that you haven't been allowed to give the evidence of so many thousands of your people being killed." The judge

*The Trident Three standing outside court after a landmark victory*
*(Angie Zelter centre). © David Mackenzie*

was furious. This was the advantage of representing yourself, because a lawyer couldn't have done that. And I think that those kinds of comments that we were making throughout the trial really helped the jury to see what was happening.

*What did you do after the Hawk action?*

I started Trident Ploughshares. We did lots of actions and I got five months in prison on remand for an action against part of the Trident system. Three of us got a boat and launched it on Loch Goil where a Trident testing barge is moored. We took the boat across to this barge, which is actually a floating laboratory where they do acoustic tests. It's a major link in making Trident workable. So we climbed out of the boat, found a window that was open, got in, and then just emptied the whole laboratory, just threw everything into the loch. And then we took our hammers out and started hammering on various bits of equipment and cut various wires. We made the laboratory unusable, taking out a vital link in the nuclear weapons testing system. And when we'd finished we had a picnic. It took them hours to find us, it was amazing!

*Was there no security?*

Not really, because who would think of anyone going and destroying a laboratory? There was some security nearby but they didn't see the banner for ages, then the police came up and we helped them on and said we were non-violent so they were fine. They were quite used to Trident Ploughshares actions by then.

But that was an important case because the judge found us not guilty on international law grounds. So we won on legal grounds as well as moral grounds and it generated a huge debate in the Scottish press. They didn't like that, because there was an acquittal and they thought it would open the floodgates to more activists, so they ordered a Lord Advocate's Reference. That was fascinating, because that was the first time any non-lawyer had represented themselves. It was a lengthy process to get the right to speak directly to the High Court myself, rather than having a lawyer do it, but I insisted. The lawyers for the Crown came up afterwards and said they had learnt a tremendous amount about international law.

*So you're constantly pushing boundaries, it seems, in everything you do.*

Yes, I want to make the law more publicly accessible and accountable. I don't think you should be allowed to be tried in a court when you don't understand what's going on. There is too much jargon used. Why can't they speak in plain

English, why do they have to use Latin terms which most people don't understand?

A lot of people ask me why I'm so interested in the law; they say surely this is a moral issue, not a legal one. But there is no legitimacy to law if it has nothing to do with common morality. That's what allows it to work. It is meant to protect the vulnerable and provide an impartial process for resolving conflicts in society – something that is being lost. I don't believe in prison and horrible punishments for people, I believe in reform and other ways of dealing with crime. But I still believe society needs to say very clearly what's acceptable and what isn't. And that is based on morality. It shouldn't be about the interests of corporations or governments, and I think we've all lost sight of that, totally lost sight of that. We have all these hundreds of laws being passed by our parliament which have no legitimacy from the majority of the public's point of view. The police aren't tackling the real criminals; they are not arresting people planning mass murder, which is what the deployment of Trident is all about. If it was an individual planning mass murder, they would prosecute them, but because it's a government and supposedly about "defence", they do nothing.

I've been doing a lot of actions at Aldermaston and Burghfield and having long conversations with the police about their role. I believe that police liaison is very important. The police are not my enemy – the system might be, but they are my police force and they are ostensibly there to prevent crime and protect me. Therefore my question to them is: why are they allowing these nuclear bomb-making factories to exist? So I challenge them to take it up within the police force, to question the legality of what is going on inside Burghfield and Aldermaston.

*How have they responded to your ideas?*

I've had quite a lot of respect from certain police officers. I've been in prison cells and had police inspectors, chief inspectors or detective sergeants coming into the cell and shaking my hand and saying they agree with what I do, though they can't say it openly. That's very nice, actually; I like that, because you feel something might change within the system.

*You then spent some time in Palestine. How did that come about?*

I first went to Israel being unaware of Palestine in any real sense. I'd married a Jewish man and when my daughter was born, we named her after my husband's aunt – she'd been killed by the Nazis and it was kind of a memory of her. I had relatives by marriage that were living in Israel and I'd always been interested in meeting them, so when the kids were quite young I went over. Whilst I was out there I met some Palestinians, and they offered me a drink of coffee, so I sat down and had a talk with them. Some very good Israeli friends of mine were quite shocked that I was sitting down with these Palestinians, having coffee. So that was my first introduction to this divide within Israel.

The next time I went to Israel, I met members of the Israeli Peace Movement and was also asked to be part of the start-up of the International Solidarity Movement (ISM). Over several visits as part of the ISM it became clear that some of the villages asking for solidarity and an international presence needed a longer term presence, not just a few days or weeks. So I went back for six weeks and whilst there talked with an Israeli who was married to a

Palestinian. She was telling me about her friend's village, where a young teacher had been shot – he'd noticed that the Israeli Army was coming so he went to call the kids in, and as he was going back into his house he was shot in the back and almost killed. He's now in a wheelchair paralysed from the waist down.

Neta, this Israeli woman, wanted a project to be set up full time in this man's village. Half the land in the village had already been taken over by the biggest settlement area in the West Bank and they knew that the Israelis had plans to take even more. They desperately wanted us, so with Neta's help I set up the International Women's Peace Service, Palestine. I got two other people to work with me, we recruited 16 people, we raised enough money to pay for the first three years and the project is still continuing.

*Were you scared when you were there?*

When I'm in the middle of something I don't tend to get scared, because you just have to work out what you're doing. But we were in a hotel once where there were bullets going up and down the street. The Israelis were invading a part of Bethlehem, crushing cars with their tanks, and we were just to one side. I knew that I didn't want to put my head out of that window, but I wasn't that scared. I get angry rather than scared. There was one incident where there was an out-of-control Israeli soldier who was starting to shoot live bullets at our group. I just got everybody to sit down, then I got another Israeli soldier and said to him, "Get that guy out, he's totally out of order. We're just sitting down, we're not going to move, he'll kill somebody in a moment." Luckily he agreed and moved that guy out.

*In a talk you gave you said that you ended up traumatised by your experience in Palestine.*

After many months of seeing man's inhumanity to man, and experiencing the hate of some of the fundamentalist Jewish Israeli settlers, I found it very difficult. When back in the UK, giving talks about what I had seen, I often found myself crying uncontrollably. I still do when I allow myself to remember those times. Quite frankly I was glad not to be allowed back into Israel and Palestine, having been deported.

*Have you been able to work on this issue from home?*

Yes. Do you remember when the Turkish ship was raided by the Israelis? They were trying to take food aid into Gaza but the Israelis went into international waters and stopped these ships from going in, they even killed a large group of Turkish peace activists – incredible that they have got away with this. So with my partner, Camilla, I started a Palestine Links group and our group is now linked with a town in the West Bank called Azzoun. Some children from Azzoun recently came to our town and stayed for five days. They were just kids, one of whom had already been in prison and was quite traumatised – they were all traumatised in various ways – but they had great fun. And the main thing was that they were able to move around. I think people forget how, if you take away the right to move freely, how much that impinges on your life. People can't go to the next town, they can't go to university, they can't meet their relatives – because they're hemmed in by the Israeli forces and the apartheid wall, they are living under a terrible military occupation. So they had a great time just being able to walk around a town, up the hills and along the river and they were taken up to Aberystwyth to see the sea.

*I feel almost tired listening to all the different things you've done over the past 30 years. How do you prevent yourself from burning out?*

By recognising when the burnout's coming. If I get depressed and feel burnt out I turn to friends and family. It's relationships with people that keep you going, really. But also in the process of campaigning you can have a lot of fun and you meet lovely, humane, wonderful people. And I think that's essential. I think a lot of people outside think, "Oh you're campaigning against something really serious like climate change or human rights abuses in Korea or Palestine or whatever, so how can you have fun?" Actually you need to enjoy yourself if you are going to work on these things. And the fun is in meeting wonderful people all around the world and feeling part of that big human family.

And even in the worst situation or places you would meet these incredible people. There was this amazing Israeli woman I met – her parents had been killed in the holocaust and because of that experience she hates what's going on with the Israeli occupation of Palestine and works with the Palestinians, trying to get them hospital treatment, or providing essential items. You meet people like that and think, I'm not doing anything like that! So it's the people you meet. And nature is wonderful... going walking. I grow organic vegetables too. At least at the end of a day's work you can see the allotment is weeded or you see some crops coming. Or the slugs coming. [Laughs.] And when I was younger, having the kids – that was so positive.

*Is there one thing that somehow ties all your campaigns together? Some underlying principle?*

The thing that ties everything in, when I really think about it, is a sense of global citizenship. I am not a white woman living in the UK – I am a human being living in the world and I feel connected to everybody. So when people ask me why I'm involved in a certain issue I think the only thing that I can conclude is that if I were in that situation, then I would want support. I would want somebody to understand it from my point of view.

I think a lot of our problems are about nationalism or religion, and I don't belong to any one religion because I couldn't bear to think that my religion was better than anybody else's religion. And I don't like to say that I'm British – that's not how I define myself. I am a global citizen living in Britain and, essentially, I think we all should be living in the way that we know is right, in a way that does not harm others.

*Angie Zelter (centre with hammer) preparing for an action against a Trident testing barge on Loch Goil. © David Mackenzie*

# Twyford rising

Poet **Emma Must** on how her attempt to save an ancient landscape from destruction left an indelible mark.

I have done two real things in my life. The first was to act, with many others, to try to stop the hill where I used to fly my kite as a child from being bulldozed. The second has been to learn how to write poetry, partly to try to write about that experience.

The hill was Twyford Down in Hampshire, in southern England: a mile long sweep of rolling chalk in an Area of Outstanding Natural Beauty. With its two Sites of Special Scientific Interest and two Scheduled Ancient Monuments, it was, theoretically, as protected from development as any place in Britain could possibly be. Unfortunately, however, the Down stood in the path of the proposed "missing link" of the M3 motorway, designed to cut seven minutes off the journey time between Southampton and London. It was just one of over 600 new road schemes announced in 1989 by Margaret Thatcher's government, described at the time as "the biggest road-building programme since the Romans". In 1992, following public inquiries, legal action in the High Court and representations to the European Commission, construction work on the road began.

## Beginnings

My involvement started in the winter of 1992. I had recently finished my English degree at Leeds University, and was living back in the south of England. I knew about the plans to build a road through Twyford Down: I'd followed it in the papers while I was a student, seen the pictures of the massive human "X" on the hill in the run up to the 1992 general election, and despaired that the Tories had been re-elected and that this meant the road would go ahead. I was working as a library assistant at the Children's Library in Winchester. My daily commute took me past Twyford Down, across the water meadows at its foot, past the Itchen River with its trailing lengths of green weed and its white swans. Superficial work on the road had already begun – the scraping off of a few feet of topsoil, leaving exposed a white face of chalk, like a blank page, where there should have been grass. I was in tears every day, twice a day, as I went past it on the train. I made phone calls: to Friends of the Earth, to the Twyford Down Association, to any organisation that might still be trying to stop the road. Nobody was. They had tried, they said, but construction work had started; they had conceded defeat. Yet it seemed to me that very little of the Down had yet been destroyed. That mile-long hill of chalk, those tens of millions of years of geological history, several thousand years of human history, and however many thousands or millions of tonnes of chalk – that landscape of my childhood – were all, in fact, still there. Surely this madness could still be stopped?

## Touch paper

A local poet friend of mine, Andy Jordan, who also cared passionately about Twyford Down, told me that there was a small group of young people camped on the hill. They were the Dongas Tribe, named after the deep gullies (ancient drovers' tracks) cutting through the hill. These gently-spoken folk with beaded hair and colourful clothing advocated a way of life in harmony with nature and had been camped on the Down since the summer of 1992, living in tipis and benders made from willow and tarpaulin, warmed by woodburning stoves. Around the camp fire, drinking endless cups of tea with Sam and Stef and Paul and Howie and Alex and Fraggle and Heather and the others, I cannot tell you how warmed I felt to have found, at last – after all those fruitless phone calls – a group of people who actually still cared.

Importantly, too, I met Becca Lush, a woman then in her very early twenties, whose energy was to prove so essential to the campaign. She told me about a group of people in Winchester itself – the Friends of Twyford Down – who also still believed that the road could be stopped. I went to one of their Friday evening meetings in the town, met Chris Gillham and the others, and that was it – my touch paper had been lit. I never looked back.

### "Yellow Wednesday"

The events of the next half a year at Twyford Down could fill a book. One day stands out in particular.

On Wednesday 9 December 1992, I walked up to the Dongas after work and saw that the green and white hand-painted wooden sign at the entrance to the camp had been broken in two. I knew then that something awful had happened. I would later find out that Winchester College, who owned part of the land on which the Dongas Tribe were camped, had obtained permission through the courts to evict them. (This day became known as "Yellow Wednesday" on account of the guards' fluorescent jackets.)

My memory of what I saw next is hazy – and this memory merges into those of the next two days – but I remember injured, exhausted people covered in mud, some with slings and neck braces; piles of smouldering sycamore and hawthorn; people perched precariously up trees; and a compound made of coils of razor wire glinting under new arc lights, with tens and tens of yellow-jacketed security guards linking arms inside. I learned that the handful of people who'd been camped on the hill as the dawn broke that day, and the few others who'd been able to be contacted (mobile phones were not widespread in 1992), had thrown themselves in front of both machinery and security guards hour after hour. It had been a running battle. That night there was a total lunar eclipse, the darkest in over a decade. And a party. We went over and under the razor wire and into the compound, and danced on the turf of the Dongas one last time. I spent the night at the camp, and went straight from there to work in the library the next day, smelling of wood smoke. It was an extremely tough decision to go to work and not to stay to physically defend the hill. I had still taken no direct action; I had never lain in front of any bulldozers. I think I was afraid to. And I needed my job.

It's hard to over-estimate the national significance of "Yellow Wednesday". It is hard to remember, now that we have seen images of Swampy and Animal down their tunnels at Fairmile, and the massive tree-sitting protests at Newbury, that before 9 December 1992 the spectacle of hordes of yellow-jacketed security guards versus direct action protesters was not a familiar sight. This was a turning point in the British environmental movement.

## A physical thing

On a personal level, there is no question that witnessing the aftermath of "Yellow Wednesday", and "Black Thursday and Friday", albeit from the periphery, galvanised me into further action. The Friends of Twyford Down, still believing all was not lost, networked like crazy to get as many people as possible onto the hill to protest about the blocking of a footpath by the razor wire of the workers' compound and a temporary metal gate. Very temporary as it turned out, because the gate was soon pulled off its hinges and wrestled back and forth between the protesters and the security guards in a kind of tug-of-war. Once the gate had been removed, the guards blocked the path by linking arms, and we went over the fence into the compound by laying bits of old carpet over the spikes. We'd run in as far as we could then lie on the grass till the guards carried or dragged us back out. Then we'd do it again. This was the first direct action I had taken. I lay on the grass of the footpath until two security guards picked me up, one taking both my arms and one both my legs. I made myself as heavy as I could, letting my body hang down in an arc. I really remember the physicality of this. I remember feeling pleased that I was tall and heavy and hard to shift. It was an absolute turning point for me. I know it sounds obvious, but direct action is a physical thing. It is of the body. You have to come to it in your own time. That was my time to come to it.

## Doing it all

Early 1993 was frantic: a mix of actions and rallies, public meetings, and ferocious networking. And all of it generated and loosely coordinated by a very small handful of people, meeting every Friday evening in the Friends Meeting House in Winchester. I remember the energy fizzing out of the gaps between the wooden planks of the walls of that building. We planned. We organised. We did everything we could think of to get as many people as possible onto the hill to physically stop construction work on the road, to keep Twyford Down in the news in the aftermath of "Yellow Wednesday", and to try to keep the political tide turning in our direction. Simon Fairlie and the *Ecologist* magazine let us use their office, and Twyford Down Alert! was born. We produced flyers for actions, faxed out press releases, networked, networked, networked. These were the days before widespread use of email, when social media had not even been dreamt of. It was a question of making hand-drawn, photocopied flyers and setting up phone trees and holding those planning meetings in Winchester at the end of every week. I think we only had about four hours' sleep a night for several months. We organised tens of actions – big and small – from a human chain of hundreds of people passing chalk from hand to hand to "rebuild the down", to chaining ourselves to bulldozers to hold up construction work for a few hours, to getting sympathetic politicians to come and speak in the cutting, to invading the cricket pitch of Winchester College, to planning a march where we all carried black wooden crosses with the names of the wild flowers and birds to be lost from the hill.

## Greenfly

One notable action, in May 1993, was "Operation Greenfly", which brilliantly disrupted the Department of Transport's plans to build a temporary metal Bailey Bridge to enable a fleet of large earthmovers to enter the construction site. Their plan, named "Operation Market Garden" was hampered by

*Operation Greenfly (Emma is second from the right with a cement bag under her jacket to keep warm!).*

a swarm of 200 human greenfly, perched all night on the girders and cross-pieces, banging out tunes, huddled inside anything we could find – a hessian cement bag in my case. In the early hours there were more than 50 arrests. The police cells of Hampshire were filled with many unlikely suspects, ordinary people with respectable jobs, including, to my certain personal knowledge, teachers and nurses, an astrophysicist, a magazine editor, and me, still – just about – a children's library assistant.

*Injunction*

In the spring and early summer of 1993, the Department of Transport took out injunctions in the High Court, preventing 77 individually-named protesters from entering the construction site. The names had been gathered both from arrests and from surveillance work by Bray's Detective

Agency. We had been followed and photographed for weeks. We were already planning a "Requiem for the Landscape" protest at Twyford Down on the 4th of July, but the imposing of the injunctions meant many of us would risk imprisonment if we walked on the hill.

A group of us sat on Twyford Down in the sunshine and calmly discussed our options. Several of us felt we must break the injunction to highlight how wrong the Roads Programme was; many, especially those with families and children, decided the risks were too great. So, on 4 July 1993, with a blue sky curving over what was left of Twyford Down, in the middle of a jubilant day of speeches and music and a march involving about 600 people, some of us crossed the construction site fence and walked again on our hill.

Several of us wore our Action File numbers, from the individual dossiers of protest activity compiled by Brays Detective Agency, pinned to our chests. I was Action File 36; Becca was Action File 14. There is a photo of the two of us, holding hands in a line of protesters, dancing on the chalk. I have flowing dark hair and am wearing a bright red T-shirt emblazoned with our "Twyford Rising" logo of a sunrise over a curved landscape; Becca has her hair pinned back and is wearing a flimsy floral summer dress. We look carefree and happy, and almost childlike, as if we were dancing to "Ring-a-ring o' roses".

*Emma (second left) and Becca (centre) breaking the injunction. 4 July 1993.*
*© Anna D*

Later that month I was at home, in the evening, in my tiny flat in Southampton and there was a ring on the doorbell. A jaunty young man with a flat-cropped haircut handed me a weighty packet of papers in a reinforced brown envelope. Inside was a bundle of photos of me protesting on Twyford Down and a letter telling me to come to the High Court that Friday. This was the summons for breaching the injunction. I felt numb, cold, and very alone.

*Prison*

We appeared at the High Court: the Twyford Seven. The court was packed. We all read out statements, linking arms, though I was so overwhelmed that one of the boys had to read mine out for me. At the end of the day we were all committed to a month in prison. The boys were sent to Pentonville, Becca and I and Raga Woods to Holloway.

I remember the journey from the court to Holloway Prison in the police van and not knowing what to expect; being strip-searched when we arrived and feeling very awkward having to walk around in front of strangers in my pants; being separated from Becca and moved almost daily from cell to cell; sharing cells with decent, harmless, vulnerable women who were in prison often for the most trivial offences – parking fines or not having a TV licence. I remember the shocking quantity of drugs available in prison – both smuggled in and routinely dispensed to inmates via the evening drugs trolley – and the visible mental distress of a number of women. The worst aspect for me, by far, was the noise: the constant, incessant blare of radios.

Despite all this I did not once feel threatened. Prison mostly made me feel fortunate to not be on drugs or mentally ill. And we were let out after just 13 days. At one point Becca and I managed to get ourselves an appeal. They dismissed our appeal, but in doing so Lord Justice Hoffman said: "These are two frank, straightforward, sincere young women. There is nothing irrational about their conscientiously held views. Civil disobedience is an honourable tradition. They may in the end be vindicated by history."

My family is fragmented, and not especially close, so I was surprised – and pleased – when my mum not only came to our court case, but to visit me in Holloway. She was present when we were released and appears in a lot of media photos, wearing a green "Twyford Rising" badge. My dad and my brother visited me in prison too. I was touched: they had gone so far outside their comfort zones to support us.

*Going national*

The campaign to save Twyford Down was to become so much more than a local protest to stop one hill being destroyed by one road. It would re-energise and galvanise a national grassroots movement against the whole of the British Roads Programme. Twyford Down would become a symbol for the potential destruction of that programme: if a road could be built through Twyford Down, a road could be built anywhere. We had to stop this from happening.

Even in early 1993 we were becoming more aware of the national picture. We learnt from figures published by the (then) Council for the Protection of Rural England (CPRE) that the Roads Programme threatened a list of protected sites which read like the lyrics of "The Twelve Days of Christmas": 2 National Parks, 12 Areas of Outstanding Natural Beauty, 30 National Trust properties, 160 sites of Special Scientific Interest, 800 Scheduled Ancient Monuments. We would repeat these figures like a mantra over the coming months.

A van load of us travelled up to Birmingham in January 1993 to a conference of grassroots activists opposing road schemes in various parts of the country, hosted by ALARM UK – the National Alliance Against Road-building. Becca and I swore a solemn pledge after the conference – under a full moon – to do everything we could to keep fighting and to stop not only the road through Twyford Down, but these other hundreds of roads too. We pledged to get as many people down to Twyford Down as we possibly could. We swapped amethyst stones. We were deadly serious. It all sounds a bit hippy-dippy now, but it was something about their representing the earth, the land, I think. We also gave an amethyst to Chris Gillham and asked him to join us in our pledge. This extraordinary, middle-aged IT expert from respectable middle-class Winchester, who had opposed the road for years and years and years, manfully accepted, even if purple gemstones weren't perhaps quite his thing.

The protests at Twyford Down took on a national flavour. We organised a National Gathering in early March – with 400 or so people from all over the country converging on the town and the hill. Road Alert! was formed, in an upstairs room in a Southampton flat overlooking a park with a magnificent cork oak, whose branches swept the ground in an enormous circle. Road Alert! moved direct action networking onto the national level, mirroring the national networking of ALARM UK with its more conventional campaign focus.

## Quiet victories, noisy defeats

The up-shot of all this effort throughout the 90s – by these hundreds of people working together to stop something so fundamentally wrong – was that whilst we didn't stop the road through Twyford Down, we did stop most of the Roads

Programme. By 1998, of the 600-odd road schemes proposed by Margaret Thatcher nine years earlier, only 37 remained. What's more, the new Labour government at the time laid out proposals for legislation on sustainable transport. In a BBC *Panorama* programme in 1998, the former Transport Minister, Steven Norris, described this reversal of the Roads Programme as the biggest change in any policy in any government department for 40 years. What had generated this change was a series of "quiet victories" – including at Oxleas Wood, Norwich, Birmingham and Preston – and "noisy defeats" – including at Twyford Down, Solsbury Hill, Honiton and Newbury. And the mix of tactics: doing whatever was necessary at a particular time (always, crucially, stopping short of violence). Finally, it was the range of people involved: from pleated-skirted Tory ladies to young people with beaded hair and colourful clothes, living on the land and playing their hypnotic earth music. Such a mix is hypnotic indeed.

The anti-roads movement, and perhaps especially its direct action aspect, would go on to spawn or re-energise campaigns on numerous related issues, including Reclaim the Streets (advocating community ownership of public spaces), climate change, aircraft noise and new runways, and criminal justice.

In terms of new roads, the pendulum has swung quite a long way back from the heady green days of the late 90s. The Campaign for Better Transport has identified proposals for almost 200 new road schemes at local and national level, including a number of schemes we stopped in the 90s. This represents the first intensive wave of road-building plans for 20 years. It seems to me that the chief problem we face is that massive road construction projects are seen as a way of stimulating a flagging economy, and sod the costs: both financial and environmental. Smaller-scale projects that benefit the environment: better buses, smart tickets, cycle lanes, pedestrian-friendly cities, are not perceived as politically exciting. The challenge is to show that they can be.

## Endings

Writing this article, my emotions have been as close to the surface as the white chalk under the short grasses and shallow soil on Twyford Down. I have cried often. A newish friend of mine, from a different country, who was barely even born when we were trying to save Twyford Down, told me recently that he thinks I've been stuck there – in that chalk cutting – for 20 years. In many ways I agree with him. A part of me will always be stuck there, as will a part of so many of us who tried so hard to stop that curved green hill being turned into a black-floored valley: those who took direct action and those who devoted years of their lives to try to stop it ever coming to that point. I hope one day I'll be able to pull myself free enough from the cutting to move on. I'm not there yet.

I want to end with a word of caution. When you act to try to stop something that you know without question, in the depths of your very being, to be wrong; when you throw yourself at it with your whole heart and body and soul; when you do this in concert with others who feel the same, it *is* going to make waves, to make change happen. It is inevitable. This is because the people responsible for the things you are opposing will not care half as much about the issue from their side as you do from yours. Most of the time most of us bumble around doing stuff that doesn't really matter very much at all. The world operates by bumbling. And bumbling around is very important: you can't hurl yourself into things all the time – campaigning can be exhausting. But if you feel strongly about

something, then you must act. I have done nothing as real in
my whole life since.

## Motorway

There's no unbroken arc of chalk,
a curve of sky across its back,
nor grasses stippling the space between.

It is wanting swans beneath its foot
and sycamore and hawthorn.
There's nothing in the way of flowers.

There are no bodies curled in pits,
no disarticulated bone, nor any wrist
still crossed behind.

The place is bare of amber beads,
quernstones, loomweights, brooches.
Worked bone is long fragmented.

There are no nights
when all the noise is night
and hill.

What there is is whiteness rubbing off
on cuffs of afternoons as we fetch
blocks of chalk from grasp to grasp

along the filling line.

**Emma Must**

# Progression

Anti-racism activist **Zita Holbourne** on police brutality, the London riots, and the Olympics – and why she will never be silenced.

*Interview by Angharad Penrhyn Jones*

*What was your first experience of racism?*

I remember my mum being called a monkey and told to go back to the jungle. I grew up in the 70s and 80s, mainly in London. People coming to the UK during the 50s and 60s, particularly from the Caribbean, faced horrific racism – the "no blacks, no Irish, no dogs" that we're now seeing a return to. There may have been equality policies and laws in place, but the racism still continued. And so I really had to fight racism and sexism, but I think the racism was more in your face, and you couldn't ignore it. You didn't get called names because you were a girl but you definitely got called names if you weren't white.

Even in the labour market, when I started work, there was discrimination. And at first I didn't realise that my experiences were to do with discrimination – I thought there was something wrong with me, that I wasn't doing things the right way and should try harder. It wasn't until I became more politically active that I really started to reflect on previous experiences and recognise what it was about.

*So you've had to re-read your past, in a sense.*

Yes, you recognise that things happened not because you're a failure, but that there were barriers. You realise that actually what you've achieved is really good considering what you were up against.

*When did you become an activist?*

It was really when I became a parent that I became totally committed. I grew up in quite a political family, which helped. My parents supported the anti-apartheid campaign so I was raised with an awareness of campaigning. I had an aunt who was a councillor, family members who were involved in trade unions. My mum was very good at asserting her rights. Sometimes it seemed like every week there was some battle where she was asserting her rights, so I learned from that as well.

*Did you find it embarrassing at the time?*

Sometimes I did. But watching her fight back and listening to the lectures that she gave people if they said something racist – that was a really positive thing. Subconsciously you're learning from that – it stays with you even if you don't quite understand it. And when you're older you put it into context.

*It normalises the idea of standing up for yourself and speaking out.*

That's one thing she was very, very good at. [Laughs.] She didn't hold back in standing up and speaking out for herself. So when I had my son, I felt really emotional. Obviously everyone feels emotional about having a child, but I felt really emotional about what his prospects were, what he would have to go through, whether he would have to experience what my mother and I had experienced. So I felt that if I campaigned for better rights and equality, it would give him and the next generation a better future. Not me alone, obviously, but I could do what I could for my child, to bring him up with positive values and instil confidence in him.

*Your son is 19 now. Does he respect your political work?*

Yes, he does. He doesn't want to be a political activist, but he's actually very good at asserting his rights and standing up for himself. And although he won't tell me very often himself, I find out from other people, like teachers, that he does talk about what I do.

*In your poem "Progression", which I watched you perform online, you talk about the fact that you've never fitted into the Oxbridge, establishment ideal. You're black, you're a woman, and a single mother. And yet you say you've got a strong belief in your own strength and your own voice, even though you don't fit the mould. You say that you won't be silenced. Where does this inner strength come from? Is it from your mother?*

That's an interesting question... [Laughs.] I think part of it comes from anger, anger at discrimination and injustice. There's a saying that what doesn't break you will only make you stronger, and that definitely applies to me because I don't get broken easily. I get down, I get upset, I get hurt by things, but my response to that is not to sit in a corner and cry. I might have a cry about things but I will get up and fight back and think, right, what can I do to change this? What can I do to bring others together and mobilise people to make sure it doesn't happen again?

*Just this morning I was reading an essay by a feminist who was saying that anger is underestimated, that even though anger is seen as an unfeminine emotion we actually need to get more angry and channel it in productive ways. But you say in the poem that people can find you aggressive.*

There's a stereotype that's applied to black people and black women that says that if we assert ourselves we're aggressive and angry. However, if it was a white man behaving in that way he would be seen to be very assertive and progressive. So it's another negative stereotype.

*And does this apply to black women in particular? This idea that you can't be cool and rational?*

It's an attempt to stamp down on black women when they're speaking up. It's an attempt to oppress people, to suppress what they're expressing. So if you're challenging discrimination they'll try and turn it on you and say, "Well, you're being very aggressive and unreasonable." So they'll try and reflect it back on to you. It's an attempt to silence you, and shut you down.

*You now work as a trade union rep. I watched a film recently about the Trades Union Congress and noticed it was predominantly male and white. What do we do to promote diversity within the labour movement?*

The further you go up through the structures of the trades union movement, the more white and male dominated it is. We've got a woman General Secretary of the TUC, which is progress, and in my union, our national president is a woman. So it's not that there aren't any women in senior positions, but it is dominated by men.

When it comes to the Congress, unions send delegations. How they decide who goes is different in every union. But you know that there are going to be men jumping up and down to go and put themselves forward. And if they hold certain positions that get allocated a seat to go to that conference, or there's a vote for it and they get more votes because all the other men vote for men. It's a self-perpetuating situation.

The other thing about women and the trade union movement is balancing carer responsibility. It's not just childcare – women tend to be primary carers for disabled relatives, elderly relatives and so on. So that is another barrier, because it might not be easy for women to attend these conferences. And also, the TUC Congress starts at the beginning of the academic year, so who's likely to stay at home and see the children settling into their new school or their new year? It's going to be mothers.

So it's a male dominated unit. And certainly it's very white as well. There are few black people in senior positions.

*Are you doing anything personally to try and fight that?*

I have been at the forefront in my union in tackling under representation of black members, which includes building black structures at different levels, creating and delivering education programmes to empower black members to get involved and to tackle the barriers to participation, mentoring black reps to get more involved, and giving encouragement and support to black members to put themselves forward.

My union has set up regional black members networks – I

was involved in establishing the first one and they recruited an Equality Co-ordinator to oversee the work.

*It must be a difficult time in your job with all these austerity measures.*

It's challenging because it's attack upon attack upon attack.

*Tell me about Black Activists Rising Against Cuts (BARAC).*

I founded BARAC with Lee Jasper in the summer of 2010. And it came about because I'd done a lot of work on tackling cuts, both relocation and job cuts, programmes that had happened in the civil service previously under Labour. And they'd all impacted disproportionately on black workers. When I say black, I use the word to encompass anybody from the African and Asian diasporas, anybody who identifies with the political term and defines themselves as black. I knew that from the previous round of cuts there had been a huge disproportionate impact. And with the Tories getting into power we knew that what was coming was going to be really horrific, much worse than anything we'd yet seen. I saw a need for a wider campaign, because this is not just about jobs, it's going to impact on services and on communities.

*Could you explain why black women are targeted disproportionately by the cuts?*

There's a disproportionate impact on women, and a disproportionate impact on black people, so it's a double whammy. Which is why they are the hardest hit. The public sector is the largest employer of black people and of women, and the voluntary sector employs a lot of black women as well. The reason why there's more people in the public and voluntary sectors is because of discrimination in the private sector – you can't even get a foot on the ladder in the first place.

A lot of voluntary sector organisations are focused on specialist advisory services, whether it's legal aid, race monitoring units, translation services, women's refuges, all of those types of things. So the cuts are having an impact on black women as service users as well as workers.

*Black women are three times more likely to be unemployed than their white counterparts.*

Yes, and once black people lose their jobs, it takes them much longer to get back into work because of discrimination in the labour market. And that's amplified by austerity, because there are very few jobs around so you're competing with far more people to get those jobs.

*You're telling me these things in quite a matter-of-fact way. I'm sure you're used to explaining these things calmly. But when you think about it, it's horrifying.*

It is horrifying, yes.

*So if I were black, I would be three times more likely to be unemployed. Not five per cent more likely, but three times.*

In local authorities where they've made redundancies, there are examples of women making up five per cent of the workforce but 45 per cent of the cuts. That shows you the clear disproportionate impact. It's institutional racism.

*Another statistic that I came across: black people are seven times more likely to be stopped and searched than white people.*

Well, young black men are up to 33 times more likely to be stopped and searched, depending on where they are, yes. So it's even worse a statistic than you've got there. It's because of racial profiling. Young black men are negatively stereotyped, they've been demonised by sections of the press and politicians. You look at what happened when the riots took place in London in 2011. They blamed young black people in particular, and they gave them disproportionate sentences.

*Has that been proven through studies?*

Oh yes. There've been investigations into it. The TUC did an investigation and so did the *Guardian* and loads of others. After one week of the riots, BARAC were doing meetings up and down the country, we were talking about the fact that the areas where the vast majority of the riots were taking place were officially declared deprived. So the media focused on black people, but actually there would be a disproportionate number of black people in those areas because of the deprivation. Black people tend to live in the poorest places geographically, because of discrimination in society and because the labour market has an impact on the wages they earn.

*So the riots were to do with poverty.*

The riots had nothing to do with race or colour. It had to do with poverty and class. However, the riots were sparked by the killing of another young black man by police and there had also been huge cuts impacting on young black people where the riots took place.

*Do you think the way the media reported it ended up fuelling racism?*

Yes, definitely. And it's not just the media. If you saw the emergency debate in the Houses of Parliament, all of the mainstream parties were demonising young people and they were saying they were feral, wild, out of control. Rather than looking at the underlying causes. Well, first we have to go back to the fact that Mark Duggan, a young black man, was shot dead by police. And he was one in a series of young black men who'd been shot dead in a short space of time leading up to the riots. The police treated the family very badly. Refused to engage with them. And the vigil that took place when the riots started was predominantly made up of women and children. So that was the context in which these riots happened.

But I would say that the riots were uprisings. And I've been criticised by a certain section of the press, and right wing people, who refuse to see them as uprisings. But it was undoubtedly a form of protest – even though it was not the same sort of protest that I am involved in as a trade union and community activist, I think it was a response to the issues. There was anger building up because in Tottenham, where Mark Duggan was shot, some 20 youth centres had been closed down. The libraries were being shut everywhere, services for young people were being cut. Tuition fees were going to be tripled for university and there were no jobs. One in two young black people are out of work. Over a million young people out of work but one in two young black people out of work in the UK.

*Zita speaking at a BARAC event. © Barry Hamilton*

*So 50 per cent of young black people are out of work. It's difficult not to become angry when you're faced with that situation.*

There would have been some people who just got caught up in what was happening but yes, I think it was a response to those things. And yes, people went and took trainers and TVs, but remember it wasn't just young black people who did this, but people of all different ages and different races. But what is forced on young people all the time, through advertising, is that they need the latest pair of trainers, the latest electronic gadget.

*And yet they haven't got the money to buy these things.*

Yes.

*Was that a stressful time for you? As you say you were travelling around the country talking about this subject, getting attacked by certain people for using the word "uprising".*

I suppose it's always stressful and upsetting when people are critical but lacking in understanding of what you're saying and when they refuse to understand it because they've got set ideas that they're not going to budge from.

If you're self-conscious, worried about how you're going to be judged, you're never going to do anything. When I first saw racist and offensive comments posted about me on the internet I was quite horrified and embarrassed by people's comments. But you have to rise above it, get quite thick skinned. Trolls are trying to distract you but you can't let your focus slip, otherwise they've won. You can't let them drain you of your energy.

And what's the saying? If you're being criticised, it means you're doing something good, you must be doing something right.

*Is that how you deal with the backlash, the abuse – by reminding yourself that at least it's being discussed?*

Yes. There is that section of society that's right-wing, that's racist. And so we have to tackle that, and challenge that every day because there are myths and lies being peddled by the government, by politicians, by sections of the press every day, and we're trying to counter them continuously.

*Do you ever feel overwhelmed by the scale of the challenge?*

If I were to stop and ask myself, "Can I do this, can I achieve this?", then I suppose I would. But I just keep going, doing what I can do, trying to get as many other people involved as possible. I don't work by myself, as one individual. I work with a network of people, as a trade unionist, as a community activist, in BARAC, in my union and the TUC.

*Tell me more about your poetry. Is that an important form of activism for you?*

It was never intended as a form of activism. Originally I wrote because poetry is therapy, a self-healing thing, it gets things out of your system. I feel better after I've written a poem about something. I'd never thought about going out and performing it when I first started writing over 20 years ago, so I went to some open mic events that were going on and did a few performances. And then some auditions came up for a poetry collective and I went along to the audition and became part of that collective. It was a black collective – a lot of it was around race but also around social issues that were impacting on our communities, and topical issues. And there would be Caribbean food, speakers or musicians as well, so it was a really nice atmosphere. Then there would be discussion and debate.

If I look back on a lot of my poetry, actually a lot of it was political, I just didn't know it, because I was talking about my experiences as a woman, as a black person, someone facing discrimination and challenges.

*It's where the personal and political come together.*

I was performing poetry in the Houses of Parliament last night in the discussion about the immigration bill. And a couple of weeks before that I performed at the National Diversity Awards, and the week before that I was performing at the "Miami 5" vigil outside the US Embassy. So I end up performing at quite a few political events. [Laughs.]

I'm constantly writing about things that happen around us every day, in terms of cuts and protests and the campaigns that are going on. I don't really write lovey-dovey poems. Only ones with a twist in them. [Laughs.]

*So to go back to the riots: I wanted to ask you about police brutality and racism because I know you've been campaigning on this issue. You spoke at a rally to commemorate Trayvon Martin. Could you talk about that case and the solidarity between you and the movement over in America?*

Well, Trayvon Martin was killed by a man who was a Neighbourhood Watch representative in a gated community where Trayvon's father lived in Florida. Trayvon, a young boy, had gone to the shop, was walking back to his dad's house with a bag of Skittles and a can of iced tea and this Neighbourhood Watch guy set upon him and actually called the police. Basically, because he was a young black boy with a hood on, he was deemed to be suspicious, even though he had every right to be there, because he lived there.

It was because of his colour and his clothes. This whole "hoodie" thing really infuriates me. My son has always worn hooded sweatshirts. They're comfortable, they're practical, they're warm! I've heard people say, "Oh no, I've stopped my child from wearing those hooded sweatshirts, he wears a nice smart shirt and some jeans and not tracksuits." I'm not going to make my child wear something different – why should he have to wear something different? Why shouldn't he put a hood on his head in the winter to keep his head warm?

*Do you worry about what could happen to your son – he's 19, black, wearing a hooded top?*

Yes, I'm always worrying about him. I drive him crazy, checking where he is. Yes, something could happen because he's been demonised, because of racism and stereotyping and because of what he's wearing.

*Tell me more about Trayvon Martin.*

He was shot dead by this neighbour and then the guy was free for four months. They didn't try and find him, they didn't care because the Stand your Ground law in Florida allows you to shoot somebody dead if you think that they're threatening you. They didn't even question him – it was actually through widespread protests in the USA that they took him in for questioning, eventually. Here in the UK we were looking at this and thinking this was horrific. But also what black communities here related it to is the "stop and search" and the deaths at the hands of the state of young black people. We haven't got the Stand your Ground law, but it's the same kind of principle.

This could be our child, these sorts of things are happening to our children. So we did that protest and then Occupy in America organised a speaking tour for the family to get solidarity and support for the parents and Trayvon's brother and decided to bring them to the UK. BARAC works alongside Occupy here and also Occupy Faith. In fact, we've worked with Occupy to try and bring the black community and Occupy together because it is predominantly white.

*It's been criticised for that.*

The joke is that black people don't do camping and cold.

[Laughs.] It's not happening, they're not getting out there and camping in the cold!

*[Laughs.] Ah, so is that why Occupy is a predominantly white movement?*

[Laughs.] It sounds funny, but that's one of the reasons! But the main thing is that in the Occupy movement you had quite a lot of young people turning up who might have been living at home. If you've got responsibility for a home and children, and you've got a job, you can't just go off and camp. And it goes back to black people facing all the cuts and discrimination – there's lot at stake. It's different if you're coming from a middle-class background and you're being supported. I'm not saying it was totally middle class but there was an element of that.

*You need a buffer in your life to do something like that.*

Exactly. And black people couldn't give up their jobs, they wouldn't be able afford to give up their jobs to go there.

*Or risk being arrested and going to prison.*

Yes. Reverend Jesse Jackson came over to the UK a couple of times and he's always supported us, so we took him to Occupy and also co-organised a Martin Luther King Day event with Occupy London which brought black communities and the Occupy movement together. Occupy in America got in contact with Occupy London and wanted to bring Trayvon Martin's family over. When his parents were here they also met with Doreen Lawrence [mother of Stephen Lawrence who was murdered by racists], and they spoke with her and she gave her support and solidarity too.

*What happened to the man who killed Trayvon Martin?*

He's still free. There was a murder trial this year, and we had a protest outside the USA Embassy and then one outside Downing Street to respond to global racism and injustice. Then they found that [Trayvon's] killer was not guilty. He got off scot free, because that law made it legal for him to kill. So there is now a boycott campaign in Florida and wider. They've asked us in the UK to support the campaign.

*To boycott it as a holiday destination, for example?*

Well, everything. Boycott Florida full stop. Stevie Wonder was the first one to come out in support, he wasn't going to perform in Florida or anywhere else that has Stand your Ground law. Then following him loads of artists – rappers, R'n'B artists, pop artists – said the same. So black activists in Florida are asking the international community to boycott the cruises, the theme parks, the products that are produced and sold in and exported from Florida. And actually we've seen that just the other day they said they're looking at reviewing the Stand your Ground laws and making some changes. I think that wouldn't have come about without that pressure from the campaigns and the boycotting.

*Is it true that the killer not only walked away, but that he was given a lucrative book deal?*

Yes, it is. He says that he's turned it down since then. But whether that's true or not, or whether it will emerge in some shape or form later on, I don't know. Either way, I think he's going to make loads of money out of it. Whether it's a book deal or some other engagement that he gets, he's going to live out his live comfortably as a result of it. It's disgusting.

*You mentioned Doreen Lawrence. Let's talk about political policing. We know now that police infiltrated the Lawrence family, spied on them, in an attempt to discredit them. What do you make of this rise in political policing, if that's what is happening?*

Well, it's being driven by the government. When the Tories came in, we saw instantly that there was a change to policing at protests and demonstrations. And look what happened at all the student demos. I've spoken at a lot of student demos and spoken at rallies and each time I've experienced brutality by the police. Either to me or to people around me. Students were abused and attacked, with batons, by mounted police. I was charged at by mounted police at one demo. I'd brought my cousin with me who'd never been to a political protest. She wanted to hear me speak. I was trying to get to the platform where I was due to speak but the police had cut off entrances either side of Whitehall, so we couldn't go down to where we needed to be. We were all just standing around waiting to see if the police were going to let people through, when out of the blue, with no warning, no announcement on a loudhailer or anything, they charged at us. I had my back to the horses and my cousin grabbed me by my arm and dragged me with all her force onto the pavement so I missed it by inches. I would have been trampled otherwise.

I also went on a protest outside my local council when they were setting the budget. I had a police officer headlock me and knock me in my chest, pull my head wrap off my head and kick me. So I've experienced it firsthand but I know people who've experienced it a lot worse. Look at Alfie Meadows, who suffered a brain injury and had to have surgery in hospital for what they did to him at Trafalgar

Square during a student demo. Things have definitely got worse under this government.

*So did your cousin say she was never going to go on another protest?*

Probably not, no, she wasn't happy at all. She found it quite terrifying. She was in shock after, actually.

*I'd like to refer to Christopher Alder's case and his sister, Janet. Could you say something about her fight for justice?*

I really admire Janet Alder. I think she's very inspirational. But I'd say that the reason she's inspirational is because she's fighting for justice. She didn't set out to be an inspirational activist – she's had no choice. And the same applies to so many families like hers, that have had no choice but to fight for justice. She's been fighting and campaigning because she wanted to see justice for her brother.

Christopher was a British soldier who died while in police custody. Several years later the family discovered that they had not buried Christopher, they had buried a black woman, Grace Kamara, who was much older than him and a different gender. It was when her family came to find her, because she hadn't been identified, that they discovered him in the mortuary, not her.

*They buried the wrong person...*

Yes. And then they weren't held to account for what they did, for that mix-up.

*There haven't been any prosecutions?*

No, they investigated it all and concluded that there was no realistic prospect of securing a conviction – and so no prosecution was ever brought.

*They were recorded making monkey noises while Christopher was dying.*

That's right; vile racism. And that's just one example. It's horrific what's been happening. And the way families are treated afterwards.

Sean Rigg was another person who died in police custody – in this case, at Brixton Police Station. Sean Rigg had mental health problems. He was supposed to have a programme of care and support and he was known to the police, they knew that he had mental health problems. So they shouldn't have taken him – they didn't follow procedures. They should have contacted his support workers when they found him. There was no reason for him to die. And his family, his sisters and his brother are having to fight for years and years.

My union is very supportive of justice campaigns and tries to give assistance and support where we can. BARAC has got more and more involved in supporting justice campaigns. So although we were initiated to campaign around the disproportionate impact of cuts, actually our remit has gone wider, to be about racism, injustice and cuts.

*Could you tell me about the role you played in the People's Assembly?*

I've been part of the People's Assembly since it was established. The aim of it is to mobilise people in their local communities, so assemblies were set up all over the country in different cities and towns, with the aim of bringing together everybody who's been impacted by cuts. And the majority of people in the UK are impacted by cuts in one way or another. It's a tiny minority that have got all the power and all the money.

*The one per cent...*

Yes. So it's about trying to bring people into the campaign who haven't been involved before. Not been active, not in a union, never been to a political meeting. To try and get into those communities and try and bring all those people together. So it's a broad coalition of lots of different organisations and campaigns and individuals.

*Do you find them exciting and energising, these events that bring local people together?*

I think all those events are energising and exciting, yes. Because it's upbeat, isn't it? You've got passionate speakers, you've got inspirational people. But I think what's important is what happens after. We need to reach those people that haven't been reached. Because if we don't engage with all the different communities and don't involve them, then we don't have the impact that we need to have to make a change and those hardest hit are still impacted.

*I was really inspired by your Olympics campaign. You overturned a decision by the Olympic committee to refuse media accreditation to the* Voice, *the biggest black newspaper in the UK. Could you talk about how you achieved that?*

That was a moment of anger that achieved that. [Laughs.] Another one of my moments of anger. I was so furious!

Basically, I'd had a series of racist incidents, the week that

I started that campaign, cases I was dealing with and racist comments on Facebook. And then I heard that the *Voice* newspaper did not have media accreditation, they did not have a pass, to go into the Olympic Games and report. And that was the last straw for me. Because the BBC had some 120 passes. Are you telling me the BBC couldn't give up one pass for the *Voice*? Think of the amount of black athletes, including British ones, competing.

But also, the readership of the *Voice* here has an interest in Caribbean and African teams. It's the biggest black newspaper and you're telling me you couldn't give them one pass. That they're not allowed to go into the Olympic arena.

And also there were a whole lot of other injustices around the Olympics that I was campaigning on. So it was also yet one more thing in terms of the Olympics that infuriated me.

And so, something seized me. I needed to do something there and then. And it was about midnight. So I opened up my laptop and I did an online petition on Change.org. Because it was midnight I didn't consult anyone – I didn't pick up the phone and speak to anyone from the *Voice*. I thought no, I'm just doing it. Didn't really think about it at all to be honest. And when I woke up the next morning, I think there were four or five hundred signatures.

There were international signatures. Also, politicians and celebrities were signing the petition. And what I'd done before going to bed was stick it on Facebook and Twitter. Then I got bombarded by the press. Boris Johnson [Mayor of London] came on board and Tessa Jowell [Shadow Minister for the Olympics].

Change.org is a really good petition site. It has campaign officers, and if a petition is doing well it will work with you. And the petition just grew and grew and grew. It got to 4,000 or something. It was interesting because it got lots of press coverage in the USA. American black media say they have that same barrier with accreditation in America at big events. So they grabbed the story because they could relate directly to it.

*How did you feel when you heard the Olympic committee had done a U-turn?*

I was really happy. [Laughs.] But I was also quite amazed because we'd just decided we were going to hand the petition in to the Olympic committee. I was doing things all the time – contacting local politicians, sharing the petition far and wide, but it grew legs, and the *Voice* put it up, the *Guardian* covered it, there was some BBC coverage, so it got quite good coverage in the UK and wider. So in two and a half days... I hadn't expected they were going to do a U-turn that quickly.

This is what people power can do. So we need to apply this to a lot of other things, because this shows you the power that we have.

*Why were you infuriated with the Olympics in general?*

There is an international movement against the Olympics because of what happens; it always has a negative impact on communities. There was a huge industrial estate in the Olympic borough where people were cleared out. Businesses that had been owned by families for generations had to move out.

I actually live in an Olympic borough, and in the run up to the Olympics and during the event there was a lot of disruption. When the Olympics were on, we were even policed crossing the road in Stratford. There were some businesses outside the Olympic Park, people selling coffee, a newsagent, a flower stall, things like that, and they were forced to relocate. The Council said they would have to move temporarily but they could come back. But they never did come back. The man who sold coffee had one of those mini-vans and he sold coffee to people that were commuting. That was his business. And they put him the other side of Stratford outside of Starbucks. What chance was he going to have? People lost their livelihoods.

Then there was the Carpenter's Road estate, which overlooked the Olympic estate, and tenants on the three top floors of each of the tower blocks were turfed out of their homes so that the BBC and Al Jazeera and other stations could take over. They wanted to gentrify that area and knock down that estate, so for the whole year since there's been a campaign to defend the Carpenter's Road estate. People have raised their children and grandchildren on that estate, these are people's homes, their roots.

So they took the people off the top floors, saying they could come back, and then the tenants found they couldn't. The BBC security took over the buildings and then celebrities would come in to look down at the Olympic park, and they were trying to stop tenants from coming into their own homes. They'd say, "You can't come in for half an hour because the Queen's come." There'd be people coming back with their babies, their shopping, after a long day at work, and told they couldn't come in.

Also there were the missiles on the roofs that terrified people. One site was in Leyton, which is one of the entrances to the Olympic Park. Of course it was all social housing where poor people live. They didn't put missiles on the roofs of rich people or private houses. They put them where lots of people live – tower blocks. It was insane. So they had military police on the roof and private security on the door. I spoke to some of the tenants, and everyone we spoke to said they found it terrifying, horrible.

I worked on a documentary about the Olympics and we went to look at the buildings that had missiles. When we [the film crew] were in a taxi the police drove up behind us and said they wanted to question us. We'd been looking around the back of the tower block to see where the police were, and we'd spoken to a few tenants, and just because of that they came up to the taxi driver and said, "There's a call out across the whole Met police and you're going to be stopped all day long, just to warn you, your number plate has gone out to the entire Met police." So essentially the military police called the Met police on to us. To get out from where we were we had to drive back down past the tower blocks. There was a line of police vans there who'd all come out after us. The whole thing was shocking.

*The issue of corporate sponsorship riled people too.*

Yes, the upshot is that it was only big business that made any money out of the event. Well, look at the rules. You couldn't go into the Olympic Park with a Pepsi, because Coca-Cola was a sponsor, and you couldn't wear Nike trainers, or T-shirts that had a political message on it.

They said they were going to set up a big market that was going to have a massive footfall, they said local businesses were going to make a fortune, so people re-mortgaged their homes and took out loans to buy products to put on these stalls. And then they changed the route so nobody ever went past that market. There's a Caribbean restaurant opposite the Olympic Park, and the council came down one day and put four trees in front of it so that nobody would see it. It just happened to be in a prime position opposite the park so they went and grew those trees in front of them. No warning, no advice, no consultation.

And then they put a guide together on the facilities around the Olympics and didn't advertise anything about local businesses. Green Street is known internationally because it's a road specialising in Asian shops: clothes, jewellery, food, a community market. The original old shopping centre – they didn't even advertise that. Such a missed opportunity. When you think about the opening ceremony and the celebration of all things British, and actually there's amazing British Asian or Caribbean things on the doorstep and they want to hide it. And then they build Westfield, a massive new shopping centre with 300 new shops. It's disgusting, it's all about money.

*What gives you the energy to fight when you're faced with these sorts of injustices?*

What motivates me, I think, is what's gone on before. History. The things that people went through before us, people who sacrificed their lives, who fought horrific discrimination. And now we have that same responsibility to create a better future. We are actually in a situation now where we pass to our children a worse future than was passed to us by our parents.

But think about apartheid in South Africa, segregation in America, the transatlantic slave trade, the enslavement of black people. People talk about the holocaust which was horrific but they forget how many millions of lives were lost through the slave trade. The horrific racism the first-generation immigrants had to go through. Paul Stephenson [civil rights campaigner] spoke at a seminar last week about the Bristol Bus Boycott in 1963, when people protested against a bus company's refusal to employ black and Asian drivers. In fact, Paul Stephenson was one of the people who inspired me to become an activist when I was 19.

*Tell me that story.*

I was at art school and I did a work placement with the *Caribbean Times* working as a photographer. And one of the stories we covered was about somebody who'd been murdered in Brixton. But it turned out that Paul Stephenson had been a good friend of this person, so I went to Bristol with the reporter to interview him. At the time I didn't know who Paul Stephenson was – I knew he was a community activist but I didn't know about the Bristol Bus Boycott. I didn't know anything.

I arrived, Paul picked up me and the reporter in his car, took us to his home, and the first thing that struck me was the pictures of Muhammad Ali and his children and him. And if you love Muhammad Ali like I do, to see him in somebody's front room in Bristol was like, wow! He'd worked with Muhammad Ali for five years. He then took us to the rich area of Bristol, the poor area where black people lived, and told us the history of the slave trade in Bristol, and the bus boycott. He took us to a Caribbean restaurant, a Caribbean pub, made sure we were fed. And his humanity was the thing that really struck me. What he saw was not a hack and a photographer from a newspaper – he saw two young black people who were the future. He spent his whole day with us, dedicated his day to us. He talked the whole time, and whether he intended to give us a history lesson and inspire us I don't know, but he did.

And the next time I met Paul was on the bi-centenary of the abolition of the slavery act, but he had no memory of that day.

*But it meant so much to you...*

It did. You know how things happen when you're younger that have a huge impact on your life? You might not consciously dwell on it at the time but that memory stays with you.

# For these are all our children

Human rights lawyer **Shauneen Lambe** gives an email interview about working with death row inmates in the USA, and why she loves representing marginalised young people in the UK.

*Interview by Angharad Penrhyn Jones*

*When you were 24, you went to the States as a law student to work on death row. Could you tell me about that experience?*

I left university having no idea that I was going to become a lawyer. It was something I decided to do after a friend in London offered me a chance to support defendants and their families through court proceedings. Then one night, as students do, I stayed up all night watching telly. There was a British guy on death row in Georgia and he was due to be executed. His name was Nicky Ingram and he had a British lawyer, Clive Stafford Smith, who got him a stay of execution for 24 hours. I probably hadn't moved from the telly when he was executed 24 hours later. I thought it was so cruel, that he was given that glimmer of hope, just one more day, before the state took his life. I wanted to go and help.

To work on death row in Louisiana was an amazing experience. With hindsight I loved my time there. I feel so privileged to have been allowed into all the lives that inhabit the cities and swamps of that humid state. By the end I would feel comfortable walking around the sketchiest of projects or the dingiest of trailer parks. My clients would call me from prison: "My Momma said she saw you walking around the project again. She was worried that you wouldn't be safe. I told her people were watching out for you." Or: "My grandma says you staying in that seedy motel in town, don't stay in that place anymore, that place is dirty, my grandma says next time you come you can stay with her."

I was struck by the oppression and the poverty and how America was a country of polar opposites. From poor schooling, to poor health care, to almost absent opportunities: for the vast majority of the people I worked with, the hurdles to a better life, to the American dream, were insurmountable. You could become a sports star, a hip hop star, a drug dealer, or find yourself a minimum wage job – those were the choices. When I left the southern United States in 2003, I felt that I was leaving the hidden America, the side that people do not know exists. It's easy to be dazzled by the glitter of the stars and stripes.

As a teenager, I was no more politically active than anyone else. But when I met those families, when I knew the people behind the stories, when I saw their hardships, I couldn't leave it, or them, behind. When the odds are stacked against you there is no equality. It is impossible for anyone to truly believe that the children I met, who began selling drugs at 11 to help their families, have equal opportunities, or indeed any opportunities at all.

*You must have found the work frustrating, and harrowing.*

It was tough. One of my young clients got a 198-year sentence when he was 18. He said he wished he'd been shot on the street like a dog. The trajectory of his life was predictable – a drug dealer had used him at an early age, and he'd just been drawn in; the path was set for him.

The hardest case for me was being parachuted into the middle of the trial of Ryan Matthews. Ryan was 17 at the time he was arrested and charged with capital murder. We came in to try and stop the jury from sentencing him to death after they had found him guilty of first degree murder. During what I remember as a three-day frenzy we cajoled and persuaded his family, who we had only just met, to reveal their intimate secrets and feelings so that we could parade them before the jury. In other words they were expected to beg the jury, the same one that had just found Ryan guilty of first degree murder, to spare his life. Unsurprisingly it didn't work, and I remember sitting behind his mother, Pauline, when those 12 people came back from their deliberations and told the court that they had unanimously decided to kill her child. It was the hardest day of my working life. The irony of the situation is that had Ryan been sentenced to life and not death, he would not have been entitled to legal assistance. With this assistance he was able to prove his innocence and was exonerated completely five years later. In 2008, Ryan's sister Monique asked me to be her bridesmaid at her wedding, Ryan was the groomsman and we walked down the aisle of the church together.

I survived Louisiana with my sanity mostly intact. With hindsight I can see that I was a young woman in an alien environment who may not have been equipped to deal with the work I was undertaking, but at the time that was my challenge: be stronger; be better; be good enough. I used to feel so sorry for those guys on death row who would wait patiently for months for a lawyer to come and visit them – and they would get me!

*Baroness Helena Kennedy, one of your patrons, said that Just for Kids Law is a most remarkable new kid on the block, an inspirational social invention in an area where innovation is rare. How did your experiences of poverty in the Southern States feed into the work you do at Just for Kids Law here in the UK?*

For me it was a natural progression. Most of the children that I work with in the UK are struggling with huge adversity. I have never seen a child get an education in prison. I have never met a child who found positive opportunities in prison. I have never come across a child whose mental health has improved after a period in custody. So why do we keep on using it? It is because we have no answers. It is easier to keep them out of sight, out of mind: we don't have to try and untangle the complex problems that many of those children pose.

In this country we see the hypocrisy of the wealthy paying for their children to go to private school to enable them to get into university and to secure good careers. They don't have enough faith in the state education system to put their children through it, yet they expect state-educated children to succeed. Do they not see the contradiction? Why don't we provide a greater investment in those communities, releasing a little from the high achievers? Instead we lock them up – I have never met a child from a well-off family in prison.

In the States, it appeared obvious to me that if there had

been an earlier effective intervention in the lives of people we worked with, they may not have ended up in that situation. Once you are in the system it's really hard to get out. The idea behind Just for Kids Law is if you intervene at the first point of crisis, perhaps you can stop it from spiralling out of control. I started thinking like a doctor who understands that prevention is better than cure and that young people need more than legal representation to re-stabilise them. You might get them off but unless you address the troubles in their lives by fighting for their education, housing and benefit rights, they will be back in court. So that's what we do at Just for Kids Law.

The typical trajectory for a young person at Just for Kids is that they come to us in crisis; they might be out of school, homeless or in the criminal justice system. We try to stabilise that immediate crisis and then we look for the underlying reason for their situation. If there is more going on than the immediate problem we will work with them through those problems. Once that person is stabilised, we help them figure out what they want to do and help them engage in positive activities, such as working with a mentor, or going into education, training, or work experience. Then they're invited to join our Ambassadors group, to become politically active and to engage in changing society.

*What are you most proud of, in terms of the work you've done as an organisation?*

One of the projects I am most proud of is our Youth Ambassadors programme. We set this up after the riots in 2011, when we began to hear from the young people how unfairly they felt they were represented in the media. Every month, 20 or so young people get together in a law office and sit around a board table. The collective problems encountered by the young men and women around the table are unimaginable, but these people, from across London, sit down not to discuss their own problems, but to try to solve social issues. The police might warn you that some of the young people are dangerous, and the government would tell you that they exploit the welfare state. But these young people never miss a meeting, and in their free time they go home and design logos for the group, vision and mission statements, T-shirts. These kids are much more engaged, active, and socially aware than I was at their age.

I was so proud when the parents of Joe Lawton [the 17-year-old who killed himself after being detained in the police station] told me that Joe's friends had felt empowered and stronger by being involved in changing the law to protect 17-year-olds. They had suffered a terrible loss but because they were able to petition and campaign they became involved in the process that eventually led to the High Court declaring the practice unlawful. Nick and Jane Lawton said these kids saw that change was possible with a collective voice, and though they have lost a good friend they believe they are part of creating a better world – which, of course, they are. For me, nothing could be more rewarding than that.

*What in particular motivates you to help them? Why young people? Do you identify with them at all?*

I suppose the reason I do it is that I don't accept this imposed social hierarchy. I want to tear down the veil of self-deception, to tell the truth to the complacent, the cynical, the lazy. "What if this was your child? Would you let this happen?" I say again and again to social workers, judges, prosecutors. "But it's not my child," they reply, until sometimes they find that it is.

I see my child in all the children I work with and I see myself in each and every one of the parents. And yes, sometimes I see myself in the young people we work with. I so admire them: when they overcome adversity, when they succeed, when they work so hard to achieve their goals. I remember the spoiled teenager I was, and it makes me want to work even harder. That sense of how lucky and privileged I was growing up carries through into everything I do. At Just for Kids Law we aim not only to make sure that our clients are treated with the dignity and respect that any human being deserves, but that they are treated in the way we would want our own children to be cared for.

*Some of the things you see clearly make you angry. Does your work take a toll on your personal and family life?*

My friends laugh at my ability to turn the atmosphere in any room with another of my tales, but when you live your life so close to other people's pain and heartache you also appreciate how lucky you are, and you celebrate that every day.

I sometimes wonder if there was something different about me that allowed me to make this my life. I always had an innate sense of justice, but other than that I suppose it is just about persistence.

I think there was a time when I believed that this work was taking a toll on my personal and family life, but I am beginning to think that the opposite is true. There is no doubt that I don't deal with stress in the best way, and there is a lot of stress in my work, but I am working on how to make that better. Having a child made me realise that only I can make myself the kind of parent I want to be; it is my responsibility to ensure that she isn't stressed, short-fused, anxious. I think just identifying the positive events in your day can convert pessimism into optimism. The thing I most want for myself and those I love is a happy life.

*You've said in the past that it's difficult to be a compassionate lawyer in this country. Why is that?*

One of the things that most upsets me is when people who are working with vulnerable children, those who most need our help, do it as a "job". Financial constraints should never stop a professional from acting in a child's best interests.

When I left my work as a barrister in the Temple to go to Louisiana, I had been trained to "not get emotionally involved with my clients." I remember mentioning this to Clive when I first arrived in New Orleans, and he laughed at me. He said, "How are you going to persuade a jury to spare someone's life unless you are emotionally involved?"

This was one of the first things Aika, my co-director at Just for Kids, and I agreed upon when we first met. There is no doubt that this can make the work harder, but ultimately I think it also makes it more fulfilling. We recently had a group psychotherapy session at work which explained the difference between empathy and compassion in a working environment. That was a real breakthrough for me. Empathy is a an amazing social skill enabling you to understand the lives of others without having to experience what they have been through; but if you empathise too much it can become a little solipsistic. I knew I could either spiral into the pain of the people I was working with, or withdraw, as I didn't want to feel it. Compassion, it was explained, has some distance to it, enabling you to understand and respond to someone's pain but to see it as belonging to someone else. This has been really liberating.

*In a speech you gave recently, you mentioned the words on the Old Bailey: "Defend the children of the poor and punish the wrongdoers." You said that the government is failing our children. Could you say more about that?*

It is not just government that fails our children: we all fail them. Look also at the words of James Baldwin that we use as our motto: "For these are all our children. We will all profit by, or pay for, whatever they become."

The parents I know do not give up on their children: they will use all the resources available to them to ensure they can help that child. Parents often take responsibility for their children's actions, blaming themselves for mistakes their children make. Shouldn't that be true of society, too? It is our collective responsibility to ensure that all children are given the best shot, the best opportunities, and investment of resources.

For me, there is nothing more depressing than

*Shauneen speaking at a legal aid rally outside the Old Bailey in 2013. ©Fleur Hallett*

meeting a young person who has overcome enormous hardship, got themselves amazing A levels and a place at a prestigious university, who is then told that they can't take up the place because, unbeknownst to them, their immigration status is unstable. They are children; they should not be punished for what their parents have failed to do administratively. That is not just wasting valuable potential but is likely to lead to complete disenchantment.

I felt the same way about the two 17-year-old boys who took their lives after they spent time at the police station without any adult assistance. If there hadn't been an anomaly in the law that excluded 17 year olds from the safeguards that were available to every other teenager, their lives might have been saved. And that "might" is enough, even if there is a cost involved. Both of those young men were huge assets to their schools and communities, and they would have carried that on into the world.

*Who or what inspires you?*

I am inspired daily by the young people we work with. They are brilliant – enterprising, adaptive, interesting and tough. And challenging. Everything young people should be. Sometimes it can be uncomfortable to hear what they have to say, and sometimes we don't like the way the message is presented, but that shouldn't stop us from listening.

The kids we work with feel maligned by the media and politicians, but this is not a new story. I remember reading an article by F. Scott Fitzgerald about the flapper generation and how they were perceived to be a symptom of a depraved immoral generation with no respect for society or their elders. Now they are romanticised.

I am inspired by writing, by poetry. I look up to political figures like Robert F. Kennedy and Aung San Suu Kyi, but

I am inspired by people closer to home, too. Ruth Rogers was a role model to me when I was younger. She owns the River Café, and when I was young I worked as a waitress there. I was so lucky that she took me under her wing and supported me in the work I wanted to do. She is an amazing mother, committed to her family, a supportive partner and an incredibly successful business woman. She allowed me to believe that it is possible to do all of those things well.

To work for Clive Stafford Smith was also inspiring: he is undoubtedly the best jury lawyer I have ever seen. But he is also a remarkable person. I recently discovered that he voluntarily paid tax on something that is tax-free because he believes it is a civic responsibility to pay tax. Most people think of ways to avoid paying tax, and I think someone like Clive, who dares to be different, begins new conversations and creates change. It was the same with Guantanamo Bay: he wanted to help those guys from the beginning. The world was reeling from 9/11, and he said, "What about those guys?" At the time I thought he was crazy, but he was right, and much of the world now agrees with him.

*What are the wider implications of the recent cuts to Legal Aid? Why have you been out on rallies demonstrating about an issue which is hardly talked about in the mainstream press?*

Earlier this year I was in Myanmar [Burma], a young democracy evolving out of a brutal military dictatorship. There they are excited about the rule of law, about building a legal aid system based on human rights, while here it is being systemically torn down.

I think it is so important to have a court system that is

independent from government. And everyone should have access to justice, not just the wealthy or those who have the right papers. There are too many horror stories in our history – stories of power being taken away from the people and the state no longer being held to account – for us to be complacent.

I have been encouraged by the response of the Courts and the media: many, many people believe that this is the wrong way to go. I hope the government has the sense to listen, for all of our sakes.

# Still here

**Angharad Tomos** writes about being imprisoned for her campaigns to protect her native language.

It was pitch black and I was amazed it was so easy. Up and up the ladder I went, up into the night, like one of the angels on the stairway to heaven that Jacob had dreamt about. How high I could go before being zapped by radio activity, I wasn't sure. Up we went, one following the other. We arrived at a ledge and decided we'd climbed far enough. It was devilishly cold.

An hour later, we were frozen solid. Five of us stood on the ledge, our teeth chattering. I'd never been up a TV mast before. It was slowly dawning over London and I could see Crystal Palace below me. What a view! To think one had to do this to demand a Welsh language TV channel. My family didn't even have a television set. But all my life, I'd wanted to take action with the Welsh Language Society, and this was my chance. I'd just turned 18, had been at university for five days, and was eager to play my part in the revolution.

Suddenly we spotted a policeman on the ladder,

"We're from the Welsh Language Society, and we demand a Welsh TV channel!" my friend shouted.

"Yes, we've been informed," he replied. "But all I want to know, love, is when you're coming down."

"We're staying here indefinitely!" I shouted. "The Welsh language is dying!"

"And I'm dying for a pee," murmured another friend. "We'll have to go down."

"We're coming down now!"

And down we went. Straight in front of Bow Street Magistrates.

I was young, and very impressionable. "Whatever you do, don't get bound over," my friend Teresa advised. She was more experienced – a ripe 19 years old. She was my mentor.

"This being your first offence," the magistrate announced, "you're being bound over to keep the peace for 12 months."

"I refuse," I said.

"I sentence you to five days prison. Next."

In the Black Maria outside HMP Holloway, I still expected my parents to intervene and save me. Five days later, they did. They gave me and Teresa a terrific welcome, and took us home.

My home in Wales is a magical place. It is also invisible. It's a secret world that no one else knows about. I have a very good idea of how a white, middle-class person in London lives – what they wear, drink, read, what music they listen to, what their views on politics are. I read about them all the time in newspapers and on TV programmes. But they know nothing of my way of life, and my culture.

I first encountered this ignorance in prison. I was treated like an alien.

"Wales? Why are you here? You painted road signs? Why? 'Cause you want them in Welsh? What's Welsh?"

I'd show them Welsh text in books. I'd even say a few words in Welsh.

"That's funny, that is," they'd reply. "I can't understand a word of it."

"You wouldn't – it's another language."

"Yeah, but I understand Pakis talking, and Afro girls – you're different."

I gave up explaining. I had learned from a young age that Welsh history and culture is seen as inferior, and even irrelevant.

I wasn't taught Welsh history at school; we had to follow the British syllabus. We'd plod through the wives of Henry VIII or the causes of the Napoleonic wars, and ignore what had happened right on our doorstep. My knowledge of Welsh history came from folk singer Dafydd Iwan, who wove politics into his lyrics. These led to many conversations around the dinner table.

"What's Penyberth, Dad?"

"A place in the Llŷn. It was an important cultural centre, but the RAF destroyed it to build a bombing school, despite half a million people protesting."

"That's terrible"

"Three activists set fire to it – and gave themselves up to the police."

"Were they jailed?"

"The jury in Caernarfon couldn't decide if they were guilty."

"So they walked free?"

"No, they were sent to the Old Bailey and got nine months in Wormwood Scrubs."

"What's Tryweryn?"

"A village in Meirionnydd that was drowned in 1962."

"Why?"

"Liverpool wanted water, so they drowned a whole village, and a community was destroyed."

"That's wrong – did you protest, Mam?"

"No. I had four children under seven, and was expecting the fifth."

"Who are the Beasleys, Dad?"

"A young couple who demanded their rate note in Welsh. They refused to pay, and the bailiffs took all their furniture away."

"So they didn't have any furniture?"

"Not for eight years, and then they won their fight."

"Where is Trefechan bridge?"

"In Aberystwyth. That's where the students blocked the traffic and started the Welsh Language Society."

"I'm going to be a member"

"Not until you're 18."

But I became a member at 14, and had a crash course in organising meetings, raising funds, corresponding with the Council, raising awareness, writing articles for the press. Yet what I really wanted to do was take direct action. I knew this was the most effective political tool. By the time I was 15, the coup in Chile had happened, and I'd stuck a poster of Che Guevara on my wall, next to Ffred Ffransis and Dafydd Iwan, who'd been imprisoned for their activities.

I loved the romance of it all. I didn't take drugs, but I was addicted to history and guerrilla fighting. My grandfather had been a conscientious objector and a great socialist. I wanted to play my part, to have my own adventure.

When I received my O level certificate in English, I handed it back to the headmaster, demanding it in Welsh.

"You'll be in jail, soon enough," he said, unimpressed.

HMP Holloway was only my first experience of

incarceration. My local prison was HMP Risley, Warrington (there being no women's prison in Wales), and over the years I became familiar with Drake Hall, Styal, and many others. Before I went to prison, all that counted was the fight for the Welsh language. Prison changed my politics and expanded my world view. Socialism was theory for me before I went to prison, and I hadn't given much thought to the class system. When I was criminalised, my eyes were opened. It was like visiting the underworld. Everyone in prison was working class. Petty theft and drugs were the main offences, but these were disenfranchised women struggling to survive.

"Any kids?" is the first question you're asked by inmates.

"No."

"It'll be easy for you then."

It was always going to be easier for me. I was in prison out of choice, and that makes a world of difference. I was nicknamed "Queen's Mum" because I had so many letters and telegrams of support. I was still considered "weird", of course. My protest background was less difficult to understand, as they'd seen Greenham women come and go, but they didn't know what to make of my cultural identity. They also assumed I was educationally subnormal.

When you're admitted into prison, they ask if you're illiterate or not, and you're given a chance to go to the Education Room once or twice a week to learn to read and write. Being in my second year in university, with exams on the horizon, I needed all the study time I could get, so I sat in the Education Room every afternoon. People concluded that I was extra thick, and as I was unable to converse fluently in English, the image stuck. I found this humiliating.

My lecturers warned me that I was destroying my chance of a career. But my career was in direct action. My friends and

I would stick our arrest warrants on the wall as marks of bravery. And whether it was painting English road signs, occupying holiday homes, climbing masts, breaking into transmitters, intruding on the Houses of Parliament, or painting Nelson's Column with the slogan "Tory Betrayal" – it was a step nearer the goal.

Some ask now, didn't I consider the consequences? But what about the consequences of *not* acting? When the campaign for a Welsh TV channel was at its peak, Margaret Thatcher came to power. Although the allocation of the fourth TV channel in Wales for Welsh-language programmes had been included in the Queen's speech, that promise was broken. Gwynfor Evans, the president of Plaid Cymru, the Welsh Nationalist Party, declared in July 1980 that unless the government stuck to its original promise, he would fast to death. Why should anyone make a fuss about me daubing a bit of paint on Nelson's Column, when Gwynfor Evans was prepared to sacrifice his life? The magistrate sentenced me to three months imprisonment for that action, but I considered myself lucky.

It's chilling to think that, within less than a year, Bobby Sands and nine others would die following a hunger strike. But Gwynfor was saved. The government finally made a U-turn (the only one that Maggie made), and S4C was born. I remember going next door to watch the first transmitting of the Welsh TV channel. It had all been worth it.

Yet there was so much more to campaign for. Nelson Mandela was still in jail. The British Army still occupied the Six Counties in the North of Ireland. Greenham Common was seeing the first cruise missiles. Then the milk quotas came, and Maggie took on the miners. Campaigning became a way of life.

"When are you getting married?" my friends would ask,

their bellies swollen with a second or third child. Married? There was too much to be done! We had to free Wales first. In the meantime, I wrote children's books and novels for adults. I was my own boss, and writing and campaigning went hand in hand. Once, I went on a protest in the morning and wrote about it in the afternoon.

But the situation of the Welsh language was changing in front of my eyes. My great aunt was in a home for the elderly, where everyone spoke Welsh. But in the primary school it was a different story. There were three newcomers there when I was a child, all English. When I returned to the same school in 10 years, half of the class were from English-speaking families.

It's called progress. All over the world, people are moving from the country to cities. The old way of life changes, languages die. One of the slogans of the Welsh Language Society is, *Rhaid i bopeth newid, os yw'r Gymraeg i fyw*. "Everything must change, if the language is to live." And everything *is* changing, but in the wrong direction. In a capitalist society, the Welsh language makes no sense: it's not cost effective, and it's troublesome. So the fight for the Welsh language is a fight for everything I believe in, and against the forces of darkness.

A language is not only a vehicle for communication; it represents a unique way of seeing the world, of making sense of everything around us. A language is an integral part of our intellectual and creative heritage. The bureaucrats' reply to us is that only 20 per cent of the people of Wales speak Welsh – but that means nothing to me. As I said in my first novel, *Yma O Hyd* [Still Here]:

"Was it my mother's fault that she taught me a minority language, and made me associate the Welsh language with the best things in life, until I could never separate myself from it? And yet, it wasn't a minority language at home, it wasn't a Twenty Per Cent language. It was a Hundred Per Cent language, and no one thought twice about it."

Everyone in my village speaks Welsh. I speak Welsh in every aspect of my life. "But you understand English!" the Bureaucrats wail. Yes, I do. I have an A level in English; I'm a writer who's travelled; I've read all the major works of English literature, and I love them passionately. But speaking in English does not come easily to me: whilst I'm eloquent in Welsh, I have only half the English vocabulary, and I'm painfully conscious of that.

So when people accuse me of hating English, I set them straight. It's not about hating anyone. I hate a system that disregards other people's way of life. And there are communities all over the world who can identify with our struggle: wherever I've travelled, wherever I've spoken about the colonisation of Wales, people nod their heads, and we find that we have a common bond.

Sometimes I wonder why I turned out this way. None of my four sisters turned into rampant protestors, despite

*Angharad being escorted by police during a Language Act protest, Aberystwyth, 1986. © Marian Delyth*

having the same upbringing. I wasn't an agitator from birth. On the contrary – I was an obedient little girl, wanting to please and do the right thing. I never questioned the rule that girls could not wear trousers in school, nor that we were forced to take cookery and needlework classes while boys were taught interesting things like woodwork and metalwork.

Taught in school that I lived on the periphery of Great Britain, taught that I was of no real importance or use, being a woman *and* Welsh *and* rural, I could have easily turned out quite different. But whilst I received my official education in English (in a school where 99 per cent of the pupils and teachers spoke Welsh as a first language), I received my unofficial education through the Welsh Language Society, who taught me that women had a crucial role to play in building a better future.

Needless to say, I could never have done it alone. Left to my own devices, I'd be knitting socks in my slippers in front of a fire. It's the comradeship that keeps you going. I've campaigned with some people for 30, 40 years. We've forged deep friendships.

And when we did come together on Trefechan Bridge in February 2013 to celebrate 50 years of direct action for the Welsh language, we had a fine record to look back on. Bilingualism is taken for granted now; we've had three or four Welsh Language Acts through parliament. We've even had our own Assembly since 1999. We did secure a Welsh language television channel. Welsh medium education is being taught in many schools. There is a lively Welsh publication market and a Welsh music scene. So much has changed. As Engles said, "An ounce of action is worth a ton of theory."

A month after the Welsh Assembly was opened, I finally got married. By 2003, I was a mother. That gives you a different perspective. Before you have children, you do it "for future generations." When you become a parent, that future generation has a pair of bright eyes that greet (and challenges) you every morning.

Eventually, the inevitable happens, "Mam, what's Tryweryn?" my son asks me, and after a small hesitation I recount the story of the drowned village.

"That is *so* wrong," he replies. "Do you know what we should do?" He tells me about his plans to challenge injustice, and how to set the world right.

He keeps me going with his enthusiasm. He challenges his grumpy mam who's grieving for a lost way of life. I've filled his head with tales of heroes, and for him, nothing is impossible. I follow in his wake, and remember the quote I saw on the walls of the Scottish Parliament, by Alasdair Gray: "Work as if you live in the early days of a better nation."

And that's what we'll do, me and my son – together.

# In defence of life

**Eileen Chubb** on blowing the whistle on abuse in a care home and how, despite paying a huge personal price, she refused to give up the fight.

*Interview by Angharad Penrhyn Jones*

*How did you get into the caring profession?*

It was accidental, really. I'd worked in retail, started off as a Saturday girl and was given my own shop when I was 17. I was good at my job so they gave me a bigger shop and it just went on from there. But I was bored, it wasn't challenging enough, I wanted to do something else. And the first shift that I did in the first care home – I loved it from the first minute. It was just the best job in the world and I miss it. I miss the fact that you can make the difference in someone's life, the difference between heaven and hell. I loved the job because whatever I gave to those people they gave me a hundred times back. It's like you're in an exchange. It was so rewarding.

I found I had this ability to put myself in their position. I can sit at a table with six people with dementia, and even if they're all talking about different things and not making any sense, I'm comfortable with it. The very fact that someone's listening to them, it makes them feel like they matter. So I found I had this ability to communicate with people and find a way in.

*So you could tune in to them.*

Yes, and in the care home they used to say to me, "Oh, this lady's really violent, we've decided to give her to you because you're so good with the violent ones." I'd think to myself, I've never come across anyone who's violent, I've only ever come across people who are frightened. And they used to label people as violent because nobody else could find a way to care for them.

Sometimes people were crying because they couldn't find their children, who they thought were little. And the staff would just walk past them. I used to say, "She's crying," and they said, "Well, their children are not little so it's not real." I'd say, "It is to her." So I'd take them into a room and I'd open their album and we'd go through all the old photographs. It was just a gentle way of reassuring someone who was distraught and bringing them back to the world again.

*It's a very intimate job, isn't it?*

They were like family, I spent more time with them than my own family and I really cared about them.

*At what point did your internal alarm bell start going off? When did you start getting suspicious about the way the residents were treated at Isard House?*

I'd been working there a little while and I'd been promoted and put in charge of another unit. The unit I had previously been working on was taken over by another team leader, who was best friends with the deputy manager of the home.

Everybody who was engaging in abuse knew somebody in a position of power to protect them – that's the way it works. But, it was about six to eight months after I started working there that I thought things weren't totally right on one of the units.

*What happened?*

A resident had walked across the room and this carer was watching the telly, and because the resident got in the way of the telly she got up and screamed at her – Grace, this elderly lady. I can remember seeing this carer's face and for the first time in my life, I thought, "Oh my god, she's evil. She's absolutely evil." She didn't realise she was being observed. She was my line manager. And I thought, "Oh my god, what am I going to do?" I can remember feeling absolutely sick.

The person who was screaming and threatening the resident was the best friend of the deputy of the home. I had no idea what to do

*How did the resident react to being threatened?*

She was crying her eyes out. Grace was one of my favourite residents. I loved them all in their own way, but Grace was the resident who looked after everyone else. Often you'd find her in her room, getting all her clothes out and putting them in piles. And I'd ask her, "Grace, what are you doing?" She used to say, "I've got too many things and there might be people who need it more than me so I thought I could share them." She'd give you the clothes off her back and she was the most amazing person. She never complained, and she made me laugh all the time. And somebody treating her like that was just... I couldn't believe what I was seeing. I think I was in shock.

The manager came in shortly after that and she was very friendly with the deputy manager so I just didn't know what to do. In the end I knew I'd have to risk it and so I went to her. She said to me, "I'm glad you told me, you're not to speak to anyone else about this." She said we'd gather evidence against them and make sure they were sacked and wouldn't be able to work anywhere else. At the time, that seemed reasonable to me. I thought the manager would do something. So when things were going on, like assaults, or people being drugged on illegal drugs that were stockpiled from dead people, I used to take the MR [medication record] sheets down to her. When I saw wrongdoing I would report it to her. This went on and on, and people were really suffering, and I asked her why it was taking so long to act on this. She kept telling me that we didn't have enough evidence.

*How did it affect you, seeing people you cared about being mistreated?*

When I think back, I don't know how I stood it. The only reason I stayed there was because those were good people I cared about. And I didn't realise how I was at the time, but my husband would tell you. I'd come home after a shift and we'd be watching the TV and he would say something about what had just been on, and I hadn't seen or heard a word of it. I forgot his birthday for the first time in my life. I was just in turmoil and every day that I went in there, more stuff was happening. There was a part of me that was suspicious of this manager, wondering why she wasn't doing anything. But I was thinking surely she wouldn't defend that abuse.

The worst abusers, I realise now, are manipulative – they manipulate everyone around them – and so I felt totally isolated. You're kind of in this bubble, where you're thinking,

"When are you going to act? When are you going to act? People are going to die for god's sake". And people did die. I'll have to live with that because I trusted this manager. If I hadn't trusted her and gone outside, people would have been saved, and that is something that I'll have to carry. The sorts of things that I was seeing to this day I cannot even talk about it without getting upset... [Starts crying.]

Every kind of abuse, every kind of hitting, pushing, making people so afraid they were like cringing animals in the corner. Their clothing, their money, their jewellery taken. Screamed at, just left neglected, lying in a bed, calling out, 18 hours at a time until their skin broke down and the smell of death on that unit – I've only got to close my eyes and I can smell it.

*In your book you talk about how people had bed sores that were so severe that the flesh had been eaten away down to the bone. And then you saw acid burns from urine, and medication burning people's faces.*

Yes, to me it was like a torture camp, I wouldn't have believed it was possible in this country. I wouldn't have believed that people could defend that kind of thing. I realise now that reputation is money. And that to admit that there was that kind of abuse going on was a threat to profits. But the longer she left it, the worse it got. And the worse it got, the more she had to defend what she knew and when she knew it.

*The stakes were getting higher all the time.*

All the time. And I just couldn't imagine that anyone in the world would do that. I must have been totally naïve. People were just deliberately mistreated. They were assaulted, they were stolen from, they were drugged up to the eyeballs on drugs that weren't even their own, they were left without food and drink. The worst cases were put in the back room. It was called the quiet lounge, and if they were put in there, they never came out. It was at the end of a corridor. When you walked through the home, you walked through most of the areas, but this room was right at the back, so nobody passed by, you couldn't hear the screams from that room. And that's why it was chosen. I used to run down to that unit constantly, trying to catch the main abuser, opening doors when I knew she was in the room with somebody, trying to protect the people while I was waiting for this manager to act. The more it went on, the worse the toll it had on me.

Then one day, a young carer, a boy from the unit where the abuse was happening, came to me and said, "I'm seeing terrible abuse down there." I remember thinking, "Oh my god, I'm not on my own, somebody else has seen it, they'll get rid of them now." And I said to him, "You've got to go to the manager. You've got to tell her what you've seen," and when he said the words, "But I am, and I have been going, and we've all been told not to speak to each other," that's how I found out that there were seven of us. And all of that time, all of this had been going on and there was enough evidence. I went home and that's when I spoke to my husband Steve about it for the first time.

*You hadn't spoken to him about it?*

No. I came home after each shift and my head was in another place.

*So you weren't actually able to communicate?*

I couldn't even talk about it when I came home.

*Was it because putting into words would make it too real?*

I think I was in shock. I was in shock from the first incident that I saw. I didn't think that at the time but looking back I can see that I was suffering a kind of trauma. And the more I was seeing, the worse it got.

After I'd told Steve, I cried my eyes out all night. And he said to me, "You've got to go outside with this." So I said, "I could lose my job and we'll never have any money." But he told me to go to the social services, as it was then. So, the next day I went back into work and it was as if that young carer had snapped me out of a bubble. I'd been in a nightmare and I didn't know where to turn. In that instant something came into me and it was an anger. I wasn't the sort of person that would go round shouting or protesting. I'd never complained about anything in my life, I'd never written a letter of complaint, I'd never even complained about crap food in a restaurant.

But in that instant, it wasn't even anger I was feeling, because it was ice cold. And I remember looking at the manager and thinking, you've got blood on your hands. People have died, and you knew, and you could have stopped it. And it was just a cold rage. I knew what I had to do. I wasn't scared any more. I'd been in hell because of this, seeing this every day and knowing I couldn't protect those people. Knowing that people had died because I'd trusted that manager.

In that instant I knew I had to go to social services with statements from all seven witnesses. So after collecting them, I went in and said to the receptionist, "I have statements here, there's seven of us in all, and widespread abuse is happening in this home and people have died and people have suffered and they're continuing to suffer and the manager's covering it up." She tried to take the statements from me but I couldn't let go of them. I said, "If you don't do something, we're going to go to the media. There is no power on this earth that's going to stop us putting an end to this abuse – these people are going to be held to account and there's no-one or nothing that's going to get in our way, not now."

I wasn't scared, then. I didn't care about anything anymore because I got pushed across a line in that minute when that carer came to me and said what was happening. I could not see anything that I wasn't willing to do to get this put right. That's the moment the old me died. I can't even say it was rage, like screaming and shouting, because it wasn't, it was quiet.

So social services brought down the head guy and I can remember the relief. They called the police, they went into the home on the Wednesday morning and they took out the main abuser straight away. She had a circle of abusers around her – that's how they operate, they surround themselves with the worst, and that's what she did. She was surrounded by five or six other people.

*So it was completely institutional.*

Yes, it was. So we were lucky that the head of the inspection team came down immediately. Knowing the abusers couldn't hurt anyone else was just... I slept that night, the night they arrested her. Because every hour and every minute she was in that building, it made me feel physically sick to think what she was doing. She lived in the building so she had access day and night to those people.

*Do you think that was deliberate on her part?*

Yes, because if you put people to bed, if you get those people up, there's no one else to witness the bruises, the skin breaking down. It's to do with control.

And the abusers knew immediately that we were the whistleblowers, even though social services wouldn't have told them because whistleblowers are supposed to be protected. I didn't know that we were whistleblowers, I'd never even heard the term before. But, of course, because we'd gone through line management with our concerns, as soon as we went outside they knew it was us. They made our lives a misery and it was like another nightmare starting.

*You were physically attacked, weren't you? You were scared for your safety...*

It grew into such a crescendo – we were totally ignored at first, and then they ended up spitting at us and saying that they'd get us in the car park. And one night, one of my residents, Molly, fell. I was checking her to make sure she was all right and the next thing I know my head came forward so hard that I hit her chest and I realised something had hit me in the back. One of the people had picked up a chair and smashed it into my back. I just started crying. It wasn't just the pain – I thought, how could you do that to somebody, with their back to you, somebody you'd worked with?

*In your book you describe them as "the mob". Would you say it was a kind of herd mentality? You'd pulled away from the herd and they hated you because of it.*

Yes, and I think there were people there who'd also seen things and maybe they'd convinced themselves that it was all right not to say anything, I don't know. But it was absolutely horrendous, this hostility to us. And it grew and grew.

*But when you finally left BUPA, the management went into the home and gave everyone chocolates.*

Yes. The day we were driven out they brought in a box of chocolates for all the staff, chocolates for each member of staff.

They protected the abusers and they crucified the whistleblowers. Our lives were made a living hell. Every day we had to go in there. I remember thinking, oh my god, I've got to do a shift. Because you were frightened in the car park if it was dark. You felt under threat every minute, to the point where you were shaking.

*Were you protected by anyone?*

No, there was nobody. We went to everyone. So after three weeks of this I rang Dick Turner, who was the head of Social Services Inspectorate. I said, "Can you get someone senior from BUPA to meet with us, because we can't go on like this, we've got to have help." And it was getting to the point where we were locking ourselves in the rooms with residents because we were frightened when the mob came through the unit – they'd start slamming doors and screaming and the residents would start crying. Maggie was the only one who had a mobile phone and I can remember her ringing Dick Turner asking him to come over, which he did, and then later on he arranged for us to have a meeting with BUPA. But I would never have imagined that anything like that could happen. The only question I ask myself now is, how did we last as long as we did?

The thing is, we'd told the secret, we'd broken the code. Maybe that's what it is with care homes and abuse – it's a conspiracy of silence. Looking back, that's what our crime was.

But the worst abuser of all, in my view, is the "look the other way" abuser. It's the person who's in a position of power to do something and decides to look the other way.

*It makes me think of the Jimmy Savile case, and other scandals, where hundreds of people knew that sexual abuse was happening and were guilty of not speaking out. And Harold Shipman, of course [doctor charged with mass murder of elderly patients]: there are parallels.*

Oh, yes. People did try to say something about what Harold Shipman was doing, but they were swimming against the tide.

*The abusers in the care home you worked in, Isard House, were also administering potentially lethal doses, like in the Shipman case.*

Yes. Before we left the building they were burning medical records in a bathroom on Unit 3, trying to destroy evidence. So that night, when the manager went home, I went to the office and we took a file at a time and we photocopied them – there was a photocopier upstairs and we went up the back stairs hoping that nobody had seen us. And I smuggled the medication records out of the office underneath a pile of towels. It was the scariest thing I'd ever done. But those medication records proved there was abuse. They were giving 180ml of anti-psychotics to somebody who was only prescribed 20ml. It was all there, in black and white.

At the time it never occurred to us that BUPA would go to the lengths they did to suppress all this evidence. To this day, even though I've written a book about this and spoken to the media, they've never been able to do anything because they know everything I say is true. And that is the worst crime of all. They could have saved those people and stopped further abuse, but at that point they became complicit, tried to cover it up. So even though the management knew those people were dangerous, they allowed them to have contact with vulnerable residents.

The main abuser was then employed in another BUPA care home. It was more important for the company to protect its brand than to stop abuse from happening. Because by admitting that abuse had taken place, they would have destroyed their reputation.

So they accused the seven of us of lying. And the 27 relatives and other witnesses who came forward as a result of the inquiry – they were also accused of lying. And they said that the social services team, who thoroughly investigated it and upheld it, were liars as well. So, I realised that you could have had Wembley Stadium full of witnesses, you could have had everything on film, even then they would have said the camera was lying and the witnesses were lying. It was horrendous, the level of denial.

*It was strategic denial.*

It's about protecting the image, protecting the brand, even if it costs people's lives

*It's the corporate mentality though, isn't it? There's a fiscal duty to satisfy shareholders by maximising profits.*

Because of the way BUPA is structured, there aren't even shareholders we could have appealed to. There are just a handful of people on the board who get £2 million bonuses.

*And the chief executive is on what, £7 million a year?*

Yes, about that. And Val Gooding, who was then the chief executive, her bonus alone was the entire training budget for BUPA. At the care home, we had 70 pence a day for food for each of the residents, so the staff used to have a whip round to go to Iceland to buy in some more supplies. We had to use our own money. I was really honoured to work with people who, even though they were on £5 an hour, were willing to dig into their own pockets. And when I think that this is a multi-billion pound company... they don't deserve to have good staff, they don't deserve to be there at all.

*So this isn't just about individuals and their personal acts of evil: it's about the system.*

Yes. BUPA have a lot of power. We didn't realise that Val Gooding was really close to the Health Minister at that time, Alan Milburn. Members from BUPA's board were sitting in the House of Lords. What we learned in the months that followed is that this world is run not by politicians and governments – it's run by corporations. The abuse of power is massive. And people who stand up to the big companies: they try to crush them, totally crush them. Val Gooding is currently advising the Home Office on their whistleblowing policies. Des Kelly was the BUPA director of care homes and is now a government adviser on elderly care, he's the head of the national care forum, he was given an OBE for services to the care industry; Val Gooding was given an MBE for services to the care industry. Des Kelly represents all care providers at government level. He sits on the CQC [Care Quality Commission] advisory panel; he tells the CQC how they should be inspecting care homes today.

At the time, I wouldn't have thought it was possible, but knowing what I know now, and being there on the inside, and seeing what happens to people who try to speak out – it's absolutely scandalous. If we take the worst kind of person who's failed in their job, like Cynthia Bower at Mid Staffs Hospital, what we do, as a country, is we allow people like that to be in charge of all hospitals. They put Cynthia Bower in charge of CQC so she was overseeing all hospitals. We reward people for the wrong reasons. Des Kelly is rewarded for what he did. He's now listed in the 10 most powerful people in the care industry.

*Whereas the ordinary people who stand up and say there are human rights abuses happening, like Julie Bailey, who exposed horrific malpractice at Stafford Hospital – they have their lives destroyed. She's lost her home, her business, there's been a witch hunt, and she's had to go into hiding.*

And Sir David Nicholson [chief executive of NHS England] is going to retire with a massive pension. What I would ask the people of this country is: is it right that people like Julie Bailey are living in a caravan in a secret location? Is it any wonder that whistleblowers are too scared to speak out? But they couldn't keep us quiet.

Every time I go out on a stage in front of thousands of people, I just close my eyes beforehand and say, "For Edna." She was one of the women who was abused in my care home. And then I just go out there and forget that I used to be

*Eileen (left) with Edna.*

a shy, timid person, and I say that I'm only here as a witness. I just keep doing it and now we're on the brink of forcing the government to do something out of shame.

I learned so much as I went on. We were campaigning and demonstrating and every day we went to Bromley Council, we wrote to every member of the Council. I used to get sick from licking envelopes. [Laughs.] It was like a factory, and I think we got pushed so far that all of a sudden I couldn't see the barriers anymore. They weren't sticking anything in my way, and we weren't going to shut up for money. You know, we had nothing. One of the other whistleblowers was evicted from their home – we suffered terrible hardship. Not being able to turn your heating on, sitting in the house with your coat on.

*You had to sell your possessions in car boot sales to raise money to survive, didn't you?*

Yes, and we'd give it to the one most in need that week. Relatives of the victims came forward and gave us stuff to sell and that was priceless to me, that they supported us and thanked us for what we'd done. Because they knew we were the best carers in that building, and now none of us could get another job. You'd ring up for a job and they'd say, "Are you one of them people? Oh sorry, the job's just gone." Nobody wants to employ a whistleblower, because if they see something wrong, they're going to report it. So I think that probably says more about the care system than anything.

I was so naïve. I can remember we all went up to London, the seven of us, and I remember this Australian tourist taking our picture outside the House of Commons. I thought the House of Commons was where you found all these important people who did the right thing when people told them what was wrong. I was so stupid. Corporations like BUPA run that place, not us. It seems you have to have a lobbying firm to have influence, you have to offer a politician a job. I remember the photograph, and I look at it and I can see we thought, "Oh, we've come to London and the government will sort all this out now." We must have been mad.

*It's a very common misconception that we all have to an extent, that it's just a case of giving the right information to the people in power, and justice will be done. But actually, that isn't necessarily how it works.*

No, it's not. It's so corrupt. The people of this country need to rise up and open their eyes to what's going on here. I mean, we wrote to every member of the House of Commons and every member of the House of Lords. Five people replied. Nearly 1000 letters we delivered by hand. Five people replied.

*Is it partly that people don't have enough respect for the elderly? Is it that we don't think they really matter?*

We do live in a world that idolises youth. This isn't a cuddly cause. If you look at any charity event on the telly, or anything that has great big award ceremonies, it's always about children. But there are other vulnerable groups too.

*Dementia is something we don't necessarily want to face up to, especially since we know that it's on the rise. We could all end up in that situation, in a care home, dependent on our carers. Do you think as a society there's some sort of collective denial about this issue?*

I think that there is an element of the taboo of our own mortality. People would rather push it away. That's why what

I'm doing is sometimes hard, because people don't want to recognise the work of the charity and they don't want to look too much at this issue. But I just think that maybe we need to look at the care system and a priceless generation. A generation that's come through a war and that never complains about anything. The most common thing an elderly person would say to me is, "Oh, I don't want to make a fuss, plenty worse off than me, duck." Or, "Don't tell my family, I don't want to worry them, they've got enough to worry about." Things like that. This is not a generation that's complained.

*There was one story in your book that really brought tears to my eyes - well, there were many, actually, but one that I think of now was about an elderly man who had survived the Second World War. He was really suffering in this care home and he told you that...*

He said that during the war, he wouldn't have swum out to the boats that came to rescue him, if he'd known where he was going to end up... [Starts crying.] The thing is, when I first went in to work there I never understood that someone's life was less valuable than any other's. A child's life, the man down the road. A human life is a human life, it's priceless, and it doesn't matter how old that person is or where they are, or what's happening to them, we can't allow this to happen to people.

Now, if a child was placed in a nursery and that child was abused, there would be an outcry, and rightly so. However, if it happens in a care home, there's this tendency to say, "Oh well, it serves the relatives right for putting their parent in a care home." Now, to look after someone with dementia at home, is a terrible toll on people and they don't get any support, any help. You've also got women working now. My grandmother lived with us, but 20 or 30 years ago women didn't work the way they have to work now. And I'm not talking about working out of choice; I'm talking about working because they have to, to survive. So you haven't got the situation where people can stay home from work and look after an elderly person.

*The other thing I'd like to ask you about is the fact that care work isn't seen as a proper profession – it's not taken seriously, even though it's highly skilled work and very challenging. That's not reflected in the wages, it's not considered to have professional status. And it's mainly women who do it. Do you think if it was a male dominated profession things might look a bit different?*

That could well be the case. I mean, yes, it's mostly women who do the work. And if you say you're a care worker, you might as well say you're a cleaner. But I've seen care workers who would put nurses to shame. At the end of the day, nurses are now doctors and care workers are now nurses. I think that needs to be recognised. And I believe passionately that good care workers should be recognised and that the bad are taken out of the system.

*Can care and profit go together?*

I don't believe so. I've been in council run homes where the building is shabby but the care is excellent because they tend to retain the staff for a long time, they're better trained, better paid, and they know their job well. I'm not saying that there aren't problems in some council run homes, but I think profit is at the heart of this problem. If the choice comes between someone's life and profit, profit will always take the dominant position. And the fact is, that's all very well if you're selling handbags and doughnuts, it doesn't belong in a situation where people's lives are at stake.

*And you're speaking as somebody who's seen the evidence on the ground, because you've been in 300 care homes all over the country. Can you talk about the undercover work that you do?*

Going out with somebody else's identity and memorising phone numbers and fictional relatives is everyday work for me. When I first did it I was really scared, but I've never come close to being caught – except once when I forgot who I was! [Laughs.] But I'd been in 10 care homes that day, and I was a bit tired.

"Tales of the Uninspected" was my first really big initiative. We take all the inspection reports on a care home that we've got information about – mainly from staff, sometimes from relatives – we look at all the secret reports that are not published and all the FOI information. I do Freedom of Information requests en masse.

You go in to these homes and you have to open your eyes, use your brain, and be willing to tell the truth afterwards. Sometimes I've gone into a care home two or three hours after the CQC have been in there and it's as if they're talking about another home. Sometimes I've had to double check the address. The difference between what I'm reading and what I'm seeing is scandalous.

*Why do people not recognise you when you go in? You're quite a prominent figure now in this field.*

I have marvellous volunteers who help me with this. A group of actors over at Twickenham have taught me about using wigs and make-up and how glasses can change the shape of your face. And the funny thing is, people see what they want to see. That's why I can go into care homes, even when I've been on *ITV News* the night before. The thing that gets me into the care home is their one weakness – money. They see a customer. And that's how I get in.

*How do you fund your campaigns?*

When we started Compassion in Care, we didn't realise that other charities take money from the care industry. That was the first big shock to us. So we made the decision straight away that we would never take money from the industry or from government, because that way we only serve the people in those homes. If we have some public donations, great, otherwise we just scrimp by. And that's how we've gone on for 14 years, really. We are now a registered charity, and we aim to break the chain that allows abuse to happen. The links in that chain are complacency, ignorance, denial and silence. Silence most of all.

We campaign massively on whistleblowing issues – we go out in the street dressed up as judges with placards and all that kind of thing. I go round the country and I talk about whistleblowing and abuse and I raise awareness at local groups who then go on to campaign and to visit care homes. So it's a growing tide of people power.

We work closely with the media, who have helped me save lives every day when the authorities have not been there. It's the media that will shine a light on these things. That's a terrible indictment of the authorities, but it's true. I've gone directly to the CQC about particular care homes and they've just ignored me. Therefore I put that particular care home on the next television programme, I've done that many times.

*And then you see results?*

And then you see results. Sitting behind a desk and saying how shocking this is – that is not going to change anything. You need to actually get out there on the front line and do something.

Sometimes I think, why am I doing this? I never set out to do this – it's just that what happened in Isard House and the two or three years that followed... you get pushed so far across the line that your eyes are opened, and it's terrible, but you can't close them again. Most people go through life with their eyes closed to what's going on in the world and they worry about their designer handbag label and their next pair of designer shoes or stuff that's totally useless in the end. And I used to buy stuff when I had a job. [Laughs.] Sometimes it's a very lonely place to be, because you hear people talking about things that matter to them, and it's not their fault but you think, "Oh my god, if only you knew." People go through life in a daze with their eyes closed, thinking, "Well I can't really do anything, it's too big, everything that's wrong in the world, it's too big for me, I'm only little me on my own."

But if you take just a little stand on your one thing in your one corner, if everybody did that in their corner, we would be living in paradise. That's all it would take. It would be to just say, I can't change everything, I can't bring down the government or anything else, but I can keep going on this and I can keep making sure that Edna and Grace and Dot and Reg are never forgotten. And if I save one life before I leave this world, that's worth it, because every life matters. I've lost my job – we lost the employment tribunal – I have no money, but I'd do it all again in a blink of an eye. I wouldn't do anything different.

*In your book you say that if you hadn't spoken out, a part of you would have died.*

There's no doubt about that. It's like something fundamental that makes us human. The capacity to love, the capacity for good. To deny, and turn a blind eye to, what I was seeing in that home would have cost me more than it would have cost me to speak out. I did what was right. I have no doubt and I've never had the slightest hesitation.

*I've read that whistleblowers often suffer from post-traumatic stress disorder.*

Whistleblowers are subjected to terrible suffering because they speak out in defence of life. They speak out in defence of people who could have been our mother, our father, our child, our brother with learning difficulties – vulnerable people. That's why they're suffering. And we have to say, it's got to stop. If it doesn't stop, it will be us tomorrow, it will be our loved ones. And only when some injustice happens, or someone you love is abused or neglected, or is involved in an accident that could have been avoided – then you realise the only thing that stands between you and that terrible injustice, is the whistleblower. What I'd say is: stand up for these people, these witnesses. And this is what I'm fighting for.

# Fire in my belly

Filmmaker **Franny Armstrong** on how she pioneered "crowdfunding" to make a climate change blockbuster, and why films are a powerful political tool.

*Interview by Angharad Penrhyn Jones*

*Was there a particular moment in your life when you decided that you wanted to change things, that you wanted to have an impact?*

I remember when I was eight, my dad took me on my first flight, to New York. He'd made a film called *Global Report* for the BBC and was showing it to potential distributors. I had the dual experience of witnessing – for the first time – extreme wealth in New York, and also watching my dad's film about this very poor family in India selling peanuts. They were talking about how much money they live on, and it was less than my pocket money. I remember saying to my dad, "Why can't I just give them my 60p? I don't mind." And he said, "Well, you could, but that's not going to solve the problem, and there are lots of other families living like that." I remember him explaining the whole concept of inequality.

It was a bit of a rude awakening, experiencing the extreme

wealth of New York and the extreme poverty in his film at the same time. It really hit me.

*You then became concerned about animal rights while you were at school.*

Yes. When I was 11 I persuaded my mum to let us go on holiday to a farm – I wanted to be a farmer or a vet when I was a kid, because I loved animals. My sister and me were up every morning at five a.m., milking the cows, shovelling the slurry. We had a favourite cow – the only brown cow in a herd of black and white Friesians – who for some reason we called Piggy. One day she tripped and stood on her udder, and made a very small cut – about half an inch long. I said to the farmer, "What's going to happen, is the vet going to come?" He told me that it would cost £37 – I remember the exact amount – for the vet to come out and put a stitch in the cut. So he was going to cut his losses and send her for slaughter. In other words, my favourite cow was condemned for the sake of £37. I couldn't believe it, £37 for somebody's life! And so from that point on, my sister and I were vegetarians.

*Did you try to persuade everybody else to give up meat as well?*

I became absolutely militant, actually! [Laughs.] Our brother and father soon followed my sister and me – they're both still veggie now. It was funny, a few years ago, when I joined Facebook, that was the first thing my old school friends said to me, how militant I'd been at trying to persuade them all to go veggie. But I have to say, some of them turned out to still be veggie, 25 years later.

*I read an article you published where you say that you became fed up and frustrated by having circular conversations with people about these issues that you cared about, and trying to have an impact one-on-one.*

Yes, I remember those teenage years, going round and round in circles, having the same conversations, not making my points exactly how I wanted to make them. And that's the genius of film. You can keep working for weeks or months or years, however long, to make the perfect point in the perfect way. You can decide who's going to say those words and how they're going to be said and what's going to follow it and what music you're going to use. And you can have such a powerful impact. Plus, of course, you can potentially reach tens of millions of people with a great film, whereas you can only reach, say, one or two people a day, talking one-on-one.

*What was your first campaigning film?*

It was called *Truth or Dairy*, and it was about veganism. My flatmate was then the President of the Vegan Society and she was saying that what they needed was a campaign video, but they couldn't afford to make it because video equipment was so expensive – tens of thousands of pounds. Nobody had video cameras in those days, this was around 1991. So my sister and I asked our dad if we could borrow some of his equipment – by then he'd left the BBC and set up his own production company. We had one friend who was a cameraman, and he recruited his other friends from film school, and then we got Benjamin Zephaniah to present it.

*How did you take to filmmaking?*

I loved the whole thing. The creativity, working with other

people who had great skills, feeling like I was doing something positive with my time, finding myself in unbelievable situations like filming the lead singer of M-People in a park explaining why she's a vegan and her suddenly bursting into song. I also didn't realise how much filmmaking I'd picked up during my childhood, when I was my dad's little assistant. He was forever saying things like, "Plug in the microphone and check the levels, Franny," and talking about wide shots when we were watching *Doctor Who*.

*Was your father encouraging?*

Hell, yes! He was so happy when me and my sister showed an interest. He still is, that I'm following in his footsteps.

*So how did you move on to do the McLibel film, then, your first really big campaigning documentary?*

I thought I was going to be a musician, as I was playing drums in a pop band, The Band of Holy Joy, and we had a record deal and were going on tours and all that exciting stuff. I was also studying zoology at college – though I was the world's worst student, as I was always away with the band – and after that I went to a tiny island off Tanzania to work on a coral reef mapping project. While I was there I was thinking about what I should do with my life, thinking that maybe hitting things rhythmically was not going to be satisfying enough, when my friend wrote to me about the McLibel trial. It was just the most inspiring thing I'd ever heard, that two people were daring to stand up to McDonalds. And it was unsurprisingly my dad who came up with the idea. He said, "Why don't you borrow my camera and make a documentary about the trial?"

*It was good advice...*

It was. So we met Helen and Dave, the defendants in the trial, and tried to get a documentary commissioned. And we found out that we were competing with lots of production companies. There were eight in total, including big names, trying to get a commission from the main broadcasters. But McDonalds was threatening legal action constantly – the BBC, Channel 4, the *Guardian*, the *Sun*, they'd all had legal run-ins – which created a climate of self-censorship where nobody wanted to criticise McDonald's, and nobody would commission a doc about McLibel, despite it being the most brilliant story. So the other eight production companies dropped out, and that left me!

*For you to document it and try and put it out there was a risky thing to do.*

It was a risk, that's true, both in terms of the ever-present possibility of legal action from McDonald's and the fact that we didn't have a commission, so we didn't know whether anyone would ever see the fruits of our labours – obviously YouTube and all the rest didn't exist then. And when we finished it, people wouldn't touch it in the beginning. It took a brave distributor, Journeyman Pictures, to stand next to us. The first broadcast was in Australia on SBS – it took another eight years before it made it onto BBC2.

*What was the high point of filming the trial? I'm sure there were many, but what sticks in your mind particularly?*

Well, I was remembering one moment recently – it was a kind of precursor to the world we're in now, of instant news and Twitter. As well as doing the documentary, we also set up a website, McSpotlight, all about the trial and McDonald's, which was getting massive amounts of traffic. At one time it was in the Top 10 most-visited sites on the web! On the day of the verdict I was going to be in the courtroom, so I told the web team, I'll run out, and call you on my mobile phone – which was very new then – and I'll tell you what the verdict is so you can get it up before the news. The news was on at, say, one o'clock – in those days you didn't have rolling news – and we thought we could be the first in the world to get the verdict out. So we started hyping this, saying, if you want to know what happened, keep checking McSpotlight. We had the verdict up within a couple of minutes of it being announced, long before any of the mainstream news!

*What was the hardest thing about the trial?*

Everything was hard. Having no money, trying to understand the complexities of the trial, persuading people to work for free, the constant threat that we might be next for McDonald's' legal action. Plus it went on and on and on – Helen and Dave told me it would take about six months but the main trial took three years, and then with appeals and stuff it ended up taking 10 years of my life. Not full-time, but two years full-time, with no money, living in a grotty flat, lugging all the equipment on the tube – you wouldn't believe how heavy the batteries were back then – and having no broadcaster backing me. These days it's quite common to make a documentary because you want to, to crowdfund the money and then afterwards try and sell it. But this is back in the day when the only way people could make documentaries was through commissions on TV. And we decided we were going to do it anyway. But I really had no idea, I didn't know anything about the film world and I didn't really watch documentaries, I didn't even have a telly. As time went on and on the years started to pass, I was wondering, is anybody ever going to watch it?

*In the end it was seen by around 26 million people – remarkably – but if it had been commissioned, it would have been seen by how many? One million, perhaps?*

Yes, maybe two. And a really interesting thing is that Channel 4 made a drama about McLibel based on courtroom reconstructions. When they broadcast it they got around 400,000 viewers but then their powers-that-be decided they weren't going to distribute it internationally. So that was the end of that. Whereas my *McLibel* documentary was taking off all around the world at film festivals and cable TV and DVDs and even in the cinema in Australia and America. And straightaway the feedback we were getting was incredible – people saying they were boycotting fast food or changing their kids' diets or starting their own campaigns or whatever. And that's one of the things that drove us all, everybody who was involved in the film, the website people, the volunteers at the trial, we all worked *so hard*, because we just felt this is the opportunity of a lifetime, to have this kind of an impact.

*The UK government did change its policy on advertising to children as a result.*

Yes. Basically a new law came in saying junk food can't be advertised during children's programmes. That's the best thing that happened. But lots of other positive changes happened as well, to do with animal welfare, organic food, lots of things. McDonald's changing its practices. Somebody told me that there was an internal marketing meeting at McDonald's about 10 years after the trial – this is a first-hand witness – and somebody at McDonald's was saying that the moment they knew they had to change everything about their business, was the McLibel trial. After McLibel they really crashed. Loads of restaurants all around the world closed, some countries closed to business.

*After all this you ended up living in a very remote village in India making a new film. How did that come about?*

I read a newspaper headline in the *Guardian*, over somebody's shoulder on the Tube, which said, "Villagers in the shadow of the dam prepare to drown," and I immediately thought: that's my next film These people were putting their lives on the line over a dam. I knew that dams were an important environmental issue but I didn't know anything about why that was. I flew out to India the very next day and found the village.

*I found* Drowned Out, *the film you made about that village, incredibly moving and powerful. There was something almost biblical about these people standing up to their necks in water, chanting. Being forced out of their village due to a giant engineering project. And of course it's not just about India. I suppose you know that in Wales in the 60s a village was drowned to create a water supply for industry in Liverpool, and the whole community had to move out. The school went underwater, the chapel, everything. So it's a story about people fighting industry and big business – or that's one of the things your film examines.*

It's about a lot of things. Once I got there I started to understand that there are multiple themes. That's what I liked about the film; it wasn't just a simple story and it wasn't just about the villagers versus industry. I had an interesting lesson, actually, when we finished the film. We sold it to a channel in America, and they wanted a shorter version. This was my first experience of working for somebody else, and they turned my film into a narrative about poor people losing their homes to support India's development. So it's a very straightforward "price of development" film. And I was saying, "No, that's only one part of it." There are so many other questions, such as: do dams ever work anyway? There are all these different layers to the story, but they turned what I felt was a very complicated, interesting, nuanced, multi-faceted story into this very simple black and white narrative. And I had no say. That was the first and last time I ever worked to a commission.

*Franny filming a man rowing past a submerged temple in India for her film* Drowned Out.

*Your next film, about climate change, became a global phenomenon. When did you first learn about climate change, or environmental devastation?*

At school, when I was about 12. I remember learning about the "greenhouse effect". I can still picture the scene of the classroom. I know what stool I was sitting on, and which teacher it was – Miss Field. It was just a normal school day and everyone else was just taking notes and being normal school kids, but for me it was a massive moment. I mean, if we destroy our life support system, how can we survive? Straightaway I got that. So then I was always interested in it. Over the years the science developed: it started off as the "greenhouse effect", and then it became "global warming", and then "climate change".

I always had at the back of my mind that this was the most important subject of our time, but I didn't know how I could make a film about it. There were a lot of documentaries about climate change, and they were broadly the same: scientists explaining things, shots of hurricanes. I decided that I wasn't going to make another one of them, but I wasn't sure what else to do. And then one day I was talking to a friend – we were a bit pissed, which probably helped – and she was asking what I was going to do next and she said that the oil industry was an epic subject. I suddenly remembered this film *Traffic* that I'd seen recently by Steven Soderbergh, which has five or six human stories on all sides of the drug industry. There's a politician and a drug user and a drug dealer and a policeman. Nobody is black and white, everybody's complicated, everybody's got their own motivations, everybody's interesting, and you're rooting for everybody. And at the end of these 90 minutes you've learnt more about the drug trade than you'll ever learn from a hundred documentaries. And I just thought that is the way to do climate change.

*So seeing an issue from lots of different vantage points.*

Yes, exactly. But not having good guys and bad guys, trying to find all good guys or all interesting guys, all loveable. So as soon as I had that idea, that was the beginning of the road.

*You'd already decided that you weren't going to work with broadcasters again after your experience with* Drowned Out. *You wanted creative control.*

That's right. And that's not only about being able to choose the right music – can you believe they put panpipes over *Drowned Out*? There aren't any panpipes in the Narmada valley! It's also about being able to say politically what you want to say. Then there is seeing how many people had watched my *McLibel* documentary, compared to the Channel 4 drama about the trial. So it's that combination of making it as powerful as you want, because nobody is telling you to water it down, and getting the most number of people to watch it. Both of those things working together.

*Why did you decide to use a crowdfunding model to finance the film?*

We didn't decide to use crowdfunding as there was no such thing back then. My dad and me, and Lizzie, the producer, met in my flat and decided that if we were going to make this film, we needed a lot of money – by our standards. £400,000 was the original budget, because we wanted to go off to all these countries, and include animation, etc. I think *McLibel* cost less than £20,000 and *Drowned Out* certainly cost less than £20,000, so it was a huge leap, though it's still a very low budget by filmmaking standards. So we needed to get that much money but we didn't want a commissioner. How were we going to do it? It was actually quite obvious. Get lots of people to give us a bit of money. So we kind of invented crowdfunding there and then – although other people also claim to have invented it. Anyway, it was different to what is now known as crowdfunding, because now it tends to be about donations, and ours was about investments.

*So the people who donate money are like stakeholders.*

Yes, you own a little percentage of the profits. And it worked really well. The first thing we did was invite around 20 people we knew to a meeting where we showed a few clips of my other films, explained the idea – and people started getting their chequebooks out! One of the things that was so great about it was that if you try and get a commission, you're going to have a year of writing proposals, having meetings, waiting for answers, doing taster tapes, and waiting for some random person who's going to make the decision about whether your idea is a good idea or not.

*The gatekeepers...*

The gatekeepers, exactly, who are all pretty much of a type. White, middle aged, middle class, male. Whereas with this, we had the idea, we set up the funding meeting, everybody gave us the cheques, and the next day we bought a camera. And the day after that, we went to find the Indian guy who became one of the main characters. We just set off straightaway. We didn't have the whole budget, we didn't have £400,000 in our bank account, just the beginnings of it. But, straightaway, people were going, "Oh, my business partner might be interested in this, can I tell them?" And it just spread.

It wasn't on the internet for years, that's a really key thing. In the beginning we only had face-to-face meetings, or one-on-one phone calls, with potential funders, and that was because we wanted to get access to film with the oil industry and we needed to keep an element of secrecy about what we were doing until we'd finished the filming.

*It's great to see how crowdfunding has really taken off.*

Yes, it's unbelievable. In our original funding document, we said, "We would be very happy if, as a side effect of [*The Age of Stupid*], we inspired other filmmakers to copy this funding model, take on the big issues, sidestep the corporate control of the media and get millions of people watching films that matter." And now Kickstarter – which is just one of more than 100 crowd-funding platforms – say they have 10,000 film projects a year! So things have changed from all three angles: from the funding point of view, the access to equipment, and the distribution, where people can even watch films on YouTube.

*Tell me why you think film is such a great medium for communicating an idea.*

I think the history of cinema has shown that the 90-minute film format is the ideal medium to take people from a position of knowing nothing about a subject to being really engaged and hopefully even inspired to act. You can be moved, you can be educated, you can go from being a complete ignoramus to a passionate campaigner, in an hour and a half. I'd argue it's much more powerful than, for example, spending that time reading a government report, or a book, or accessing a website, or frankly any other medium, because of the emotional pull of real people, music, graphics – everything in the filmmaker's arsenal.

*When you were making* The Age of Stupid, *you and Lizzie Gillett, the producer, went to Nigeria, but you were strongly advised not to go by somebody from the SAS.*

Yes, we went on a course on how to deal with survival situations, and that was his advice: don't go. And all my family and were friends were saying that too.

*You were almost taken hostage. Would you say that you're fearless?*

No. [Laughs.] But Nigeria, that was like... OK, we really want to make this film, we think it's really important, and someone in the oil war zone of the Niger Delta is going to tell the story in the best way. We really want to do that, so how can we minimise the risk? It's a cost-benefit thing – so we decided to go for a really short time, and get trained up in how to deal with situations. We weren't going in recklessly. And I wouldn't do it now I've got children.

*So your instinct for a good story and to campaign for justice now has to be weighed up against the fact that you have children. The balance has changed.*

It's just the balance, yes. Because now, if I was weighing that up like I was before, I'd have to also put my children into the picture. And I wouldn't leave them. It doesn't mean I'm not going to make lots of political films; just I'm going to make them in different ways that don't involve me going to the Niger Delta.

*Were you pleased with how* The Age of Stupid *turned out?*

Oh my god, yes, it blew my mind. My whole life I've had this burning desire... every morning I would wake up with this feeling that I wanted to do something good. A fire in my belly. I didn't want to die having not contributed something good to humanity. And after *Age of Stupid* and 10:10 I noticed that that feeling had gone away, simply because I feel that I have now contributed something. If a bus was coming at me now, in my last moment I think I'd think, "My life wasn't pointless." And then, "Aaaaaaaargh!"

*So you can relax a little bit now.*

[Laughs.] Yes. And having children – it all worked out well, thankfully. I was getting a bit old and I was wondering whether I'd ever be able to have kids. I'd always wanted to have them, but I wanted to do something good first. I started with *Age of Stupid* when I was about 33, and then it ended up, like all films, going on much longer. Then straight after that we then went into doing 18 months' more work promoting it, because the climate summit in Copenhagen was coming up. And we also founded 10:10 just before Copenhagen, and that extended for another year, and the whole time I was thinking, "I'm getting old, I'm getting old."

*And now you've met a filmmaker and you have a family.*

Yes, I was very lucky, it all worked out in the nick of time.

*Going back to the film: some of your shots are beautiful. The sequence where you film the changing of the seasons outside the train window in France – it's just unforgettable. You illustrate how the four seasons are disappearing.*

Every shot in *Age of Stupid* has been obsessed over. Getting that sequence – that is obsessive behaviour. [Laughs.] We went back to the Alps something like seven times to get that right. When I watch our *Making Of Age of Stupid* film – which is up on YouTube – I'm amazed at the lengths we went to.

*But the screening that you did before you introduced the drama element into your film – the screening to all the stakeholders – that was a flop, wasn't it?*

It was a flop, yes. [Grimaces.]

*So you and Lizzie had to show something you'd worked your socks off to make, travelling all over the world and to one of the world's most dangerous countries, and it didn't work as a film. Tell me about that, because that was a really exposing thing to do.*

Many filmmakers don't like to show their work in an unfinished state, but I've always thought that, if you can bear the pain, it ultimately makes a better film, as you get people suggesting improvements you hadn't thought of. But this test screening was particularly excruciating not just because most people hated the film, but because many of them had invested their hard-earned cash in it.

Most people gave up on us at that point. Even people who were heavily involved, they just went, "That's a flop then, that's it." But this one guy, Bruce Goodison, our executive producer, took me to the pub and said, "Come on, we've got to save it, what are we going to do?"

*And that's when you introduced the drama element and completely turned it around. I've been told that you have a talent for persuading people to work with you. You persuaded [film director] Ken Loach to do court reconstruction scenes for McLibel, and [actor] Pete Postlethwaite to play a big part in Age of Stupid. How did you pull it off?*

Ken Loach was interesting because we were absolutely nobodies back then. We'd never made a documentary, and we asked him to come and help us by directing some courtroom reconstructions. He was one of my heroes and I never imagined for a second that he would say yes. He agreed to do it because of the story, of course. That was a very influential moment for me. I remember the feeling when a fax started coming through from him and I was trying to read it as it came in. Him saying yes made me realise that you can ask anybody anything.

*So that made you more confident about approaching Pete Postlethwaite.*

Yes. His is a good story because when we decided we were going to add a drama element to the documentary, and it was going to be an old man in the future, I immediately knew I wanted Pete Postlethwaite to play him, because he was my favourite actor. The other people on our team said, "You don't do it like that, you've got to get a script and then you get a casting agent blah blah." But I was like, "No, I'm sorry, I want Pete Postlethwaite." [Laughs.] So I Googled him to see if he was interested in climate change and the very first article that came up was his local paper, the *Shropshire Star*, with an article about how he was trying to get a wind turbine in his garden, and a quote from him at the end saying it's everybody's responsibility to do everything they can about climate change.

At first I thought that was an amazing coincidence, but as I got to know him and he did loads and loads of promotion for the film, I thought, it's not a coincidence. I loved Pete Postlethwaite as an actor, because he has this great integrity which shines through every performance. And guess what? If you've got a lot of integrity and intelligence in this era, then you care about climate change.

*Can you talk about Postlethwaite confronting Ed Miliband [the Secretary of State for Energy and Climate Change at the time] during the UK premiere?*

That all started when we failed to get the film into Sundance, where we'd planned to launch it! [Laughs.] We thought we'd better come up with something even better and so ended up organising a megatastic premiere – building a solar-powered cinema tent in Leicester Square, linked up live by satellite to 71 cinemas all over the country, making it the Guinness World Record's biggest ever premiere. Ed Miliband's office phoned up and asked if he could come along. Once we knew he was coming, we thought, right, we need to take advantage of this opportunity, because we knew there was going to be tons of press there, because of the celebrities we had coming along – sad, but true. And so we racked our brains and asked everyone we knew for ideas. There was a big campaign about coal at that point and lots of activists were focusing on the Kingsnorth coal power station, taking direct action to try to prevent it being commissioned. Someone came up with the idea that we should do a pledge and Pete Postlethwaite should say, "If you commission the coal power station then I, Pete, will never vote Labour again." We thought that was a brilliant idea. So I took it to Pete, and straight away he agreed to do it. He said, "I've got a better idea. I'll threaten to give back my OBE." The premiere was coming up, and we'd put our hearts and souls into it, and I had this sudden realisation that we were going to ambush Ed Miliband live – me and Pete. I was actually quite terrified about the whole thing, as was Pete. I remember us sitting on a bench outside the cinema tent sharing a can of Guinness to steel our nerves before we did it.

*Was it scarier than going to Nigeria?*

[Laughs.] In some ways it was, because it was way out of my comfort zone. I'm not really the provocateur on camera. But Pete did such a great job and Ed Miliband's face was so funny, it's definitely worth looking that one up on YouTube. But, more to the point, within a month, the government changed the UK coal policy. They didn't do exactly what we were asking for, but it was a good step forward. Later I saw Ed and I asked him whether the change in policy was due to that night, and he said, "Yes, of course."

*He was held to account in front of all these impassioned, empowered, informed people.*

Exactly. And it was the right thing to do. So that was a very important moment, using the attention created by the film to demand something specific, and getting it within a month. And once we'd realised what the film could do, Lizzie and I agreed to do another 18 months' work, right up to the international climate talks at Copenhagen, promoting the film, which was a big decision, because we'd already done four years, five years, and she was wanting to go back home to New Zealand. And I was thinking about having children. But when we were doing the screenings and seeing people's reactions, we realised we couldn't stop.

*Tell me about 10:10.*

Well, after we ambushed Ed Miliband at the premiere, I thought that would be it, he would never speak to us again. But his office phoned us up and said he was challenging me to a debate, which I accepted. So I was walking through Regent's Park to this debate thinking, I've got to come up with something good. I'd recently been to a lecture by the climate think tank, PIRC, and they'd been talking about this idea of cutting 10 per cent of our carbon emissions a year. And it just popped into my head, a campaign to cut 10 per cent a year across the whole of society during 2010.

So I phoned up Lizzie and my climate cohorts, Leo Murray and Dan Vockins, still walking through the park, and they then ran it by Team Stupid – there were 12 of us working full-time promoting *Age of Stupid* – and everybody immediately loved the idea. So I announced it during the debate with Ed that night. [Laughs.] It just goes to show what a non-campaigner I am.

*What do you mean, a non-campaigner?*

Well, I'd only just thought of it that afternoon but I went ahead and announced that we were doing it. I spoke to some professional campaigners afterwards and they said that to set up a campaign like this, you'd need £2 million quid, and at least two years to get everything in place before you launched it – but I just announced it there and then. But it worked, because I said it was happening and suddenly it was happening! And then the *Guardian* – this was the key thing – they got on board in a massive way, and it just took off. On our launch day, we had the whole of the front page, several more double pages, the entire *G2* magazine and videos and

*President Mohamed Nasheed accepts his 'Not Stupid' award from Franny Armstrong and Lizzie Gillett. The Maldives was the first country to go carbon neutral.*

audio interviews on their website. As someone who was previously really chuffed to get a short review, it was insane.

*How does 10:10 work?*

The idea is that we all make the same calculation: what's the point of me cutting my emissions by not taking the flight to go to my sister's wedding in Sydney, when Jimmy next door is flying eight times a year? My cutting has a negative impact on me but it doesn't have any good overall impact. The whole point of 10:10 is that everybody's doing it together. And suddenly we had London Zoo and Spurs and the Science Museum and 120,000 individuals, and the prime minister and all the cabinet and 15 hundred schools and almost half of local councils and Stella McCartney and Colin Firth and Oxford University and Great Ormond Street Hospital – I mean the list is unbelievable. And it very quickly spread to other countries until there were 42 autonomous campaigns and cities like Paris, Oslo, Marseille and Mexico City committed to cutting their emissions by 10 per cent. We calculated that, in the first year, around half a million tonnes of $CO_2$ were not emitted thanks to 10:10.

*It's exciting to think that a campaign like that grew out of one moment of inspiration.*

I suppose I spent seven years thinking about climate change, working on climate change, reading every book about climate change, talking constantly to people involved in every aspect of it, and so... there's that idea about how creativity works, which I now can't remember exactly, but basically it doesn't happen in isolation. To have that moment of inspiration you have to be completely and totally immersed in the subject.

*Everything came together in that one moment.*

Exactly. But only because I was immersed in it.

*You've been posting recently how the concentration of carbon dioxide has just passed 400 parts per million. The last time this happened was 2.5 million years ago, when humans didn't inhabit the plant. Is there still hope?*

I've spent my life fighting and campaigning to try to keep the planet habitable for my children, your children and everybody else's children. I want other people to come and enjoy what we've enjoyed – that's what I'm doing it for. And I want to be part of that, too, by having children and hopefully them having children. But do I think there's any hope? No. Really, no.

*It's too late?*

It's too late for civilisation as we've known it to continue, yes. Which isn't to say that humans will be wiped off the planet completely, just that – "just" [laughs] – just that there will be a catastrophic collapse causing suffering and death and horror on an unimaginable scale.

*This is the thing we've been battling for so long, isn't it, to try and persuade people that climate change isn't only about ice and polar bears, it's not just an environmental issue, in the narrow sense of the word, but it's to do with human suffering.*

There are people right now dying of climate change impacts in floods or hurricanes, of disease and starvation. The biggest climate change impact event so far is still the European heatwave in 2003, I think, that killed something like 35,000 people. That's what climate change is about, people suffering and dying unnecessarily right now and a hell of a lot more people suffering and dying unnecessarily in the coming years.

*Is campaigning on this issue a way of alleviating depression?*

I've noticed that the people I know who are trying to make the world a better place – not just campaigning on climate change, but tackling any important issue – are happier than the people I know who are not campaigning. Why is that? My theory is that we're all bombarded with these messages, climate change doom, all this doom. And if you try and ignore that and carry on as though everything's normal, then you carry a massive psychological burden, whereas if you turn and face it and go, OK, that's the problem, I'm going to put my effort and my time in trying to do something about it, then whether or not you achieve anything, you've faced the problem, and I think that you don't carry that burden.

But also, it's been extremely exciting. I've been all round the world, I've met the most incredible people, I've been in situations you'd never find yourself in in normal life – like standing in water as the dam is filling up, or standing outside the McLibel court as Helen and Dave are cheered by a huge crowd. There are so many moments – those great moments when some political change happens, or when you meet an amazing person. It's such a fulfilling way of life that of course you end up happier than if you're stuck in an office with depressed people selling advertising space or something.

*What was your reaction to the Copenhagen summit? Why have world governments failed us so spectacularly?*

There's a question, jeez. I remember before Copenhagen, the best option on the table was that proposed by the EU, which, had it been accepted – and, crucially, if the emission cuts had then been made across the developed world – would have given us about a 50:50 chance of not hitting the dreaded two degrees and passing the point of no return, whereby the warming becomes essentially unstoppable, leading to the end of life on Earth as we've known it. Imagine if the politicians were standing at the door of a plane ushering the citizens on and saying that there was a 50:50 chance of the plane landing safely. Nobody would get on that plane! And yet, we are all on that plane... And that was the best-case scenario before Copenhagen, and yet we came out with less than the worst-case scenario. I remember someone from Greenpeace telling me they'd prepared a range of responses to the different possible outcomes and that the outcome we ended up with was worse than their worst-case scenario.

So instead of giving us a 50:50 chance of keeping the planet safe, the world's governments have given us a, well, no one can say for sure, but if it's not a nought per cent chance then it's very close to it. And if that is not the most spectacular failure of global politics of all time, then I don't know what is.

*But still, you're dedicating your life to this issue...*

I'm a child of the 70s, the MTV generation that was told that the point of our existence is to go shopping. So when I came to understand that actually we are the most powerful people who will ever live – because the generation before us didn't know about climate change and those that follow will be powerless to stop it – it's like, "Hey, our lives have meaning after all!" It sounds slightly absurd, but it is absolutely true to say that the future of life on Earth is in our hands. And where previous generations managed to solve the big questions of their time – whether ending slavery or landing on the moon or overturning apartheid, or what have you – we have been handed the biggest responsibility any humans will likely ever have. Why would I dedicate my life to anything else?

Leabharlanna Fhine Gall

# Contributor biographies

Former pop drummer and self-taught filmmaker **Franny Armstrong** has directed three feature documentaries: The Age of Stupid (2008), McLibel (2005) and Drowned Out (2003). These have been seen by 60 million people worldwide. Through her company, Spanner Films, Franny pioneered "crowdfunding", which allows filmmakers to raise reasonable budgets whilst retaining ownership of their films – Age of Stupid was for a long time the most successful known example, raising £800,000+ from 300+ investors. In September 2009, Franny founded the 10:10 campaign which aims to cut carbon emissions by 10 per cent every year and which inspired autonomous campaigns in 41 countries. Participants included Adidas, Microsoft, Spurs FC, 120,000 people, 1,500 schools, a third of local councils, the entire UK Government, the prime minister and the cities of Paris, Oslo, Brighton, Marseille and Mexico City. Franny is a Londoner born and bred.

**Zoe Broughton** was one of the founders of Undercurrents, the UK's first alternative news video magazine delivering "the news you don't see on the news." They filmed, edited and trained with activists from all over the country, putting citizen journalism at the heart of many protest movements. Her film, It's a Dog's Life, an undercover investigation into Huntingdon Life Sciences animal testing laboratory won the British Environmental Media Award 'Scoop of the Year' and the International Brigitte

*Bardot Genesis Award. She also won the EarthVision Environmental Film and Video Competition for* Nonviolence for a Change, *made for the Quakers. Her undercover footage inside chicken farms was pivotal in getting MEPs to vote to phase out the battery system. She has also worked as a camerawoman for the BBC and Reuters and regularly films for Greenpeace UK. She gives talks and runs workshops for campaigning video journalists. She is a mother of two.*

**Skye Chirape** *is a visual activist who uses art to raise awareness about political and human rights issues. Currently her art focuses on homosexuality on the continent of Africa, as well as issues affecting asylum seekers and refugees. As a co-founder of Noizyimage, Skye uses cinematography, photography and fashion to bring visibility to queer Africans. Previously, with the label Skyetshooki, Skye has used fashion design to examine knife crime, anorexia, cancer, HIV/AIDS and gang culture. She showcased on London Fashion Week in February 2008. In 2009 she was nominated for a BEFFTA award and in 2008 she won a community achievement award. The philosophy of Ubuntu motivates most of her visual activism and passion for psychology: "We are because you are and therefore humanity is a quality we owe each other." Skye has completed an MSc in Forensic Psychology and currently works as a forensic psychological assistant for the Ministry of Justice.*

**Eileen Chubb** *was one of seven care workers who blew the whistle on widespread abuse of vulnerable elderly people in a care home. They were the first whistleblowers to lodge a case under PIDA (the Public Interest Disclosure Act ) and soon became known by the media as "The Bupa 7". Despite evidence of abuse being upheld by social services, their* *employment tribunal case exposed fundamental flaws in PIDA and this law's failure to protect whistleblowers. Eileen's book,* Beyond The Façade, *is a detailed account of her experiences. She founded the charity Compassion In Care which campaigns to protect vulnerable elderly people in care homes, acting on information from whistleblowers and concerned relatives. She has also started a campaign for Edna's Law, Edna being the first person to continue to suffer horrific abuse until her death, because of the failures of the legal system.*

*Eileen gives talks to many different groups around the country. She also works tirelessly with the media to expose what some care companies would rather hide.*

**Liz Crow** *is an artist-activist and founder of Roaring Girl Productions (www.roaring-girl.com), working with text, audio, film and performance as a means to trigger social and political change. Interwoven with a long career of direct action and campaigning, Liz's work has been shown at London's Tate Modern, the National Film Theatre, and Washington DC's Kennedy Center for Performing Arts, as well as on television and at festivals internationally. Her work includes* Resistance, *comprising a performance on Trafalgar Square's Fourth Plinth in which Liz appeared in her wheelchair wearing full Nazi regalia as part of Anthony Gormley's* One & Other *project, and an internationally touring film-based installation, both works exploring the Nazi campaign against disabled people and what it means for us all today. More recently, in* Bedding Out, *Liz responded to the UK Government's current benefits overhaul with a 48-hour durational performance in which she took to her bed in a gallery, livestreamed to 10,000 people in over 50 countries.*

**Kate Evans** *has been making the political personal in her cartoons and comics for the past twenty years. She was involved in the anti-roads protest movement and spent much of the 90s living up a tree. She collated the experiences of fifty activists into* Copse: The Cartoon Book of Tree Protesting. *The book pleased readers and reviewers but confused booksellers, who tried to categorise it under "humour" rather than "contemporary politics". Later works include the snappily titled* Funny Weather We're Having at the Moment: Everything You Didn't Want to Know About Climate Change but Probably Should Find Out. *Followed in 2008 by* The Food of Love: your formula for successful breastfeeding. *Kate gives comic lectures on breastfeeding and parenthood, as well as environmentalism and the art of protest. Her next book is* Bump: how to make, grow and birth a baby, *a pick-your-own-adventure guide to womanhood, published in spring 2014. She is currently working on a graphic novel about the life of Rosa Luxemburg.*

**Zita Holbourne** *is an award-winning trade union activist, community activist, equality and human rights campaigner, poet / spoken word artist, visual artist, curator and writer. She has been a trade union activist for over 20 years in the NUS, GPMU, CPSA and PCS unions and the Trades Union Congress. She is elected to the TUC Race Relations Committee, PCS union National Executive Committee and ACTSA National Executive Council. She is the co-founder and National Co-Chair of Black Activists Rising Against Cuts (BARAC) UK, and sits on the National Committee for the People's Assembly and the Coalition of Resistance. She has led, founded and is an active participant of numerous equality, anti-racist and justice campaigns and organisations.*

**Shauneen Lambe** *is the founder and co-director of* Just for Kids Law. *She qualified as an attorney in Louisiana and a barrister in the UK and started her career working for Clive Stafford Smith representing people facing the death penalty in the USA. In 1999 she helped establish the charity Reprieve and in 2006 she set up Just for Kids Law in London. In 2010 she became a World Economic Forum Young Global Leader, in 2011 a Shackleton Fellow, and in 2012 an Ashoka Fellow. Shauneen is the UK chair for Global Dignity a global movement to empower people with dignity and is on the board of Birthrights, a charity protecting human rights in pregnancy and birth. In 2013 she was shortlisted for Liberty's Human Rights Lawyer of the Year award.*

**Sharyn Lock** *was born in Australia but has made her home in the UK. Although she started out with a music degree, and has done all sorts of jobs from community development work to selling cupcakes, her heart has always been in working for ecological sustainability, justice, and peace. In 2008, with the Free Gaza Movement, she was one of 44 people from 16 different countries who broke the Israeli sea blockade to be the first international boats reaching Gaza in over 40 years; Free Gaza achieved four further successful trips. As part of a small International Solidarity Movement group, Sharyn remained in Gaza throughout Israel's Operation Cast Lead, accompanying Palestinian ambulances under attack and later documenting the day-to-day Israeli fire on fishermen and farmers. She has just finished a midwifery degree, currently describes herself as an anarcho-Quaker, and would like her gravestone to read, "I would rather fight for the impossible than accept the unacceptable!" Sharyn published* Gaza: Beneath the Bombs *(Pluto Press, 2010) with Sarah Irving, and contributed to* Freedom Sailors *(Free Gaza, 2011).*

**Emma Must** *campaigned against the British Roads Programme during the 1990s, initially at Twyford Down in Hampshire, close to where she grew up. She went on to co-found Road Alert! – a national direct action network against road-building – as well as working with both ALARM UK (the National Alliance Against Road-building) and Transport 2000 (now the Campaign for Better Transport). In 1995 she was awarded the Goldman Environmental Prize for Europe. She currently lives in Belfast where she works as a teacher whilst studying part-time for a PhD in Creative Writing, focusing on eco-poetry, in the Seamus Heaney Centre at Queen's University. She has had poems published in a number of magazines and journals, including:* Abridged, Poetry and Audience, *and* Butcher's Dog. *She won second prize in the 2013 Strokestown International Poetry Awards.*

For further information about the Campaign for Better Transport's "Roads to Nowhere" campaign, see: http://www.bettertransport.org.uk/campaigns/roads-to-nowhere

**Jasvinder Sanghera** *is a survivor, campaigner and author. She is the founder of award-winning charity Karma Nirvana, the leading national charity for those affected by forced marriages and honour-based abuse. Karma Nirvana is now in its 21st year. Her book,* Shame, *about her own experience of forced marriage, was described in Parliament as a "lethal weapon". Jasvinder has won many awards and accolades for her work, including Legal Campaigner of Year 2013, one of the* Guardian's *most inspirational women in the world 2010, Ambassador for Peace Award, and Pride of Britain Award. Jasvinder continues to campaign and work tirelessly for the protection of victims, providing support to thousands every year through the unique Honour Network Helpline. This has* *led to critical new legislation making forced marriage a criminal offence from 2014. Jasvinder was honoured with a CBE in 2013 for her ground-breaking work.*

**Mary Sharkey** *was born in 1935 in the shale mining village of Broxburn, West Lothian. She married in 1956 and moved to the small village of West Calder where she brought up seven children and was very active in community life. She moved to Livingston New Town in 1980 and started campaigning for facilities for children. She went to college and did a Community Education diploma in 1982 and then joined the local Labour Party. She was elected as a local government councillor in 1984. During this time she was involved in lots of successful campaigns, in particular the campaign to keep Union Carbide (responsible for the Bhopal disaster in India) out of Livingston. She was involved in the 1984 Miners' strike, running a strong women's group and organising food parcel deliveries to miners' families. She is now 78 years old, works for Women's Aid, and is still going strong.*

**Helen Steel** *is a parks gardener in London and a union rep in her workplace. She has been active in environmental and social justice movements since she was a teenager. The 1990s saw Helen (and Dave Morris) fighting a high profile battle for freedom of speech, after McDonald's tried to suppress leaflets criticising the company. McLibel became England's longest ever trial and was also declared "the biggest corporate PR disaster in history."*

*At the age of 24, Helen began a relationship with a close friend who was also politically active. He disappeared two years later and she spent years trying to find out what had happened to him. 18 years later Helen found out that he had been an undercover policeman, spying on her and other political campaigners. In 2011 she and seven other similarly deceived women began joint legal action against the police with the aim of preventing this abuse happening to anyone else. (Information on the case can be found at http://policespiesoutoflives.org.uk/)*

**Angharad Tomos**, *the second of five sisters, has been a writer and campaigner from an early age. She has lived all her life in Dyffryn Nantlle, which lies in Snowdonia. She was the chairperson of Cymdeithas yr Iaith (the Welsh Language Society) from 1982-84, and has edited their monthly magazine. She won the Literary Medal of the National Eisteddfod twice in 1991 and 1997. As well as six novels for adults, she has written and illustrated a popular series of books for young children. She visits schools to teach creative writing, and she has been writing a weekly column in the* Herald Cymraeg (Welsh Herald) *for 20 years. She met her Welsh husband in Nicaragua and visits the country regularly, the last time with her 10-year-old son. She lives in Penygroes, near Caernarfon.*

**Anuradha Vittachi** *fled her native Sri Lanka at the age of 13 after her journalist family was subjected to political persecution. This experience fostered her lifelong belief in the importance of responsible media to support responsible governance. She experimented with a variety of media to promote global justice until she discovered the internet. Her articles on human rights – especially on population, gender and child rights – have been published in dozens of journals around the world. Her books include* Earth Conference One *(1988), with Carl Sagan, James Lovelock, et al, on climate change and other threats to global survival; and Stolen* Childhood, *on the exploitation of children around the world. She is an award-winning TV documentary-maker on issues of* *global justice; her interviews include discussions with President Gorbachev, Mother Teresa and HH Dalai Lama. In 2006 Anuradha founded OneClimate. In 2013 she co-founded the Hedgerley Wood Trust (www.hedgerleywood.org), exploring empathy as a route to human and planetary health, where an extended version of this piece can be found.*

**Jo Wilding** *is a barrister, writer and mother of two. She made three trips to Iraq, before, during and after the invasion, for around eight months in total, and wrote a widely read blog. In 2004 she set up a small circus working with traumatised children. She made two trips into Fallujah during the siege of April 2004 to evacuate trapped civilians and casualties and escort ambulances which were being fired on by US troops. Her writing from Fallujah was published around the world. She was also involved with the breaking of the siege at the Church of the Nativity in Bethlehem in May 2002. In 2005 she was co-nominated as one of 1000 Women for the Nobel Peace Prize. In 2007 she qualified as a barrister and now practises at Garden Court Chambers in London, mainly in asylum, human trafficking and unlawful detention cases. She is the author of* Don't Shoot the Clowns, *a book based on her blog. Boomchucka Circus has continued with trips to Iraqi Kurdistan and regularly tours Palestine.*

**Angie Zelter** *is a human rights, peace and environmental campaigner. She has founded many international campaign groups, including Trident Ploughshares and the International Women's Peace Service. She also helped set up the Institute for Law and Peace. Her love of trees led to her founding Reforest the Earth and CRISPO – Citizens' Recovery of Indigenous Peoples' Stolen Property Organisation. Angie was a member of the Seeds of Hope group that disarmed a BAe Hawk jet to* *prevent it being used in the genocide in East Timor. In a later landmark trial on the disarming of a Trident laboratory, the judge agreed that the deployment of Trident nuclear missiles was illegal under international humanitarian law, and the campaigners were acquitted. Angie has been arrested over a hundred times in 10 countries, and has served many prison sentences for her non-violent resistance to inhumanity and corruption. She has received the Sean MacBride Peace Prize and the Right Livelihood Award (on behalf of Trident Ploughshares). She has edited and co-authored five books; her latest,* The World in Chains, *was published in 2014 by Luath Press.*

# About the editors

**Helena Earnshaw** was brought up in north Wales and Lancashire and currently lives in mid Wales with her husband, stepson and son.

Her first experience of direct action was taking part in a month-long student strike at university in protest against spending cuts. In her early twenties she volunteered on the Navajo Reservation in the US with a lawyer who was working to get compensation for the many Navajo affected by uranium contamination. This humbling experience strengthened her belief that it is up to all of us to work to overcome injustice. In 1995 she started work at OneWorld.net, bringing global justice issues to a wider audience. She became involved in various online campaigns, including McSpotlight, as well as in the anti-road protest and anti-globalisation movement. One of her most memorable moments of direct action was locking herself to a digger to prevent a large man using it to destroy a beautiful landscape.

She missed the mountains too much whilst living in Oxford, so moved back to Wales in her late twenties where she started writing a column for *Big Issue Cymru* and got involved in peace campaigns, protests against the Iraq War, and helping to organise Wales's first International Festival of Peace. She now works for an independent women's publisher.

It took her many years to realise that "being good" is as important as "doing good". She is inspired by Anne Frank's sentiment: "How wonderful it is that nobody need wait a single moment before starting to improve the world."

**Angharad Penrhyn Jones** is a freelance writer, and a campaigner and commentator on environmental and social justice issues.

As a teenager, Angharad successfully campaigned with her fellow pupils to overturn the rule that girls shouldn't wear trousers to school; initiated a mass sit-in at the same school to demonstrate against cuts to the education budget – a protest which then spread through the whole county; and climbed onto the roof of a Welsh Government building to protest against their lack of respect for the indigenous language of Wales.

In her twenties, she collaborated with her sister on an observational documentary series which exposed the issue of rural homelessness and heroin addiction. Described by Ken Loach as "an important social document" and referred to in Parliament, it went on to win many awards. She has been named BAFTA Wales Best Newcomer of the Year.

She has presented a Welsh-language documentary about climate change, where she interrogated the chief climate negotiator from the Bush administration, and she was also the subject of a Welsh documentary about the anti-globalisation movement. She has written for a number of publications, including the *Guardian*, *Mslexia*, *New Internationalist* and *New Welsh Review*. In 2011 she won a Literature Wales bursary to work on her debut novel and she has been shortlisted for the *Observer* Young Travel Writer of the Year award.

She lives with her eight-year-old daughter in mid Wales, and one of her proudest achievements is the part she played in preventing the supermarket giant Tesco from colonising her home town, Machynlleth. She was also arrested for taking part in a mass demonstration against Trident, the UK's nuclear weapons programme. The experience of sharing a police cell with a blind young activist was profoundly motivating. She continues to be inspired by the outrageous acts and everyday rebellions of ordinary men and women.

# Acknowledgements

We would like to thank all of the women who contributed to this book, not just for the work they put into their pieces, but for their inspiring work as activists. And thanks also to all the men and women we couldn't include but who are out there fighting for a better world for all of us.

We are also grateful to the following people for their enthusiasm, insights and editorial feedback: Anne-Marie Carty, Tom Crompton, Carl Chapple, Andrea Currie, Gwen Davies, Kate Doubleday, Julia Forster, Caroline Geary, Tanya Hawkes, Richard Hawkins, Brian Healy, Tim Holmes, Joanna John, Suzy Kemp, Jackie Pearce, Tomos, Sara, Lisa, and Gruffydd Penrhyn Jones, Rachel Lilley, Angela Llewellyn, Robin Llewellyn, Martin Padget, Claire Paszkiewicz, Geraldine Purser, Izzy Rabey, Lesley Rice, pol sifter, Janet Thomas, and Michelle Whale. Particular thanks are due to Will Bamford and Andrew Isherwood.

Finally, thank you to the Welsh Books Council, in particular Lucy Thomas, and to Caroline Oakley and all at Honno, for believing in this book.

# Walking to Greenham

*Walking to Greenham: How the Peace Camp Began and the Cold War Ended,* by Ann Pettitt

A unique first hand account by the progenitor of the march.

Coming together with a small group of friends, Ann Pettitt started a movement that changed the face of Cold War Britain. Her remarkable memoir tells the real story behind one of the 20th century's most iconic expressions of grass roots political will.

She exposes the surprising roots of the march on Greenham Common, how the Peace Camp left the marchers behind, and how those first marchers took their cause direct to the *Kremlin*. It is an intriguing and challenging look at what shaped a generation of women's lives and made them strong enough to fight for what they truly believed in.

It is essential reading for those interested in the history of popular protest and women's history.

*"...poignant and insightful"*
The Spokesman

*"an important historical document, and deserves to be read – and studied – as such. It is also 'herstory'."*
New Welsh Review

*"a riot of a read"*
Melissa Katsoulis, The Telegraph

£8.99
ISBN: 9781870206761

# More in the *Honno Voices* series

*A series of titles featuring vital firsthand testimonies from women of all walks of life from important points in history, giving an intimate portrayal of real women's lives in different eras.*

### Changing Times
*A different world –women's stories of the 50s and 60s*
Edited by Deirdre Beddoe

Life in the 50s and 60s still meant segregation and inequality for many women, but it also brought rock-n-roll, rising hemlines and the first signs of female emancipation since the vote.

£11.99
ISBN: 978-1-906784-10-2

### Struggle or Starve
*Stories of everyday heroism between the wars*
Edited by Carole White & Siân Rhiannon Williams

A vivid recreation of the lives of working class women during this difficult time of depression, dislocation and dramatic industrial and political struggle.

£9.99
ISBN: 978-1906784-09-6

# More in the *Honno Voices* series

*A series of titles featuring vital firsthand testimonies from women of all walks of life from important points in history, giving an intimate portrayal of real women's lives in different eras.*

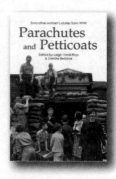

**Parachutes and Petticoats**
*Evocative women's stories from WWII*
Edited by Leigh Verrill-Rhys & Deirdre Beddoe

Women were the backbone of the country's war effort, 'keeping calm' and 'carrying on' on the frontline and under bombardment in the UK. But there were good times alongside the bad.

ISBN: 978-1-906784-11-9
£11.99

All Honno titles can be ordered online at
www.honno.co.uk
twitter.com/honno
facebook.com/honnopress

# ABOUT HONNO

Honno Welsh Women's Press was set up in 1986 by a group of women who felt strongly that women in Wales needed wider opportunities to see their writing in print and to become involved in the publishing process. Our aim is to develop the writing talents of women in Wales, give them new and exciting opportunities to see their work published and often to give them their first 'break' as a writer. Honno is registered as a community co-operative. Any profit that Honno makes is invested in the publishing programme. Women from Wales and around the world have expressed their support for Honno. Each supporter has a vote at the Annual General Meeting. For more information and to buy our publications, please write to Honno at the address below, or visit our website: www.honno.co.uk

Honno, 14 Creative Units, Aberystwyth Arts Centre
Aberystwyth, Ceredigion SY23 3GL

## Honno Friends

We are very grateful for the support of the Honno Friends: Gwyneth Tyson Roberts, Jenny Sabine, Beryl Thomas, Annette Ecuyere, Audrey Jones.

For more information on how you can become a Honno Friend, see: http://www.honno.co.uk/friends.php